A HARD ROAD TO JUSTICE

My Life as a Renegade Lawyer

Tony Dior Gaenslen

PEARL STREET PRESS

Printed in the United States of America.
10 9 8 7 6 5 4 3 2 1

Library of Congress Cataloging-in-Publication Data
on file with the Library of Congress.

ISBN 10: 0-578-69536-7 | ISBN 13: 978-0-57869-536-5

This book is dedicated to the memory of my dear friend,

DOROTHY COTTON

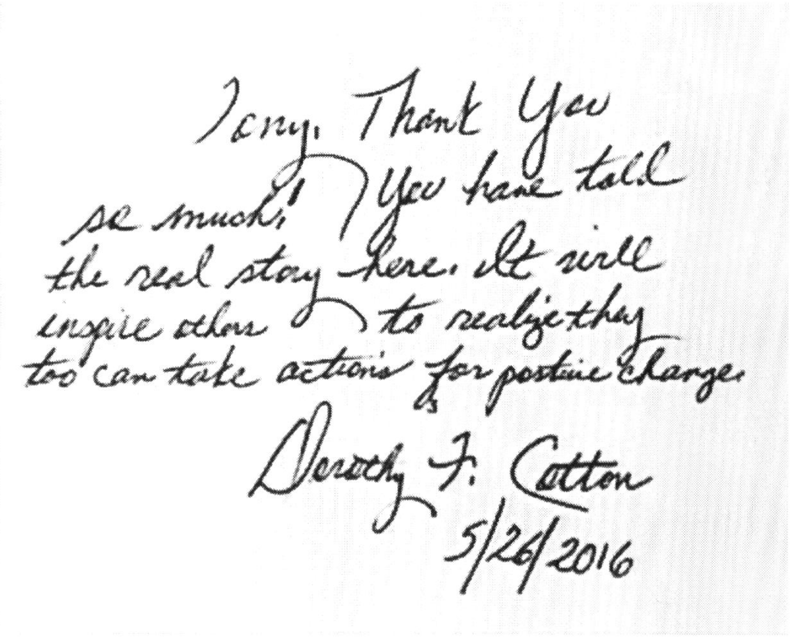

Tony, Thank You
so much! You have told
the real story here. It will
inspire others to realize they
too can take actions for positive change.

Dorothy F. Cotton
5/26/2016

Contents

Acknowledgments

THIS book would never have come into being without the inspiration and support of my wife Annie Wexler, who together with Dorothy Cotton pushed me into writing it, edited the first draft of each of its chapters as soon as they came out, and put up with me over the ten year period that separates the moment when the first gleam of possibility awoke in my eye to the date of completion.

My stepson Michael Wexler, co-editor of the book, transformed the turgid idiom of a litigating attorney into the cliffhanger prose of a Sixties activist whose decision to jump in took him from the March on Washington to a Mississippi death-row cell and the migrant fields of California.

My dear friend Joan Friedman took the vocation of editorial commitment to unprecedented heights of patience, love, perseverance, and editorial skill. The book quite literally would never have survived to completion without her dogged willingness to hang in there through revision after revision as I struggled to hone the message with which Dorothy Cotton had entrusted to me to a fine edge.

I owe a deep debt of gratitude to Robert Tubach, who faithfully translated *A Hard Road to Justice* into French. Robert had been working on a biography of William Seward, Abraham Lincoln's Secretary of State, but put it on the back burner, telling me: "Your book is actual current history." The work of a translator is often unrequited, but during the period that we worked together Robert, translating chapters as I finished writing and then revising them, became a good and true friend.

Many thanks to Anne Neiryinck for cheerfully undertaking the painstaking project of conforming the French in Robert Tubach's translation to my American English original. Thanks also to Anne as well for important substantive and stylistic suggestions which made the text a better book.

Many thanks to my friend Doug Johnston who read an early draft, making numbers of helpful suggestions that helped shape later versions.

Warm thanks are owed to Margaret R. Dakin of Amherst College's Archives and Special Collections for digging through the stacks of Amherst College's Robert Frost Library and the Jerry Cohen Papers to locate original archival records of the secret agreements and epic legislative struggle that led to passage of the California Agricultural Labor Relations Act of 1975, described by many commentators as the most progressive labor law ever written in America.

Gratitude is owed also to Peter Burford, publisher of Burford Books, without whose friendship, expertise, encouragement, insights, suggestions, and general assistance the published version of this book might never have seen the light of day.

Preface

I LONG resisted my dear friend Dorothy Cotton's repeated urgings that I write up an account of my life-long involvement in the Civil Rights movement. We had often shared stories of our lives in the movement, she as the daughter of an impoverished tobacco worker raised in the segregated South who had risen to become Director of Education, and the highest-ranking woman, in Martin Luther King, Jr.'s Southern Leadership Conference, and I as a white volunteer who had jumped into the Civil Rights movement as a student in the early 1960s and come out the other side forever changed.

Dorothy knew that I had good stories to tell. We had both been at the March on Washington; she had typed portions of King's "I Have a Dream" speech while I had been one of the 250,000 whose hearts had risen and fallen to the cadences of those immortal words. I had sat in to desegregate segregated facilities. I had lived and worked with migrant labor leader Cesar Chavez, drafting the California Labor Relations Act of 1975, a charter of liberties to provide living wages and human working conditions to the migrant workers who fill our supermarket shelves with a cornucopia of plenty. I had litigated for workplace justice against some of the largest corporations in America. And on the 100th anniversary of the Battle of Gettysburg, I had found myself in a Baltimore jail. My next stop would be on death row in Greenwood, Mississippi.

Good as these stories might be, though, I could never bring myself to believe, as Dorothy did, that they would encourage others to jump in as we had done. Mine had been but one voice among many in an entire generation of young Americans who had put their lives on the line in the fight for justice. Why did my story deserve to be told more than any of theirs?

In 2010, though, Dorothy Cotton was awarded the prestigious National Freedom Award, whose previous recipients had included the Dalai Lama, Desmond Tutu, and Nelson Mandela. She was allowed to name one official escort, and she chose me.

Not long after we returned from the award ceremony my wife Annie and I were chatting with Dorothy in her kitchen.

"I know you've told me before," Dorothy said, "but please remind me: just how did you become involved in the Civil Rights movement?"

Dorothy had never quite gotten over the fact that someone like me, Texas born and a self-identified Southerner, would throw in his lot with people who were taking to the streets and being jailed, and even killed, to enjoy rights I had always taken for granted. And so I told her the story once again.

Dorothy had tears in her eyes by the time I finished.

"You've got to tell that story, Tony," she said. "Movements aren't just made up of great leaders. They're made up of ordinary people who decide to jump in and take action for social change. The leaders follow."

Why did so many young people of our generation, of every race, color, religion, background, and gender, decide to jump in and breathe new life into American democracy? A moment in time came for each one of us when we realized we could no longer live with the silence, indifference, and collusion of our forbears in the injustices, crimes, and cruelty that scar all too much of American history. We had no choice. We had to jump in.

What goes around comes around. Once again we as a people find ourselves with our backs against the wall. Mega-predators ensconced in the great centers of power and influence—Washington, Moscow, and Beijing high on the list—ravage natural and human environments in their global quest for wealth, power, and influence. We the People, joining hands together nationally and transnationally across divisions of age, race, religion, ethnicity, gender, political identification, and social and economic status, have no choice. We too have to jump in if we are to redeem the promise of America.

PART 1

JUMPING IN

CHAPTER 1

Yale

I MAY not have been the least likely member of Yale's class of 1963 to plunge into a life of activism, but I was certainly a strong contender. I was a Texan by birth who only a few months prior had embarked on a bicycle trip through Virginia's Civil War battlefields, paying homage at the sites of Robert E. Lee's greatest victories. I perceived labor unions as conspiracies against the free-enterprise system and crossed picket lines of struck employers on principle. The idea of voting for or allying with the Democratic Party was anathema to me.

It was my assumption that I would find kindred spirits at a place like Yale. Happily dropping off my bags at Vanderbilt Hall, I set out to tour the fabled surroundings. Not far from my own new digs stood another building, Connecticut Hall, the oldest edifice on campus. Guarding its entrance stood a statue of Nathan Hale. The only volunteer to step forward when George Washington asked for a spy to report on British military movements, Hale had studied at Yale. He was eventually captured and executed, but not before issuing the defiant last words carved into the base of the memorial:

"I only regret that I have but one life to give for my country."

Something about those words struck me, something that I could not easily put into words. I stood there, deeply moved, staring into Hale's young eyes, his hands bound behind his back.

Only a few blocks north was St. Thomas More Chapel, a gallant building crowned with an elegant white steeple. A devout Catholic, I looked forward to attending services and making friends inside this holy house—and I did. A sophomore by the name of Steve Clark glimpsed my wide-eyed wonder (and insecurity) and took me under his wing. I met a coterie of other God-fearing Yalies, and my destiny seemed pleasantly assured. But life has a mind of its own.

• • •

Less than two weeks later, wending my way from Vanderbilt to Yale Station to pick up my mail, I was stunned to see what lay inside. There, on top of some bills and a letter from my beloved French "Grandpère" (Grandfather), Henri Dior, sat a newssheet entitled *The Catholic Worker.*

"This must be a mistake," I said to myself. Glancing more closely at it, I saw that it was, in fact, addressed to me. Steve Clark, it appeared, had subscribed me to the rag as a gentle nudge to reconsider my "simplistic" worldview. The lead story featured a foreman in a Chicago meatpacking plant by the name of Stanley Vishnewski, who had begun to protest the plant's sweatshop conditions.

"If Vishnewski doesn't like the place," I immediately reasoned, "let him find another job."

Back at Vanderbilt I found my roommate Mike Henderson.

"Look at this subversive crap!" I pushed the paper in his face. "How can the U.S. Mail deliver this kind of drivel?"

"Tony . . ." Mike responded empathetically. "This is America. We have something called The Bill of Rights and Freedom of the Press? Have you ever heard of those things?"

I was shocked. I knew my family was conservative, but I had no idea that there were people, and entire newspapers, espousing such radical points of view. A month later, The Catholic Worker again appeared in my cubby, and this time the lead article finished what it started:

VISHNEWSKI FIRED

"Good," I said to myself. "He got what he had coming." Yet I didn't throw the paper in the trash. The logo at the top of the tabloid depicted a grainy Jesus Christ, his arms around two workers, one white, the other one black. For some reason, I found the image strangely comforting.

Also featured on the front page was a powerful black and white woodcut by artist Fritz Eichenberg, illustrating the prophet Isaiah's

"Peaceable Kingdom," showing a lion and a lamb lying tranquilly together.

The picture's impact on me led me to search the remaining pages of *The Worker* for other pieces by Eichenberg. He was, I would learn later, a Holocaust survivor, a Jew, and a Quaker who, as an outspoken critic of Nazism, had fled Germany in 1933 when Hitler rose to power. His artwork, drawing on Jewish prophetic sources, the teachings of Jesus in the Sermon on the Mount, and the literary works of such authors as Tolstoy, Dostoyevsky, and Edgar Allen Poe, pulsates with his commitments to social justice and nonviolence and with his deeply spiritual nature expressed in vividly contrasting themes of light and dark.

From that day forward, when the paper arrived at Yale Station, I eagerly turned its pages in search of Eichenberg's works. Among the most powerful of these was an image of homeless men and women standing in a Depression-era soup line, Jesus standing quietly interposed in the midst of them.

"If Jesus were alive today," the thought struck me, "this is probably where he would be."

My affair with Eichenberg led to another clandestine discovery: a column entitled "On Pilgrimage," penned by the magazine's editor, Dorothy Day. Day had worked for something called the IWW (Industrial Workers of the World) during the 1920s. When she became pregnant in the 1930s, she had an epiphany that her child should be raised in a religious context. She converted to Catholicism, founded *The Catholic Worker*, and began publishing it as a voice for the disenfranchised, the homeless, and the unemployed. Dorothy Day had a compelling voice, and I became a begrudging reader.

• • •

On New Year's Day 1960, a college student at NC State University named Joseph McNeil was denied service at a Greyhound Bus Station lunch counter in Greensboro, North Carolina because he was black. McNeil had already bonded with three other freshmen at the same university: Franklin McCain, Ezell Blair, Jr., and David Richmond, and the four young men hatched a plan. On February 1 they sat in at the Woolworth's lunch counter in Greensboro and, when refused service, remained seated until closing time. When they returned the next day, twenty-one young men and four women had joined them. News of the "Greensboro Four" spread like wildfire; like millions of other Americans, I was soon watching the faces of the Four, then dozens, then hundreds and thousands of other courageous young people sitting in, only to be hauled away in police cars and immortalized nightly on the evening news.

By the end of March, sit-ins had spread to 55 cities in 13 states. On July 26, 1960, not quite six months after the Greensboro Four took their seats, Woolworth's desegregated its lunch facilities nationwide.

* * *

One warm Sunday in May 1963, a month before graduating from college, I bought a cup of coffee and a copy of *The New York Times* and sat down under a tall, leafy tree on Yale's Old Campus. It had been cold and rainy for a couple of weeks, but with the sun breaking through the clouds and a warm breeze blowing, it was time to take advantage of the good weather.

Settling under the shade of the tree not far from the statue of Nathan Hale, I opened up the *Times*. My eyes immediately fell on banner headlines about a Civil Rights march in Birmingham, Alabama. On the front page were photographs of black people forced down the street with fire hoses, and of a black man whose pants were half ripped off by a police dog. The policeman holding the dog's leash had let it out just far enough for the dog's fangs to rip the man's clothing off his back.

A voice shouted inside my head: "Somebody's gotta do something about this!" I didn't want to be that somebody. I was a senior at one of America's most prestigious institutes of higher learning and planned to continue on that path by attending law school in the fall. I was happy with my life just as it was, thank you very much. But that train of thought didn't last very long. The voice in my head was not only loud; it was undeniable. By the force of the inner logic that had always guided my life, I knew in my heart of hearts that I, myself, was "somebody," and thus, I had no choice.

On the spot, I decided to put off my plans for going to law school. Yes, I would join these people—whoever they were—out on the front lines who were risking life and limb to enjoy the simple things that I had taken for granted my entire life. I would become part of their movement.

CHAPTER 2

Somebody

I COULD never have gone through with my decision to become a part of something bigger than myself (even though I didn't know what that something was yet) without support. Fired up by my decision, I went to Father Neville Brazier, an English priest serving as Yale's assistant pastor. At 6' 7", Father Brazier was conspicuously tall; he was physically awkward and shy, and getting to know him personally was not easy. Once I did, though, I discovered a warm heart that cared deeply about the boys in his charge.

We became close during my sophomore year when my friend and classmate Corky Yarzab jumped to his death from a fifth-story window of the Sterling Memorial Library. A few days before the tragedy, upon returning from a movie we saw together, Corky had looked at me. "Tony, could you come on up to my room? I need to talk."

"I would but I've got papers due Monday, Corky. Can it wait?"

"Yeah, sure. No problem."

Apparently there was a problem, and when I heard that Corky had died, I knew that I had completely misread the urgency in his voice that night. It broke my heart, and I was crippled not only by grief but also by a chilling regret and massive guilt. I went to mass and confession that evening, and the priest in the confessional was Neville Brazier.

"You knew the boy who jumped to his death?" he asked. "What a sad and terrible thing. Would you like to meet me for supper after mass? We can talk and get to know each other; I'd like to help you if I can."

Father Brazier was there for me during the trying weeks after Corky's death, and we'd remained close for the rest of my time at Yale. So on that Sunday morning in my senior year I turned to Father Brazier.

When I told him of my decision, however, I was jarred to find that he vehemently opposed it.

"You're young, Tony, so you don't understand to what great lengths your parents have gone to send you here. You could be a success in life," he told me. "You have an obligation to them. God's will is for you to do what your parents have strived for. You must go to law school in the fall!"

Under almost any other circumstances I would have listened to what he said, but what the voice in my head said was even more powerful than this emissary of God. I knew that we had come to a fork in the road, and without Father Brazier's guidance and support, I felt disoriented. Vertigo. I knew I needed some sort of mentor to help me figure out my hastily prepared next steps. To whom could I turn?

William Sloane Coffin, chaplain of Yale University, was nationally renowned for his involvement in what I have come to call justice. He was a spellbinding speaker, and even though he often preached on dark subjects that presented strong moral challenges, he radiated energy, optimism, and hope. His great-grandfather had founded the highly successful W. & J. Sloane Company; his father was president of the Metropolitan Museum of Art and an executive in the family business. Coffin had been a close friend of George H. W. Bush since boyhood, and it was through Bush's influence that Coffin had been inducted into Yale's prestigious senior society, Skull and Bones.

I knocked timidly on the large and imposing door to Coffin's office. A voice from inside boomed, "Come in."

When I walked through Coffin's door, the phone was at his ear. He was trying to win an audience with one of Yale's heavy hitters, Dean Smith.

"What do you mean Dean Smith isn't in his office?" Coffin asked the dean's long-suffering secretary. "Where is he then? And just what is he doing?"

The poor woman on the other end of the line wasn't prepared for formal questioning, nor had she anticipated the good-humored insistence with which Coffin pressed those questions. When she couldn't come up with a plausible excuse, Coffin let her squirm, but only for a minute.

"You were just kidding when you told me Dean Smith wasn't in, right?" he teased. "The truth is, he's in his office, isn't he?" His voice was friendly, jovial, and amused. "I'll tell you what. Just tell Dean Smith the jig is up and that I know he's in there. Tell him that you just don't know how to put me off, and so he'll have to handle the crazy preacher himself."

The secretary was toast, and she knew it. She put the call through.

When he had finished talking with Dean Smith, Coffin turned his full attention to me, and I told him about my recent decision and Father Brazier's response.

"Father Brazier was pretty categorical," I confessed to him. "Other than being pretty sure God isn't telling me I have to go to law school, I'm not sure what to do. I want to work on something important, maybe get involved with Martin Luther King and the Southern Christian Leadership Conference. But I don't know how to get in touch with them, or whether they'd want me. I'd hoped that Father Brazier could point me in the right direction...I just don't know."

Coffin got up from behind his desk and paced beneath the cross that adorned his wall, a cross far more "stripped down" and humble than the ornate version on Father Brazier's wall.

"You see, God isn't something outside yourself, Tony," he told me. "It isn't somebody else telling you what you should be doing. When you're called to do something and you know you have to do it, that's what God and religion are all about. It takes courage to do what you're doing. And I know in my heart of hearts that you'll look back on this decision someday and you'll know in that place deep within that you did the right thing."

It was no wonder that Coffin's speeches to groups and churches were the stuff of legend; chills ran up and down my pencil-thin body. But I was crestfallen when he informed me that King and the Southern Christian Leadership Conference were flooded with applications from Northern volunteers like myself and couldn't accommodate all of them.

"Don't fret, though. There's plenty of work to be done here at home." I hadn't thought of that. "There's a place for you in the social justice movement, Tony. I can feel it. Let me make a few calls, and I'll help you find something that works. I'm here for you, Tony, and I'll be here for you when you need me again."

• • •

I don't know what I had done to earn such loyalty and commitment, but whatever it was I was grateful for it. And just as "right" as William Coffin had been, Father Brazier had been equally spot-on. When my parents learned of my decision, they wrote to say they were cutting me off financially until I came to my senses. I was not to turn to them for help, they graciously added. They eschewed my Yale graduation and did not send any presents or checks. Even worse, they wrote to my grandfathers, uncles, and aunts, imploring them to contact me with admonitions to change the disastrous course I was taking. And all of them did.

Except one. My beloved French grandfather, Henri Dior, did not join the crowd. Instead, two or three months later, on my 22nd birthday, he sent me a book with the following inscription:

Pensees affectueuses pour l'anniversaire de son très cher Tony au grand coeur. –Henri Dior.

Affectionate remembrances on the birthday of his very dear Tony with the big heart. –Henri Dior.

To this day, I treasure that inscription like a child, but at the time—with no one from my family coming to graduation—I took refuge in conveniently concluding that college graduations were nonsense, and I decided to skip it too. I was still in New Haven as the graduation parade approached Old Campus. From the window in my room, not far from where I secretly read The Catholic Worker and where Corky Yarzab jumped to his death, I could hear the band playing a stirring rendition of the Yale song, "Bright College Years," and I strutted into the street to mock the stupidity of it all. Yale's gleaming stalwarts strode into sight in their academic uniforms, a florid member of the faculty carrying the Yale University Mace, a ceremonial silver club modeled after the weapon of medieval knights. I laughed out loud, but not for long.

When the first of my actual classmates came into sight down Elm Street, I experienced a sudden and brutal change of heart. I desperately wanted to be with them, sharing the last hours of what had been a transformative four years. I ran down the street like a schoolboy, and to my joy and relief, the rental outlet for caps and gowns had yet to lock its doors. Slapping money on the counter, I jumped into my costume and raced into the parade. Finding my roommate Mike Henderson, I fell into step with him.

I was part of the Class of 1963 after all, and they would forever be a part of me.

CHAPTER 3

Gwynn Oak

TRUE to his word, Bill Coffin landed me a job as director of what was known as The Philadelphia Tutorial Project, an initiative in which student volunteers tutored inner city kids.

I packed my bags and left for Philly on a secondhand motorcycle. Three other members of "the justice department" and a couple of requisite hangers-on already occupied the apartment I had found. Ours was the top floor of a three-story walk-up at the inaptly named 1428 Diamond Street, in the heart of the North Philly ghetto. The summer sun, beating hard on that roof, broiled us from the inside. On weekdays we could escape the heat temporarily, but I was learning the same lesson yet again: that the things I took for granted growing up were not inalienable rights for every man, woman, and child. For the first time in my life I was truly poor, living like the tens of thousands of other inner city Americans in a major city with no escape from the elements, nowhere to run and hide. It was a side of American life I had never experienced before and never considered.

Occasionally, I escaped the heat by hanging out on the front stoop of 1428, and I attracted neighborhood kids by making origami from discarded paper. My specialties included a host of airplane designs, two types of water bombs, a two-seated Venetian gondola, a sailboat, a box, and a peace dove whose wings flapped when you pulled the tail.

I loved hanging out with those kids, who were mostly eight to ten years old, street smart, intelligent, lively, and fun. They delighted in the paper presents I made for them, coming back with request upon request.

When I got to know people in suburban Philadelphia and compared their eight- to ten-year-old children with those living on my block, the deck seemed stacked on the side of my streetwise, mature, self-reliant, inner city friends.

But when those same kids reached their early- and mid-teens, the picture morphed. The inescapability of their environment, the poverty, the crime, and the destitution rife in their neighborhoods ate away at their souls. The dawning realization that the American dream they saw on TV lay beyond their reach dimmed the light in their eyes.

• • •

Not long after I had become the Origami Master of West Diamond Street, word spread that a major event would be taking place on July 4 at an amusement park outside of Baltimore. I had no intention of attending until one of my fellow workers, Sharon Thornton, set me straight. "Tony, you're the director of an important agency in Philadelphia, and this is an important event. People need to know where you stand. Are you going to take part in the sit-in movement, or are you going to sit in the stands?"

I had only been director of the Philadelphia Project for a month! Coming from a politically and socially conservative background, I felt like a fraud, groping and looking for guidance every day, despite the fact that I was ostensibly in charge. Maybe this is why Sharon's comment struck a chord. The movement was growing with people from all walks of life, and they were not just sitting in, but taking to the streets and facing arrest and jail every day.

I signed on the dotted line, and on July 4, 1963, 300 of us showed up at a staging area in a Methodist church in Baltimore, arriving in buses and cars from up and down the East Coast. To my surprise, a myriad of television cameras and film crews awaited us as we filled the hallowed hall. Some were the press. Others, grimmer in demeanor, were an array of law enforcement luminaries: FBI, CIA, and local cops.

The target of the day's "event" was an amusement park named Gwynn Oak, which had opened in 1893 and been fiercely segregated since the day its shiny turnstiles were first installed. By the late 1950s and early 1960s, however, the park's exclusion of black boys and girls had become a point of contention. Gwynn Oak had been picketed before but still held fast to its antiquated policies. Now, major figures in the Civil Rights movement had zeroed in on the park, intent on breaking down its barriers once and for all. Maryland restaurants, swimming pools, movie theaters, and other public facilities also kept blacks out. If Gwynn Oak could be made an example, other Maryland doors might open too.

The men and women who demonstrated that day included prominent representatives of all the leading religious denominations. Bill Coffin from Yale was there, along with Eugene Carson Blake, Stated Clerk of the United Presbyterian Church; Monsignor Austin L. Healy of the Archdiocese of Baltimore; Rabbi Morris Lieberman of the Baltimore Hebrew Congregation; and an assortment of lesser-known representatives from the National Council of Churches.

Microphones and cameras rolled as one religious leader after another read his firebrand statements to the press. I've never had much tolerance for speeches, so I stood at the back of the hall until the last statement had been read; then it was time to board the buses. Paradoxically, since I stood as close to the back door as I could during the proceedings, I was among the very first to board, and the bus I boarded was among the first to leave for the demonstration site.

Stepping off that Greyhound at Gwynn Oak, we found a crowd of angry hecklers waiting for us. Fearing the number and mood of the hecklers (we were a minority, you have to remember), the police had cordoned them off with ropes in a feeble effort to keep us safe. Once the battle lines had been drawn and the numbers swelled to the thousands, Baltimore County Police Chief Robert Lally took to the megaphone and advised the assembled do-gooders that we were trespassing on private property and were to disperse "at once" under threat of arrest and/or prison.

The fact that I had chosen to stand at the back of the church continued to produce surprising results. As one of the first eight faces to show up, I was charged with having conspired to organize the Gwynn Oak protest, as well as with the even greater charge of "assault on the 'Southern Way of Life.'" I was shoved into a windowless paddy wagon, the door was slammed and locked behind us, and the armored car peeled away, sirens blaring.

It took forty long hours to clear up the confusion, during which I was locked in a six-man cell with forty other demonstrators, including Bill Coffin. But the protest at Gwynn Oak was not over yet. With the buses that had brought us to Baltimore long gone, I hitched a ride back to Philly with a few other jailbirds. It was late in the day by the time we got out, and knowing that federal law had recently desegregated U.S. Highway 40, we stopped in a roadside restaurant for supper.

The owner of the restaurant was not exactly happy to see our mixed-race crew.

"We don't serve coloreds here," he said.

"Route 40's been desegregated by federal law," we said. "We have a legal right to eat here."

"You may have a legal right to eat whatever you damn well please," the owner concluded, "but there ain't no one in this restaurant gonna serve it to you."

Having just spent forty hours in prison for trying to integrate a segregated amusement park, we were not about to take our hats in hand and shuffle out the door.

The restaurant happened to be a stopping place for truckers coming up Route 40 from the South. And as we sat there discussing our options, driver after driver swung through the door, sized up the standoff, and lined up along the wall by the front door.

As the situation became increasingly dire, we called the Maryland State Police.

"Route 40 has been desegregated by law," we told the officer in charge. "We have a right to be served here."

"Why y'all makin' trouble?" the officer replied in a thick Southern drawl. "This man," he nodded toward the owner, "is mindin' his own business, and y'all are stirring things up. Take my advice and get the hell outta here while y'all still can."

The atmosphere in the restaurant had become sufficiently charged that we decided this was good advice. Eight to ten truck drivers had lined up by the door, waiting for the minute we set foot into that parking lot.

"These men are looking to kill us," we said to the officer, and I'm not sure we were exaggerating. "Will you give us protection so we can get out of here safely?"

"Well, all right," he said with a distinct lack of enthusiasm. "But be quick about it."

The police held off the truckers just long enough for us to clear the doorway, and then they stepped aside. Like a track team, we ran for our lives (and car) and jumped in, locking the doors.

We were up to 80 mph on Route 40 in no time flat, but the blinding headlights of frothing 18-wheelers soon overtook us. Two of them pulled in front of us, blocking the highway ahead. A third pulled even with our car and began edging us off the road and onto the shoulder. Just as we were about to hit a ditch and flip a 360, we reached an intersection as its green overhead light turned yellow. The prescient driver of our car slammed on the brakes, skidding to a halt in the middle of the intersection and then backing up out of it.

The 18-wheelers, carried by their momentum, flew by and disappeared down the open road. We pulled into a nearby gas station so that, should the truck drivers return to beat us senseless, it would at least take place in the presence of witnesses. Ten or fifteen nervous minutes went by and no one showed up. Relieved, we turned north, heading back toward the Mason-Dixon Line, Pennsylvania, and safety.

It had been a narrow escape but a worthy one. Less than two months later, on August 28, 1963, an eleven-month-old girl named Sharon Langley became the first African American child to ride the park's merry-go-round. The park remained desegregated until it closed in 1973, after a hurricane washed away most of its rides.

Fifty years after the original demonstration, on July 4, 2013, several hundred people gathered at the site of Gwynn Oak, now a public park, to commemorate the events of so long ago. Sharon Langley came from Los Angeles to join the celebration, as did the wooden horse she had ridden in 1963, borrowed from the National Mall in Washington, D.C., where the original Gwynn Oak carousel now stands.

CHAPTER 4

The March on Washington

AFTER the march on Gwynn Oak, I threw myself into the business of the project that had hired me. Serious tensions had built up among the staff, however. About this time, I also discovered that our expenses were outstripping income. The unpleasant task of letting go some of the team fell to me.

It was not something I was well equipped to handle. Feelings ran high and office meetings were more like melees. Personally, I liked the staff, but I had no skill in mediating their differences, which were often heartfelt and passionate. Night after night, I tossed and turned in bed, turning alternatives over in my mind. The chaos among staff members had to be faced first, then the financial issues. Or was it the other way around? In the end, unable to think of anything better, I shouted above the din of one particularly raucous, bitter meeting.

"That's enough!" Since I'm usually pretty soft-spoken, a hush fell over the room.

"Things have gotten out of hand here, and we can't go on this way." I don't think anyone disagreed. "I'm shutting down the office until further notice. I'm going to meet with the Board, and I'll let you know how things shake down."

It was a dramatic move, and it didn't sit well with my staff. After the shutdown ended, few of the people I hoped would return did. Nevertheless, I winnowed the staff down to a crack team of a few good men and women, and I focused on fundraising and running an efficient and effective project. But there was something brewing under the civil surface that few, if any, saw coming.

• • •

A coalition of Civil Rights organizations was planning a march on Washington to take place in late August. It would protest segregationist laws and practices, with a particular emphasis on the South, urging the government to pass legislation eliminating segregation in public places and ensuring the right of black Americans to vote. The march would include such nationally known figures as Martin Luther King, Jr., A. Phillip Randolph, Bayard Rustin, and John Lewis.

At the time, I was active in the Catholic Interracial Council. The president, Miles Mahoney, suggested that the CIC should sponsor a bus to go to Washington, and everyone agreed. Since I was the director of an independent project and did not have to answer to any supervisor, I agreed to put the resources of my organization to work coordinating the transportation. In the end, we filled not one, but two, buses.

Miles also had the idea of inviting priests from the Archdiocese of Philadelphia to ride and march with us, the CIC paying their way. Since he had the best contacts, he placed the call. When his offer reached the desk of Archbishop (later Cardinal) Krol, the archbishop forbade any priest in the archdiocese from participating in the march.

Stunned, we discussed Krol's response and concurred that Miles should call the Chancery back to request that an archdiocesan priest at least say prayers and bless us and our buses before we left for D.C. Archbishop Krol forbade any priest from saying such prayers or offering such blessings.

Thoroughly angered by the archbishop's response, I decided we would have our buses meet in front of the Cathedral Basilica of Saints Peter and Paul anyway, and if no one from the archdiocese would pray for us or bless us, we would do the damn thing ourselves.

And so we did, Miles praying a brief and moving prayer. When Archbishop Krol arrived at the Chancery that morning to find its parking lot filled with March on Washington cars, smoke began to billow from his ears.

• • •

I remember everything from that fateful day. It was a beautiful day in late summer. Our bus pulled into its spot on Constitution Avenue in a long line of monoliths of all stripes and sizes hailing from every nook and cranny of these United States. It was a festive time. We already knew we had come for an important event, and the moment we stepped outside we felt that something truly special was afoot. Photographers and TV cameras were ubiquitous, taking pictures of us, interviewing us, making us all feel suddenly so important.

The most striking aspect of the March was how integrated it was. Even for those of us from the North, where segregation was not enforced by law but often existed in practice, the sheer number of whites and blacks marching, walking, and talking together was unparalleled. For Southerners, regularly beaten up and jailed for crossing the color line, I'm sure the experience was even more profound.

Everyone who was there that day has his or her own unique memories of the March on Washington, and for me it was lying in the grass and eating fried chicken in the shadow of the Lincoln Memorial. Like Nathan Hale's words at Yale, the lines engraved over the head of Daniel Chester French's sculpture of the Great Emancipator are etched into my mind:

> *In this temple*
> *As in the hearts of the people*
> *For whom he saved the union*
> *The memory of Abraham Lincoln*
> *Is enshrined forever.*

As I said before, I have a low tolerance for speeches, political and otherwise. Prior to King's closing remarks, the only part of the dance card that ignited much fire in my heart was the crooning of my two favorite bards, Bob Dylan and Joan Baez.

It was growing late by the time Dr. King rose to speak. And no one, not even his closest advisors—Dorothy Cotton among them—could have been prepared for what was to come.

> "I am happy to join with you today in what will go down in history as the greatest demonstration for freedom in the history of our nation."

We soon realized that we were witnessing not just the greatest demonstration for freedom in the history of our nation, but perhaps the most inspiring articulation of it.

> "Five score years ago, a great American, in whose symbolic shadow we stand today, signed the Emancipation Proclamation. This momentous decree came as a great beacon light of hope to millions of Negro slaves who had been seared in the flames of withering injustice. It came as a joyous daybreak to end the long night of their captivity.
>
> "But one hundred years later, the Negro still is not free. One hundred years later, the life of the Negro is still sadly crippled by the manacles of segregation and the chains of discrimination. One hundred years later, the Negro lives on a lonely island of poverty in the midst of a vast ocean of material prosperity. One hundred years later, the Negro is still languished in the corners of American society and finds himself an exile in his own land. And so we've come here today to dramatize a shameful condition."

I never knew that a quarter million people could be so quiet.

> "And so even though we face the difficulties of today and tomorrow, I still have a dream. It is a dream deeply rooted in the American dream.
>
> "I have a dream that one day this nation will rise up and live out the true meaning of its creed: 'We hold these truths to be self-evident, that all men are created equal.'
>
> "I have a dream that one day on the red hills of Georgia, the sons of former slaves and the sons of former slave owners will be able to sit down together at the table of brotherhood.
>
> "I have a dream that one day even the state of Mississippi, a state sweltering with the heat of injustice, sweltering with the heat of oppression, will be transformed into an oasis of freedom and justice.
>
> "I have a dream that my four little children will one day live in a nation where they will not be judged by the color of their skin but by the content of their character.
>
> "I have a dream today!"

• • •

A great ocean of sound rose up from the grounds of the Lincoln Memorial and along the reflecting pool as King spoke his concluding words, the immense rising of the hearts and minds of a quarter million people joined together as one. Of course, the final words of the speech are the stuff of history books.

> "'FREE AT LAST! FREE AT LAST!
> THANK GOD ALMIGHTY
> WE ARE FREE AT LAST!'"

As soon as we reached home, we turned on our television sets to learn that we had just won the attention and admiration of the entire world. We knew that we had been changed in some fundamental way by what we had experienced in Washington. Deep in our hearts we did believe we would overcome someday. Together we would overcome.

CHAPTER 5

Mississippi Burning

AT their 2012 annual meeting, the Catholic Bishops of the United States unanimously recommended the canonization of Dorothy Day, founder of *The Catholic Worker,* the magazine to which I had become a convert and that I read like a secret agent in my small garret at Yale. During my year at the Tutorial Project, I had been lucky enough to hear her speak in Philadelphia at a small gathering of friends. Her words on war moved everyone there to tears.

> "Once again our country is at war. Over the course of my lifetime, more than 20 million young soldiers and 100 million civilians have died in war. Today, Buddhist monks in Vietnam are setting themselves on fire. They are giving up their lives to awaken our consciousness to the deaths of countless Vietnamese men, women, and children set afire every day by our napalm fire bombs. And once again leaders on every side find reasons for going to war, bringing with it all its terrifying forms of killing and destruction."

I left the meeting with Dorothy Day inspired by her person and fired up by her vision. In the days that followed, as I pondered everything she had said, two ideas became firm resolutions. The first of these was to found a Catholic Worker inspired house in one of the hardest hit and most destitute neighborhoods of the North Philadelphia ghetto.

Through a colorful Irish building inspector named Tom O'Reilly I eventually made contact with an Orthodox Jew named Gormish, who owned a lot of rental properties throughout Philadelphia.

"Catholic Worker?" Gormish asked when I spoke to him. "You're looking to convert the people at 18th and 8th?"

"Absolutely not, Mr. Gormish," I said. "We just want to live in a North Philly neighborhood and get to know the people who live there face to face as friends and neighbors."

"At 18th and 8th?" Gormish wanted to know. "Do you know what you're getting yourself into?"

Mr. Gormish was a schmoozer if ever there was one; we were on the phone for close to half an hour. The clincher came when he discovered that I, like him, had been on my high school wrestling team.

"Sure," he finally said. "I'll let you have the place at 1807 North 8th. I'll charge you $1 per year for rent. Just make sure somebody's in it all the time. Places down there get vandalized in a minute if they're left vacant."

And so an Orthodox Jew became the patron saint of Joseph House, the Catholic Worker inspired experiment in communal living we founded deep in the Philadelphia ghetto. My own personal dream for the house was that it become a center for tutoring and learning for all the children in the neighborhood, and it did indeed become that. Over the ten years that Joseph House operated, thousands of neighborhood kids passed through its doors, eagerly scanning the *National Geographic* magazines and other books we had collected for them, and getting tutored in school subjects that gave them trouble.

Thinking through the implication of Dorothy Day's words also led me to see that I could never again think of killing for my country, with the limited exception of a foreign invader crossing into the borders of my native land, as in 1940 when Germany invaded France. In Vietnam, though, if a commanding officer ordered me to fire on native people under circumstances that I believed were wrong, I would have to refuse his order—an impossible situation.

I couldn't help being aware that in making this decision I was opting out of a war in Vietnam in which friends of mine were risking, and in some cases losing, their lives. When the call to serve in the military came, these friends, and tens of thousands of young people like them, spoke simply of "going into the service," as though serving their country in time of war was the natural obligation of any American of draft-able age.

I decided that I owed these friends of mine nothing less than they were putting on the line—their very lives. I therefore resolved that when the opportunity presented itself I would take leave from my job at the Tutorial Project and spend a year "in the service," joining the fight for justice where the danger was greatest, in the heart of the Old South.

In keeping with this resolution, I vowed to become a pacifist and a conscientious objector, a decision that would have fiery consequences. If my parents had been outraged by my decision to go into the Civil Rights movement, they were incandescent over my decision to become a pacifist. Although they hadn't come to my Yale graduation, and would skip my wedding the following spring, they caught the first plane from France to Philadelphia to pound some sense into my head. It didn't work.

• • •

In the spring of 1964, I took a month's unpaid leave from the Project and headed for Mississippi. I had made few preparations and only one decision: to walk into the local office of the Student Nonviolent Coordinating Committee (SNCC) in whatever town I ended up in and volunteer to do anything that needed to be done.

I found and stayed in a SNCC "Freedom House" in Jackson, Mississippi for a few days, meeting with the local coordinators and volunteers. On my second day in the Union's 20th state, I was given instructions to pick up a lawyer flying in from Michigan and drive him to nearby Hattiesburg. His name was John Conyers. He would eventually serve as the Dean of the House of Representatives and the then longest serving member of Congress at 52 years. Back then, he had a successful Detroit law practice and had flown in to defend one of the SNCC's key workers in Mississippi, a man by the name of Larry Guyot.

After dropping Conyers off at the Hattiesburg courthouse, I parked my car and walked over to the town square. The SNCC had assembled a large crowd including blacks from Hattiesburg, SNCC workers, and white activists from out of state.

Guyot was a well-known and highly visible Civil Rights worker. The SNCC was determined to show how much public attention Guyot, and the movement whose card he carried, truly had in Mississippi. When the trial began we all trooped in, enough warm bodies to fill the room.

I walked in and sat with the Hattiesburg contingent. We took our seats, and the prosecutor rose to address the judge.

"Your Honor," he said, "it seems we have a number of interlopers here from out of state who are not familiar with the Southern way of life and the customs of the state of Mississippi. I am hereby making a motion before this court that these people be ordered to vacate their seats and sit, as is customary here in Hattiesburg, white on the right side of the central aisle, niggroes on the left."

"So ordered," said the judge without a second thought. "All white people sitting on the left side of the aisle are to rise and move to the right. All Negroes on the right side are to sit on the left." In saying this, she hit the bench with her gavel.

Reluctantly, everyone in the courtroom who was on the "wrong side" of the aisle got up. I instantly turned to the chair of the local SNCC who was directly behind me and asked what I should do.

"I'm in the middle of organizing a voter registration drive," he said, "and can't afford to be arrested. But it's up to you to follow your conscience."

I'm sure they didn't like it. Many of the whites in that room were with "us," but everyone in the "colored" section obeyed the judge's order and moved. Rather than relocating to the "white" side of the courtroom, they stood in a line against the back wall. I alone was left sitting where I'd been.

I had no idea what to do. I knew I didn't want to obey. At the same time, I didn't want to be the only person arrested. Looking down the row in which I was sitting, there were six people between the aisle and me. If I got up and moved I would have to step over each of them on my way. And due to the narrowness of the row I would have to physically push past each one of them. In my mind, I felt that would be a subtle but indelible message, something in the order of, "Do you know what you are, boy? You're a nigger."

I couldn't bring myself to do it. I just sat there like a statue, paralyzed and unsure of what would happen next.

"Young man, stand up," the judge demanded.

"I've ordered you to leave your seat. Are you going to obey my order or not?"

"Since your order is based on racial segregation," I said, standing my ground, "I cannot in good conscience obey it."

"Very well then," the judge said. "Clear the courtroom."

* * *

Everyone, myself included, got up and shuffled out. When the court reconvened, black and white did not sit together. Only the parties to the litigation and their lawyers were allowed back inside, the visitor section of the courtroom remaining empty. John Conyers told us that he would use the entire incident on appeal to invalidate any conviction at trial.

As we gathered in the hallway, many of the people who had been inside crowded around me, thanking me warmly and shaking my hand. It was a deeply rewarding moment. Hundreds of courageous young people, men and women, black and white, sharecroppers and Ivy Leaguers would repeat scenes like this in every corner of Mississippi throughout the spring and summer of 1964. By the time it was over, Mississippi Freedom Summer would change the face of America.

CHAPTER 6

Death Row

MY next SNCC assignment was in Greenwood, Mississippi where, I would soon learn, the Old South was alive and well. In 1954 Emmett Till, a young black man from Chicago visiting relatives, had been castrated and then lynched a few miles outside of town. Till had been unguarded enough to look up at a passing young white woman, a mistake that cost him his life. Byron De La Beckwith, the man who murdered Medgar Evers, called Greenwood home. And that small, infamous town also boasted the national headquarters of the feared White Citizens Council.

Those of us who had volunteered for the front lines slept in a SNCC Freedom House, a heavily guarded "safe house" in a predominantly black neighborhood. The hours I slept behind its locked doors were the few each day that I was not intensely afraid. It was so strange being white and tightening up with fear every time I saw a *white* face approaching me, and feeling great relief when the face was black.

One face that brought relief was that of "Blood," a black restaurant owner and the only one in Greenwood with enough courage to serve both races. We "Freedom Riders" (as we were commonly called) all ate at Blood's Café, as did many of the local blacks. People like me and like Dick Frey, the white coordinator of the SNCC office, couldn't really eat anywhere else. The white establishments weren't safe, and the black restaurants couldn't run the risk of having us. Rumors abounded that Blood's landlady, a well-to-do white woman, was going to shut the place down. Blood wasn't optimistic about his chances.

One night, when several of us were having supper, a large, late-model automobile pulled up in front of the café, and three people got out. One was a well-dressed woman of about forty-five; the others were a boy of about eighteen and a girl of about sixteen. All three were white. They entered the restaurant together, the two children following their mother to the counter. She was Blood's landlady, and they spoke for about five minutes.

After the family left, we crowded around Blood, wanting to know what was up.

"I'm sure you've heard rumors that I'm going to shut your place down," the woman had told Blood. "In fact, people have urged me to do it. But I just want you to know that you have nothing to worry about; I'm going to keep your place open, and I came down here so I could tell you myself."

* * *

As we made our rounds, encouraging people to register to vote, a good many said they would be there "come hell or high water." Others were more tepid. And the majority, I think, just "yassuh'd" us as we asked or cajoled them to show up, wanting nothing more than for us to move on, so as not to be seen in front of their doors. Contingents of reporters and Northern TV networks were expected in Greenwood on the first day of the drive.

The unasked question that lay behind this reticence was, "Who's gonna be around to pick up the pieces when the White Citizens Council strikes back?" They knew the ruthless and brutal ways of the White Citizens Council—lynch first, ask questions later. And they also knew that the out-of-towners like myself wouldn't be around after the drive was over, when things got dark. Impoverished sharecroppers, they were already destitute; they were already beaten down. I was torn, eager to have the drive succeed but troubled by the consequences that would befall these people once I, and others like me, returned to the safety of our homes in the North.

Since I had a car, when voter registration day arrived, I was assigned to personally drive carloads of people from the black sections of town through the hazards of white neighborhoods and safely to the Leflore County Court House. An elderly woman was among the first to use my "Voter Uber."

"I've waited 72 years to see this day," she proclaimed. "An' I'm goin' register to vote if I have to crawl on my hands and knees."

I drove meticulously within the speed limit but was still ticketed twice for speeding by the Greenwood police.

At the courthouse, the "colored" waiting room could accommodate some ten to fifteen people. The rest of them, many elderly, queued up in the broiling heat on the sidewalk outside. Each applicant waited an hour or more for the courthouse staff to administer the voter registration test, a test which a number of them failed. This was puzzling since white folks uniformly passed and were commonly registered in a matter of minutes.

The courthouse bathrooms were closed to blacks; there were no facilities open to them within miles of the downtown. Those who could no longer wait to relieve themselves lost their place in line.

* * *

The leaders of Greenwood's White Citizens Council may have been hateful, but they weren't dumb, for at the start of the voter registration drive, Greenwood's white leadership stood by on the sidelines, making little noise and no arrests. The relative quiet slowly thinned out what had been a huge press contingent looking for fireworks, or at least a rocket. Eventually, they got tired of waiting, folded up their cameras and hopes, and blew out of town in search of more newsworthy news.

We kept on doggedly, managing to register a few voters each day. Finally, one morning, when our once gallant voter registration team—Dick Frey, myself, and twelve local blacks—were all arrested, we were charged with the mortal offense of "obstructing the sidewalk."

Dick Frey was a Quaker, a gentle, unassuming, soft-spoken young man. He had worked at the SNCC office in Greenwood for two years, living in a black neighborhood while quietly working for nonviolent change. When we were first hauled in, Dick and I shared a two-man cell in the Greenwood City Jail, whose only other prisoner was a well-known town drunk. Our jailer kept Dick and me up all night, making sure the light in our cellblock burned and rousing us any time we drifted into much-needed sleep.

Not long after daybreak the prison guards pulled Dick and me out of our cell and hauled us over to the segregated county jail where the first floor was reserved for white prisoners, the second for blacks. Dick and I fell into an exhausted sleep in a cellblock already crowded with fifteen other inmates.

Half an hour later, I awoke with a jolt of terror. In my sleep I had heard the voices of the white prisoners discussing what they intended to do with us. I hadn't picked up any of the details, but the terror clutching at my gut told me that, whatever it was, it was grim.

"If they're planning to kill us," I thought, "they might as well get a good look at whom they'll be killing while they make up their minds."

I jumped up off my cot, strode to the iron table in the middle of the cellblock around which the other prisoners sat, and began pacing the floor in front of them, making it impossible for them to continue plotting Dick's and my fate behind our backs. After about five minutes, one of them could stand it no longer.

"Miss your nigger friends?" he taunted.

By a stroke of good fortune, the seat next to him was vacant. I immediately sat down next to him, and looked him square in the eye.

"My name's Tony," I said. "I was born in San Antonio, and partly raised on a farm in Kansas. I live in Philadelphia now. Ever been to any of those places?"

Otis Nestor, the man I was talking to, did a double take, hesitating no more than a moment before replying.

"Yeah," he said. "I'm an over-the-road truck driver. I've been to all those places." Picking up on this opening, I drew him out, asking him questions about his adventures on the road. He'd been to Camden, New Jersey, just across the river from Philly, and we traded notes on the Northeast. As we kicked questions of geography around, things in the cellblock began to warm appreciably.

Other prisoners now joined in, and I soon learned that the county jail was winter quarters for the Leflore County Prison system. Around mid-April, in about two week's time, all prisoners on both floors would be transferred to the county prison farm. Although some of the prisoners were serving long-term sentences, most were petty criminals, the kind who ended up in jail for botched burglaries or attempted car thefts that failed when the cars ran out of gas.

With the ice broken, I found a measure of kinship with some of these men, and even willingness in a few of them to befriend us, now that we had acquired a human face. One of them even went so far as to say that Dick and I had to be all right since the same rotten-hearted authorities that imprisoned them had imprisoned us as well. It was a line of logic you wouldn't want to push too far, but it was far better than any of the alternatives.

After about fifteen minutes, though, Otis Nestor jumped up as though stung by a wasp.

"You don't realize just how lucky you are!" he shouted angrily. Otis had awoken suddenly to the fact that I had slipped beneath his guard.

"Listen to your nigger friends!" he shouted. "They're fucking. Listen. You can hear them. They're animals. They fuck all the time.

"You just don't got any idea how lucky you are!" Nestor shouted again. "The food they give us in this shit-hole ain't fit for a dog. We only survive because of the food our families bring us come visiting day. Yesterday was that day, but the warden cancelled visiting hours 'cause of all the shit you Freedom Riders are kicking. It's 'cause of you we'll be eating crap for another week."

I paused and listened. I did this partly because I wanted to hear whatever it was that Otis was hearing, or thought he was hearing, upstairs. I also did this so as not to anger him any further. The concrete floors/ceilings separating the whites on the first floor from the blacks on the second were nearly a foot thick; it was hard to fathom how anything short of an explosion could be heard through that concrete. And indeed I heard nothing, either then or later.

"The warden told us you guys would be landing here this morning," he continued, "and that we could have a free hand with you, anything at all, and he'd protect us from the law. Just so you'll understand what I'm talking about, I'm in here for murder." Otis paused for a moment to let it all sink in, and then pointed to another prisoner on the far side of the table.

"You owe your life to that man over there," Otis decreed.

I looked over at our "savior." His huge, black, half-crazed eyes beamed with wildly spinning fury, and so I dubbed him "Windmill Eyes." Nothing in his demeanor suggested the slightest kindness or mercy. But though he may have been mad, he was smarter by half than the other prisoners and enjoyed a measure of authority over them.

"That mother-fucking warden isn't going to cover our asses if we do in these mother-fucking pinko commie Freedom Riders," Windmill Eyes had told the other men while Dick and I were lost in exhausted sleep. "We're the ones who are going to take it in the ass if these fuckers get carried outta here feet first. We could even get the electric chair down in Parchman. Let's beat the shit out of these guys and let it go at that."

To this penetrating line of reasoning Windmill Eyes had added another much more imaginative clause.

"Remember, these Yankees are highly-trained Communist agents. Chances are, they're trained to kill. Their hands are probably lethal weapons. Whoever goes into their cell first better watch it; he's the one who just might end up dead."

Windmill Eyes' insightful thinking had slowed hotheads like Otis Nestor down long enough to talk over their options. (Otis, I learned later, was in jail for having killed a man in a barroom brawl.) It was their agitated discussion that had woken me from my exhausted sleep, giving me time to leap up and touch the better side of Otis's impulsive nature.

• • •

The rest of that day passed peacefully enough, and we all returned to our individual cells. Sometime later, another prisoner, whom I nicknamed "The Panther" because of his long, lithe strides, came around to speak to Dick and me.

"I don't care how much you're getting paid to do what you're doing," he told us. "It isn't worth it. I myself know people on the outside who are planning to kill you as soon as you get out of here. Take my word for it. When you get out of here, get the hell out of Mississippi."

Late in the afternoon, another prisoner came over to our cell.

"I'm the 'trustee' on the Leflore County Prison Farm," he said menacingly. He was about fifty years old, his skin tanned and dried to the hard consistency of old shoe leather.

"Just so you know, in a couple of weeks we're all goin' to the Farm for the summer, and I'm the prisoner in charge of the other prisoners. D'ya know what the strap is?"

I said I didn't.

"It's a leather strap with iron studs in it; we use it on the Farm to keep mother-fuckers like you in line. I'm makin' you a promise, and I'm gonna keep it. As soon as I get you down on the Farm, I'm gonna strip you naked and whip your naked ass with the strap until your blood and your shit flow together."

Since it was this individual's abundantly trustworthy quality that had earned him his position of authority on the prison farm, I dubbed him "The Trustworthy Man."

• • •

Shortly after first light the following morning, Windmill Eyes rose from his iron cot and began pacing the floor, ranting and raving. The object of his fury was again Dick and me.

"These fucking commie pinko nigger-loving Freedom Riders!" he raged. "They're in with the niggers who are running the country from Washington. What chance does a white man have in a country like this, what with niggers and their nigger-loving friends running everything? What's left for the white man? Hind tit, that's what. Hind tit."

"Don't talk to these men!" he warned the others. "They've been to college. They're smarter than any of us, even me."

It was a fascinating, though terrifying, performance. Windmill Eyes possessed the oratorical skill of a born-again preacher come over from the dark side. He had a shrewd perception of the other prisoners' emotional constitutions, knowing how to work them to higher and higher pitches of emotional arousal. His rage skillfully stoked the deepest levels of prejudice, anger, and hatred buried in our cellmates' souls. All were now carried along like storm-driven leaves blown by the swirling energies of Windmill Eyes' overheated mind.

Just when it seemed that our fate was sealed, the door of our cellblock swung open and in strode "the Angel of the Lord." This angel was a Protestant clergyman in the black garb and white collar of his trade. He was a big man, around 240 pounds. He had a large shock of red hair and spoke with a thick Dutch accent.

With the breezy manner of a North Sea wind, he made his way over to Dick's and my cell, sat down next to us, and asked us how we were getting on.

"We're okay," we said shakily.

"Anyting you want I do for you?" he asked.

"Yes!" Dick rasped. "Get us out of here. These men are going to kill us."

"Yah. I will do dat," said the clergyman unhesitatingly, as though telling Southern prison wardens how to run their establishments was the leading qualification on his résumé.

"Anyting else you want I should do?" he asked again. Other than saving our lives, Dick and I couldn't think of very much else.

• • •

Five minutes later, our cell door swung open and Dick and I were taken out—to freedom, I naïvely assumed. The warden, though, had other plans. Instead, we were taken upstairs to the private section of the colored floor, and when the door to our new accommodations closed behind us, we found ourselves in an old execution cell of the Leflore County Prison. The ring in the ceiling through which the noose had passed was still in place, and I spent long hours staring at it, thinking about the men who had lain on the same bunk on which I was now lying, readying themselves for death.

Next to our cell was a second holding tank for condemned men, the two cells together forming a miniature death row. The day after Dick and I arrived, one of the prisoners from the black lock-up, who was slated for execution at Parchman State Prison, was transferred to this adjoining cell and thus became our neighbor. He had broken down under the strain and stared at us with blank, uncomprehending eyes.

Finally, the following morning, the warden of Leflore County Prison, accompanied by another white prison official, came to pay us a call. There, in earshot of our neighbor and us, the warden described the pleasure he was going to take in watching that neighbor die the following day. He savored the preview, lingering over its details despite the moans and groans of the wretch sprawled out on the floor of the adjoining cell.

The intent behind the warden's carefully staged performance was not lost on either Dick or me. The pleasure the warden expected to derive from watching our neighbor die paled beside the pleasure he would get from watching our demise. If Dick's and my release from Leflore could be delayed for a couple of weeks, we would be transferred to the county prison farm and come under the oversight of the Trustworthy Man, who could then fulfill his promise.

In my experience, whenever Civil Rights workers had been arrested, lawyers with bail money were always right on the scene. A stay of a day or two in jail before arraignment was usual, three or four days unusual but not unheard of, and so I held tight to this glimmer of hope. The day after our neighbor was taken out to die; the morbid and creative warden filled the now-vacant cell with two black teenage girls who had also been arrested in the Civil Rights struggle.

These girls were full of life and spirit; they were fearless and free of that crippling deference to whites that scarred the lives of so many previous generations of African-Americans. With nothing else to do, we talked about our lives, dreams, and ambitions. And, in this way, we subverted the warden's carefully laid plans, turning the girls' and our death row experience into a mini Freedom School.

• • •

Ten days had passed since Dick and I were arrested. There was no bail. There was no lawyer. We had no idea why our release was taking so long, nor had we received any word of assurance that help was on the way. The county prison farm was now only a week away, and a clutching fear washed over me, locking my guts in a vice-grip. Late one night, as we sat silently listening to the sounds of Mississippi crickets, one of the girls in the adjoining cell spoke up.

"Do you know any poetry, Tony?"

I carry around three poems in my head: the first eighteen lines from Chaucer's "Prologue" to *The Canterbury Tales* (in Old English) and two sixteenth-century French romantic poems. I recited all three.

I don't think the girls understood a word of what I'd said, but a long and peaceful silence followed after I was done. At long last one of them replied, "Say them again, Tony." And so I did.

After another long pause, the same girl suggested, "Let's hold hands, Tony."

By standing in the corners of our cell, and reaching out as far as we could, Dick and I could just hold hands with each of the girls. We stood there for a long time, black and white together on death row, unsure and unsettled by what the Mississippi morning might bring.

CHAPTER 7

Free at Last!

IN the end, to the bitter disappointment of the Leflore County prison warden and the Mississippi White Citizens Council, the Trustworthy Man never did get to beat Dick and me "til our blood and our shit flowed together." Ben Smith got there first.

Ben was the senior partner of what was, at the time, the only integrated law firm in the South. Anticipating massive arrests when the Mississippi Freedom Summer got going in late June, Civil Rights lawyers like Ben had prepared legal papers to remove jurisdiction over such cases from state to federal court. When Dick, I, and 12 black SNCC workers were arrested in late March, we provided them with the perfect test case. Ben filed "Removal" papers with the Federal District Court in Greenville (not to be confused with Greenwood) Mississippi the day after we were arrested, expecting prompt action. The federal district judge had no discretion; he was required by law to sign the papers. Once he did, Ben would get Dick and me out of jail on bail immediately. The judge, however, never did seem able to find his way to that part of his desk with our removal papers on it, and so our stay in jail dragged on day after day. Ben called the court anxiously every day for progress reports.

"The judge will get to it just as soon as he can," the clerk kept telling him.

By the time a week had passed, Ben was thoroughly alarmed. He phoned the clerk of the court, scheduled an immediate "in chambers" meeting with the judge, and flew up from New Orleans to keep it. When Ben arrived in Greenville, though, the clerk apologized. The judge had forgotten that he had calendared a turkey shoot with his friends, and would be out hunting all day.

Ben went ballistic.

"That's the biggest pile of horseshit I've ever heard!" he shouted. "If anything happens to those boys in Greenwood, the judge will be on all the national news outlets, explaining himself to the entire world."

"I'm afraid I can't tell you where to find the judge," said the clerk, smiling sweetly. "But my husband is out hunting with the judge, and I could tell you where to find him. I'll draw you a map."

When Ben located the judge's hunting party in the woods a few miles outside of Greenville, he strode across an open field and shoved the removal papers into the judge's gut.

"I guess I don't have any discretion," the judge said, looking over the papers.

"That's right," Ben said. "You've got to sign."

Ben and his lawyer friends got their test. Our case would be argued all the way to the U.S. Supreme Court.

• • •

When federal marshals finally showed up at the Leflore County Jail and drove us all to the Federal Courthouse in Greenville, Ben was there, ordering people around as though he owned the place. In short order papers were signed, bail was posted, and the marshals drove us back to Greenwood, where we walked free.

Still ringing in my ears, though, was the Panther's warning:

"I personally know people on the outside who are planning to kill you," he had told us. "When you do get out of here, take my advice and get the hell out of Mississippi."

Dick and I didn't need to be told twice. We found my car and, with a black Civil Rights worker nicknamed C-Bass who had been jailed with us, headed north. All the pent-up terror of the last 11 days now rose out of the depths of my being, flooding into my consciousness with the force of a geyser. I looked anxiously into my rearview mirror as we sped toward the Mississippi–Tennessee border, daring to hope a little more with each passing mile that we would reach safety.

The full measure of the danger we had been in would make national and international headlines two months later when three young Civil Rights workers, Andrew Goodman, James Chaney, and Mickey Schwerner, were murdered near Philadelphia, Mississippi. Known as the "Freedom Summer" or "Mississippi Burning" murders, these killings were intended to send a chilling message to all volunteers planning to head for Mississippi that summer. Dick and I had escaped their fate by the narrowest of margins.

When Dick, C-Bass, and I crossed over the Mississippi–Tennessee border, we all felt an immense surge of relief. For the first time in over a month our lives were out of danger. Memphis was hardly a welcoming haven, though. There was no safe place for an integrated party to get a bite to eat or use the bathroom. We sped on through the rest of the day and throughout the night, successively crossing the Virginia and Maryland borders until, shortly after dawn, we crossed the Mason–Dixon line into Pennsylvania. Tears of joy and relief came into my eyes. I felt a strong urge to get out of the car and kiss the ground. Words I had heard not quite a year before came flooding back into my mind:

FREE AT LAST
FREE AT LAST
THANK GOD ALMIGHTY,
WE ARE FREE AT LAST!

PART 2

COLD HARBOR

CHAPTER 8

Dad, Mom, and Pearley Bee

SHORTLY before I turned four, growing up in the West Texas oil town of Midland, I spotted a black Cocker Spaniel dog on the sidewalk half a block from our house. I was fascinated. I had never seen a dog before, so I ran down the block to check it out.

"Y' wanna play with my dog, sonny?" The dog's owner, large and overweight, sat on a rocker on his porch surveying the scene below him. "Go ahead . . . her name is Nigger. Y'can play with her all ya want."

As I began to play with Nigger, experiencing for the first time the fun and excitement of having a dog, I jabbered on excitedly about all the wonderful things in my life, Dad, Mom, and especially my beloved Nanny, Pearley Bee. The neighbor cut in:

"Didn't yer mama or yer daddy ever teach y'a 'bout niggers?"

"No sir."

"Never told ya 'bout Pearley Bee being a nigger?"

"No sir."

"Sonny. Ya gotta learn to tell niggers from regular folk, white folks that is, like yer and me and yer daddy and mommy." The neighbor then launched into a lengthy disquisition on the subject of niggers, none of which I understood. As he talked on, though, I began to feel that there was something sinister about him. I suddenly remembered that my mother had told me never, under any circumstances, to have anything to do with this particular neighbor. Frightened, I ran home.

The following morning, jumping up and down on my bed while Pearley Bee dressed me, I told her all about my adventures of the following day. Quite suddenly, I got to the most exciting discovery of all.

"Pearley Bee" I shouted. "Do you know what you are? You're a nigger."

My mother, who had been folding laundry in another part of the room let out an anguished cry. Reaching awkwardly over Pearley Bee's shoulder, she slapped my face. It one of only two times in my life that my mother ever slapped me; it did not, nor was it intended to, hurt. Rather, it had the felt effect of the slap a Buddhist master might give his disciple on the brink of enlightenment. Quite suddenly I saw that the word "nigger" was the worst kind of word a person could ever use. When Dad used bad words like "Oh hell," "dammit all," or more rarely, "Goddammit," my mother would be angry for a while, but then the clouds would lift and life would drift slowly back to normalcy once again. The word "nigger," I now saw, was a bad word of a very different kind. Once you had said it you could never take it back; it made things forever different. I was frightened, and began to cry.

Pearley Bee took me into her arms, kissed me, and comforted me. Slowly my world, which had been turned upside down, began to right itself, until my mother, my father, and Pearley Bee once again took their familiar places at the center of it. Such was my introduction to the searing question of race in the Old South of my youth. I never, ever, used that word again.

• • •

My parents belonged to a social class that would have cut its food budget before doing without the services of a colored maid. In the days before modern conveniences like washing machines and dish washers, women who could afford it almost always had help with housework and other chores. Of equal importance to my parents, in the Southern society of the 1940s, was the fact that a family without a colored servant working in their home tottered on the ragged edge of social respectability. Dad would have scoured the West Texas landscape from end to end rather than allow such a fate to descend on his family or settle for less than the perfect person for the job.

And so it was that Pearley Bee entered my life. In addition to her cleaning and housekeeping duties, Pearley Bee was my nanny, waking me up and dressing me in the morning, taking me into her arms and holding me in their safety. It was she who bathed, clothed, and fed me. More often than not it was Pearley Bee who picked me up when I fell, banged my head, or scraped my knees. It was she who comforted me, kissed my head, and dried my tears.

One picture of Pearley Bee holding me in her arms has survived from my Texas childhood. A small boy a little older than me, Pearley Bee's son, stands in the foreground. Pearley Bee is wearing a white uniform, her hair neatly tied up into a bun. She is tall and has a strong face. Nothing weak or servile shadows her features. I look out of the picture with a questioning expression, perhaps feeling that the safety of Pearley Bee's arms is a better place to be than the uncertain world outside of them.

• • •

My mother's ancestral village, Savigny-le-Vieux, lies in a shallow valley shaped by gently rolling hills in Lower Normandy. "The first Diors," my mother told me many times when I was young, "were Viking settlers who came to Normandy a couple of centuries after Duke Rollo conquered the province from the King of France. They lived the hard life of peasant laborers for eight centuries."

In the mid-1800s, though, the Dior fortunes changed: my mother's great-grandfather Louis made a fortune in the fertilizer business. In a single generation, the Diors went from peasant status to being one the wealthiest families in Basse-Normandie.

Thanks to Louis' entrepreneurial energy, my mother's uncle Maurice, who inherited the Dior fertilizer factory, lived in a spacious mansion and beautiful gardens perched high on a cliff overlooking the old walled city of Granville, the fishing port below it, and the English Channel in the distance. The Diors lived the genteel, spacious, and elegant lifestyle of wealthy bourgeois in the idyllic period before the outbreak of World War I known as "*La Belle Époque*."

This prosperity lasted until the Crash of 1929, when Maurice's bad investments brought ruin to the family. For my mother, who was of marriageable age, the aftershock was devastating. Bourgeois marriages in those days depended on the size of a young woman's dowry, and my mother's had gone the way of the rest of the Dior fortune. The family of the young man on whom she had set her hopes forced him to break off their relationship. She was heartbroken.

With no money and no prospects, my mother set sail for America in the fall of 1930. She was bound for Madison, Wisconsin, where she had secured a teaching fellowship at the University of Wisconsin. She never forgot her first view of New York Harbor and the brightly illuminated Statue of Liberty, the torch in its upstretched arm pointing toward her new life and, she hoped, someone who would love and cherish her because of who she was, not what she owned.

• • •

Dad was the grandson of German immigrants, Julius and Mathilde Gaenslen, who had settled in Milwaukee around 1870. He was about 14 years old when his father asked him what kind of work he wanted to do in life.

"I don't have any idea," Dad said.

"Have you thought of being a geologist?" Grandpa asked, and explained that this was someone who went into the wilderness looking for minerals.

In that moment, Dad's life's work was settled. He would cross vast deserts, penetrate thick jungles, and scale high mountains in his quest for minerals. He never wavered, majoring in geology at the University of Wisconsin, which had one of the finest departments of geology in the country at the time.

Soon after enrolling at the University of Wisconsin Dad learned, to his chagrin, that a number of the most important geological texts of the day were written in French; he would have to acquire a reading knowledge of the language. Dad dragged himself off to face the rigors of introductory French with a heavy heart. Things quickly took a turn for the better; if I heard the story from Dad once, I heard it a hundred times:

"When your mother walked into the room, I knew I had made the right decision taking introductory French."

Dad was deeply smitten with Mom before the end of his first class. Although Mom was five years older than Dad, he was not a man to let such trivial details as age, status, or school regulations stand in the way, he immediately invited his new teacher out on a date and was soon courting her assiduously. Just before Thanksgiving break he invited her to the university prom, spending his last penny showing her a good time.

A month or so later Dad invited my mother iceboating. Mom, whose brothers never undertook the five-hour train ride from their home town of Granville on the Normandy coast to Paris without cautious planning, had inherited her great-grandfather Louis's Viking love of adventure. She eagerly accepted. Dad took her out on Lake Mendota on the northern edge of the University of Wisconsin campus. Mom had never been on an iceboat before. I doubt she had even heard of one. Dad was masterful at winter sports, a fine skater and hockey player and a fearless iceboater. As the iceboat skimmed over the surface of Lake Mendota at speeds nearing 60 miles per hour, Mom thought she had never met anyone like Dad. There was something different about him . . . something she couldn't quite put her finger on. He was . . . it was . . .

He was an American. There was something utterly spontaneous, wild, and un-European about Dad, together with a driven quality that she couldn't quite read. His very being promised excitement, the open road, face-to-face adventures with nature in faraway lands. With his energy, enthusiasm, and drive Dad could almost have been, in my mother's imagination, a reincarnation of old Great-Grandfather Louis Dior.

* * *

By the time Dad graduated from Wisconsin in the spring of 1933, the country was in the depths of the Depression and jobs ran from scarce to non-existent. He needed steady work if he was to marry my mother. The only job he found, though, was as a mucker in a lead mine in Idaho. Dad hitchhiked out in the early fall, sleeping by the edge of the road in the already chilling night weather. Once at the lead mine, he worked deep in the damp and cold of the underground mines. It did not take him long to contract tuberculosis. He wrote to his parents, and his father drove to Idaho and brought him home. Dad would spend the next three years convalescing in the north bedroom of my grandparents' home on West Wisconsin Avenue in Milwaukee.

By mid-1936 Dad was healthy again; he worked briefly as a curator at the Milwaukee Public Museum and then headed south to Texas and Louisiana searching for work in the oil business. Dad sought out buildings with oil-business tenants, climbing the stairs to the top floor and knocking on every door before moving down to the next floor, and so on down to the ground floor, and then on to the next building. When he ran out of buildings in one city, he moved on to another. After two steady months of this kind of searching, someone finally offered him a job as a roughneck wrestling 90-foot lengths of drilling pipe into place as the well went down; it was rough, hard, dangerous work. Men could, and regularly did, get seriously injured and even killed on the rigs. Dad admired the tough, resilient men who did this work. They lined up to be first for the hardest, dirtiest, and most dangerous jobs. They laughed it off when things went badly; they didn't complain when they got hurt.

Dad's experiences in the oil business shaped many of his later attitudes toward life. "Life," he would often tell me, "is like a concrete mixer. You get banged around a lot, but if your luck holds out you don't get crushed."

Like the roughnecks Dad met in the oil fields of Texas he was a stoic, courageous and uncomplaining. In the fields of geology and science he was, additionally, a bold and original thinker. He made it his business, moreover, to ensure that I grew into a "real man," developing those same characteristics in me that he had learned to admire in the Texas men who were his first colleagues.

Dad worked as a roughneck for the better part of a year and then got promoted to the job of oil scout, sleuthing to find out where rival oil companies were looking for oil, and with what success. It wasn't exactly what Dad had in mind when he majored in geology, but it provided a steady, modest salary, a car, and an expense account. Dad finally had enough of a stake to be able to marry my mother. They had waited seven years for each other.

Mom was a devout Roman Catholic. Dad was not. Accordingly my parents could not be married inside the church. Instead, they were married on September 11, 1937, on the porch of a small Roman Catholic church in Lake Charles, Louisiana, at that time headquarters for Dad's oil scouting activities.

• • •

My mother loved Louisiana in general, and New Orleans and Lake Charles in particular. There were corners of Cajun Louisiana where French was still spoken. She could walk into a store and make herself understood in her native tongue.

Mom came to have a particular appreciation for, and even love of, her

Southern friends. She found them to be hospitable and welcoming. They took a genuine interest in making the young French woman feel at home. They had time for friendship, hospitality, and personal relationships.

Dad too found their new home congenial. People were friendly and welcoming. They made his French bride feel accepted. The happiest part of my parents' married life would take place during the few years they lived in Lake Charles. They had friendships there that they kept up through correspondence over the decades after they left town, even as they moved to distant parts of the world.

* * *

I was born in the late summer of 1941 in San Antonio, Texas, my parents' only child. Mother wanted more children, but her health was delicate. She was warned that bearing more children could endanger her life. Dad did what he could to ease her grief. "With just one kid to raise, we'll concentrate on doing it right," he told her. "We'll put all our resources into raising him into someone we'll be proud of."

If Dad had one educational maxim it would have been "Throw him in the drink and watch him swim." As Dad saw it the universe had a fundamentally Darwinian character, but where his one and only son was concerned, the possibility that the kid might sink was a shadow that never crossed Dad's mind. His kid would swim, no doubt about it.

One of Dad's favorite stories ran somewhat like this:

A father is teaching his five-year-old son the all-important lesson of self-reliance. Setting Johnny on the dining room table, the father says: "Jump into my arms, Johnny. Daddy will catch you."

"No Daddy," Johnny replies. "I know you're going to drop me."

"Johnny," the father says, "You have to learn that if there's one person you can trust, it's your own father."

"No Daddy," Johnny answers. "I just know you're going to let me fall."

The father and Johnny go back and forth until Johnny, against his better judgment, jumps. The father lets him fall to the floor.

"Johnny," the father concludes, "You have to learn that you can't trust anyone, not even on your own father."

Dad always laughed heartily when he got to the end.

"George," Mom always said, "That's a terrible story."

"No," Dad always replied, "It's a good story."

* * *

Whereas Dad would have me sink or swim, Mom prayed for me, and she also took a vivid interest in developing my mind. Of all the qualities and characteristics human beings can have, the one my mother placed on a pedestal was intelligence. Absolution and forgiveness of sins was, in my mother's view, available for a wide panoply of human shortcomings. The sins of theft, embezzlement, treason, and more could be wiped away in the sanctity of the confessional. Lack of intelligence, on the other hand, was a sin for which there could be no forgiveness. It was a mortal sin in a class of its own. If you committed this sin by failing to be intelligent, you dragged your low IQ through life like the mournful chain of Dickens' Jacob Marley. Speaking of such a person, my mother would shake her head sadly and say, "Il n'est pas intelligent" ("He's not intelligent"). The unfortunate object of this observation was condemned for life.

My mother took my education in hand at an early age. Reading was its first foundation, and by the time I was three she would sit me on her lap, point to the pictures in children's books, and tell me the stories. Reading together this way was the one opportunity I had for physical contact with my mother, and she would read to me every day for as long as I would sit still on her lap. Mom had a passion for learning and a capacity for finding great excitement and pleasure in all she did, and so she made the characters come alive. In time she transmitted her passionate and wide-ranging interests to me. I absorbed them viscerally sitting on her lap no less than I absorbed them through the gray matter between my ears. By the time I was six or seven, I was a voracious reader. While I got my love of adventure from Dad, I owe my passion for learning to Mom.

* * *

My mother did not often hold me. Born and raised in a well-to-do family in France, she had been brought up in a society that turned the care of infants and small children over to servants. Moreover, her own mother's tragic illness (she had spent 19 years dying from tuberculosis in the gatehouse of her in-laws' spacious estate) had deprived my mother and her brothers of maternal care, love, and affection. Since my mother had rarely been held in her own mother's arms, she felt awkward with her own child. She spent the first part of most mornings behind closed doors in her bedroom, praying for all the people she cared about, Dad and me most prominent among them. But she left the physical aspects of my growing up to other people.

High on the list of the ways Mom approached the responsibilities of motherhood was to read all the then-current literature on cutting-edge techniques for raising children. In those days, people like John B. Watson and B. F. Skinner were creating (and riding high on) a wave of "scientific" theories about child-rearing. Steeped in scientific methodology and mechanistic thinking, Watson and Skinner had a boundless and unquestioning faith in the efficacy of a social ideology called "behaviorism" as the method of choice for raising virile, self-reliant, successful children.

Watson in particular, as president of the American Psychological Association, was the standard-bearer for a "professional crusade against the evils of affection."[1] "When you are tempted to pet your child remember that mother love is a dangerous instrument," Watson had warned. "Too much hugging and coddling can make a disaster of infancy and adolescence, and so warp a child as to make it unfit for marriage."

Watson encouraged manly encounters with a harsh world and went so far as to suggest that parents should "Dig holes in your back yard and let your kids fall in and learn about life." Mothering by cradling, cuddling, and holding a crying child in one's arms was a recipe for softness, a strategy for undermining strong character. Watson put parents, particularly mothers, on notice that excessive mothering endowed their children with "weaknesses, reserves, fears, cautions, and inferiorities."[2]

Dad, who was not given to reading learned articles about child rearing, nevertheless had a natural affinity for Watson's approach. Digging holes in our back yard so I would fall in and figure out how to get out was just the sort of thing he would have endorsed for raising a manly, fearless son. And my mother, who read all the current literature religiously, was not about to undermine my character with excesses of physical affection. Instead she poured all of her maternal energy, passion, and commitment into my intellectual and social development.

• • •

When I was three years old, I fell seriously ill. The doctor was not sure I would survive. My grandmother came down from Milwaukee to help my mother care for me. I cried desperately during those days, but not for my mother's arms. In my distress I would turn away from both my mother and grandmother and reach for the safety of Pearley Bee's comforting arms. She had not enjoyed my mother's educational or social advantages and did not follow the scientific child-rearing theories reported in journals. Instead, she held, hugged, and kissed me, and she knew how to comfort me. And so it was that at the most desperately dangerous time in my young life that she, and not my mother, saved my life.

---

1. Blum, Deborah. *Love at Goon Park: Harry Harlowe and the Science of Affection.* (New York: Basic Books, 2002)
2. Quoted in Blum, supra

CHAPTER 9

Hassan

DAD got his big break in the oil business in 1944 when he was hired by Esso (now Exxon), the largest oil company in the world, to do geological exploration work in the Egyptian desert. Mom and I crossed the Atlantic and the Mediterranean in a troop convoy a year later. Although Germany had already surrendered, we were still at war with Japan. Accordingly, depth charge drills were carried out on a regular basis. The depth charges, the size of oil drums, dropped off the stern of the ship. A minute or so later a huge geyser would surge out of the sea, rising high above the deck. I loved depth charge drills.

Dad met us at Alexandria harbor and took us to our new home. There he introduced me to Hassan, our new Sudanese house servant and my personal care-taker. Hassan was a tall man, handsome, kind, gentle, and unfailingly patient. Hassan got me up in the morning, dressed me, fed me, bathed me, packed me off to school. On week-ends and school holidays, when he went out of the house on errands, he often took me with him.

Although Dad had any number of admirable qualities, he had inherited a terrible temper from his father. Very rarely it got so bad that Dad actually smashed furniture. I was frightened of him, and when he beat my behind he hit hard. The most memorable of these incidents came when I was about seven. I had thrown a rock in play; my aim was off and so I hit my friend Peter Walker in the head. Although Peter was not seriously hurt his forehead was badly bruised, and he was bleeding liberally. Dad lost it, pounding me as hard as he could with all of his considerable strength. I still see my mother, who rarely cried, standing there with tears streaming down her cheeks crying:

"Stop, George. Stop. You'll break his bones."

• • •

Not once in the time I knew him did Hassan ever become irritated with me, much less lose his temper; he was uniformly patient and kind. Hassan gave me a bath every night, heating the bath water on a kerosene stove, then pouring it into the tub. One night, just as Hassan had the bath water ready and was lifting me in, I suddenly realized that I needed to pee. Dad was a driven man, often impatient and in a hurry. I was sure that if it had been Dad he would have been angry at the delay. Fearing that Hassan would get as angry as I imagined Dad would have, I didn't say anything about the need to pee and so got into the warm tub right away. The inevitable happened; almost immediately the warm water made me pee. Dad, I felt, would have yelled at, and perhaps pounded, me.

Hassan for his part only said: "Oh, Tony" in a regretful voice. These were the harshest words he ever spoke to me in all the time I knew him. He lifted me out of the tub, drained the water, heated up another can on the kerosene stove, and made up another bath. I had never before seen such a gentle reaction in a man. I never forgot it.

As vivid in my memory is the day Hassan and I were passing a footbridge on one of our morning walks. The bridge crossed an irrigation canal running along the edge of our town. The canal had silted up, and was being dredged by hand. The workmen stood nearly up to their waists in the water, shoveling the muck out with broad adzes. The labor contractor who had hired them, dressed in a suit and tie, stood on the foot bridge. A labor dispute of some sort was going on. The man in the suit shouted angrily at the men below, throwing rocks at them to emphasize his points. Pinned in the mud, the workers couldn't move out of the way; they swiveled this way and that, trying to avoid the flying rocks. I stopped to stare at the scene. The frightened faces of the men below, and the angry face of the man on the bridge, seared their way into my memory. I would have stayed longer but Hassan, ever protective, grabbed my hand and hurried me away from the scene.

• • •

Some 35 years after leaving Egypt, when I was in my early 40s, I awoke in the middle of the night to the feeling of a palpable presence in my room. Immediately I knew that it was Hassan, that he was dying, and that he had come to say a final goodbye. He stayed in the room for about five minutes and then faded away. Although he is gone, his memory will live forever in my heart and mind.

CHAPTER 10

Christian Dior

IN 1946, at the end of our first year in Egypt Mom and I headed for France. Dad would follow us two months later. It was Mom's first visit home since 1939 when, as a young bride, she had brought her husband home to meet her family. Shortly after she and Dad had returned to America, German armies began their sweep across Europe and much of the Western world. France had been overrun and occupied by German armies in a few short weeks. My mother's elderly father had lived under German occupation for four long years, and her brother Alexander been a prisoner of war for five. Now, seven long years of waiting to see her family had finally come to an end.

Our first destination was the home of Henry Dior, my mother's father and my "Grandpère." Grandpère had been the presiding judge of a three-judge court in the provincial capitals, first of Fontainebleau and later Epernay. He had cut an impressive and dignified figure in the days when had been greeted as "Monsieur le President," and now, in retirement, he strolled down the street at a leisurely pace in his three-piece suit with his gold chain, watch, and cane. Grandpère was the best grandfather a boy ever had or dreamed of having. He was extremely tender and kind with both my mother and me and found endless ways to be attentive to me. He was inventive, a great pantomimist, and a lot of fun.

Of Grandpère's three children, my mother, Elisabeth, most shared the interests of his lively mind. They were both quick-witted and funny. Their knowledge of Latin, Greek, ancient mythology, arcane history, and obscure passages in literature was encyclopedic. They joked and laughed as they teased out answers to the most challenging crossword puzzles the newspaper could throw at them.

The separation of the war years had been hard on them, not knowing when, if ever, they might see each other again. Now, reunited, they were beyond delighted to enjoy each other's company. I had always loved having Mom all to myself, but having Grandpère and Mom together was as good as going to the circus.

* * *

After about a month of living with Grandpère, Mom and I returned to her hometown of Granville on the Normandy coast. The old walled city of Granville rests on a stone promontory named Cap Lihou, the cape itself jutting half a mile out into the sea. Above the city walls its seven-century-old church and gothic spire dominate the horizon. Nestled far below the walls lies the port from which, for centuries, the men of Granville set out for long months of fishing on the Grand Banks.

Granville became the hometown of the Dior family when, in the mid-nineteenth century, my great-great grandfather Louis Dior moved the center of his flourishing business enterprises there from Savigny-le-Vieux. He built a fertilizer factory in Granville and moved there to manage it personally. Later in life, as Savigny's most distinguished citizen, he moved back to serve as its mayor until his death.

Granville owned my mother's heart as no other place on earth. The happiest years of her life had been spent there. Each time we visited, she told me about her favorite places in the town, those richest in memory and associations.

For my mother, given her deeply religious nature, foremost among these was the church of Notre Dame du Cap Lihou, protectress of the city and of the fishing fleets that lay at anchor in the harbor below. I grew to love Granville as much as my mother did. From her I caught the religion of my ancestors, woven as deep into the fabric of my being as it was in hers. Because she spoke of it so often, I came to reflect frequently on the thousand-year history of my Norman ancestors, their religion an anchor in the harsh evolutionary landscape in which they lived out their peasant lives. They had passed it down generation to generation to her and she, in turn, passed it to me.

* * *

Many times too my mother took me to visit Les Rhumbs, a beautiful estate perched high on the cliffs overlooking the ocean and the old town of Granville. It had been the home of her uncle Maurice Dior. Her voice crackling with nostalgia, my mother showed me the ocean-view terrace where, in good weather, the family had taken its after-dinner coffee and liqueur.

Here she had played with her brothers and her cousins Christian and Jacqueline. Hanging in my study I have a treasured picture taken at Les Rhumbs of my mother with Christian and his brothers and sister Jacqueline. My mother is about 14 years old, Christian 15, and Jacqueline 11. Mom's amused and mischievous expression speaks of a born rascal, a lover of fun, excitement, and trouble. Christian wears the long hair of a Sixties' hippie 40 years before his time. Jacqueline is poised and beautiful.

My mother and Christian Dior had different temperaments. My mother was a competitive and driven student, working hard for top grades. Christian, who was highly intelligent, never took school work very seriously and got only average grades. Later, she came to think of him as an impractical dreamer. She became critical of him as well for not putting his considerable talents to work keeping the Dior factory thriving and doing more to preserve the family's fortune both before and after the crash of 1929.

Christian, for his part, liked my mother's lively mind, quick wit, and irreverent spirit, which made her a lot of fun to be with. She and Jacqueline were beautiful, and he enjoyed dressing them up. Christian made elaborate dresses and costumes using large amounts of good quality cloth. His favorite color was pink, and he used a lot of it, set off with a variety of other colored accessories. He loved flowers, favoring scarves with floral designs.

I first met Christian Dior a few years after my first visit to Granville, when he had already become world famous. A shy, sensitive, superstitious, and highly gifted man, Christian was very kind and attentive to the young boy I was then, almost unheard of for an adult of his time and social class. He left an indelible impression on my mind.

My mother had judged Christian harshly when, after the collapse of his family fortune, he led what she thought of as the life of a dilettante, becoming quite poor and doing a variety of jobs. But he had reserves of determination and ambition that surprised her. Christian went from being utterly unknown to world famous on February 12, 1947, when he launched his "New Look" fashion collection. During and after World War II, the title of the fashion capital of the world had shifted from Paris to New York. In 1946 Christian had joined forces with textile millionaire Marcel Boussac to launch a fashion house under Christian's name. Boussac financed Christian's enterprise with the express intention of bringing the title of fashion capital of the world back to Paris. They succeeded beyond their wildest dreams.

My mother, who liked to dominate her brothers Alexandre and Michel and her cousin Jacqueline, had never been able to dominate Christian. Despite this, or perhaps because it amused him, Christian never lost his fondness for my mother. After he became famous, however, Mom felt unsure of her ground and somewhat awkward in his presence. Once when, on the spur of the moment, he extended her an invitation to have lunch with him, she ducked it because the dress she was wearing was a Dior imitation. My mother couldn't bear the thought of the amused and critical look in his eye when he saw it.

Christian Dior came to occupy a very large place in my mind. Often I have walked the paths of his family garden in Granville (now renamed "Jardin Christian Dior") thinking about the shy, sensitive boy who had walked these same paths many years before. In that garden, he thought thoughts and had inspirations that would later win over the world of high fashion, and he founded a fashion empire that would carry his name to the far corners of the globe. His life inspired me, and inspires me still.

CHAPTER 11

The Chalet de Caux

AFTER about three weeks in Granville we returned to Clamart, a suburb of Paris, to be with Grandpère. Dad had flown in from Egypt to be with us for the last couple weeks of this vacation. My cousin Catherine and her parents had an apartment in Paris, and they soon paid us all a visit. I had met Catherine a few weeks earlier in Granville, and lost no time developing quite the young boy's crush on her. I now adored my pretty little cousin, looking eagerly forward to the visit, but it took a bad turn.

Dad and Mom had bought a special gyroscope top as a gift for Catherine. Wanting to show off for my pretty cousin, I offered to demonstrate how the top worked, and I promptly broke it. Dad flew into a rage, giving me a terrible pounding and seriously frightening Catherine.

Two photographs taken that day tell the whole story. The first is a beaming picture of Catherine and me holding hands was taken shortly before this incident. A second picture, taken not long after Dad pounded me, shows Grandpère, Dad, and me standing on Grandpère's back porch. Dad looks directly into camera's lens with dark intensity. I stand dejectedly in front of Grandpère, looking at the ground. Grandpère, his usual kind and gentle expression on his face, rests two protective hands on my shoulders.

Leaving France a few days later Dad, Mom and I headed for the town of Lausanne in Switzerland, stopping there at an elegant, gleaming white, two story building. Mom and I walked its tiled floors while the Swiss sun poured through arched windows, projecting shadows on the alabaster-white walls. We stopped in also to visit one of its rooms, bright, cheerful, and inviting. Leaving Lausanne, we headed for Montreux at the east end of Lake Geneva, transferring to a cog railway train that clawed its way up the mountainside to a village called "Caux." The day was strikingly warm. The three of us sat in our hotel's lovely garden, Dad and Mom tender with each other and with me.

The following morning we split into three parts, Mom returning to the gleaming hotel in Lausanne which turned out not be a hotel at all, but a tuberculosis sanatorium. My mother's mother, her grandmother, and both of her maternal aunts had died of the disease.

Dad and I hiked together to a steep-roofed Swiss chalet where medleys of flowers bloomed in colorful array. The Chalet de Caux lay on the a slope of a towering mountain, cradled between two beneficent meadows, and fronted by a dirt road guarded by fence posts and a narrow wooden gate, just wide enough for a single person to pass through.

"In you go" Dad said, opening the door.

"Aren't you coming?" I asked, innocently.

"No" Dad said. "You're staying here." He turned and walked away.

Until that moment I hadn't realized that the Chalet de Caux was a boarding school. Dad had said nothing about it. Even if he had wanted to, I doubt he would have known what to say. Mom was sick with the illness that had killed her mother, grandmother, and two aunts. Dad had to earn a living in the Egyptian desert. I would have to become a man, and that was that.

I had always been a dreamy little boy, and now I found refuge from the world by turning inward. I spent fascinated hours lying or sitting in a field taking in the dizzying riches of small mountain flowers crowded together. Small, delicious, tiny strawberry-like berries lurked among the grasses, rewarding our taste buds with their fresh fragrant flavor whenever we came across them. The sight, taste, and smell of these flowers and grasses filled my heart with grateful awe and wonder.

Almost daily all of us children went for long walks in the Swiss countryside, awestruck by the mountains and the great pine trees towering over us. From time to time we took the cog railroad one or two stops up the near-vertical tracks, hiking back down paths leading along mountain creeks or through fields lush with mountain wildflowers.

• • •

The Chalet de Caux had its shadow side, though. The headmistress, Mademoiselle Alice, meted out draconian punishments to keep her charges in line. Two memories in particular have stayed with me over the years, one of them arising out of one of these wonderful walks. The rule was that, on the hikes that we all took together through the incomparable Swiss countryside, all the children had to stay together from the moment we left the school gate 'til the moment we returned to it. On this occasion, though, after a long walk my friend Philippe, in a fit of enthusiasm, broke from the group and ran the last fifty yards ahead of the group to the gate. For this signal offense Mlle. Alice gathered the whole school, pulled Philippe's pants down, and beat his bare backside with a hairbrush until it turned shiny pink.

Another, even more memorably terrifying event, involved two little girls aged five who consistently wet their beds. Mlle. Alice took the two girls outside, gathered the entire school body, and in front of us all stripped them naked. On a momentary impulse, she plucked a blade of grass and stuck it in the vulva of one of the little girls. We small fry stood there, stunned and unsure of what to do. One of the older girls named Marie, and a number of the other older girls and boys, soon herded us all off to the left, thus cutting short the two girls' time of shame and embarrassment.

• • •

Two miracles showed up in my life not long after I arrived at the Chalet de Caux, changing it dramatically. The first of these came in the form of a box of Cheerios that Mom sent me, delivered, it seemed to me, in a golden chariot pulled by six fiery steeds. Mom hadn't forgotten me after all. She was still out there somewhere, thinking about me, missing me, and praying for me. I made plans to hoard the box, eating just a few Cheerios a day as a way of keeping Mom's presence close to me for as long as I could. Mlle. Alice, however, decreed that I should share my Cheerios with the other children. The whole box was served up for breakfast the following morning.

The other miracle was the gleam I awakened in the eyes of a pretty little girl named Annie, and she lost no time showing me how she felt. It did not take me long to return her affection.

A tiny photographic print taken that first winter at the Chalet de Caux, and miraculously surviving six decades of moving around on three continents, tells the whole story. Annie is sitting on a sled. She is a pretty little girl, her full round face wearing an expression as mischievous and sweet as it is full of her love of life. Annie has a very affectionate nature. In her arms she clutches Minou the cat, the lucky object of her attentions at the instant the picture was taken. The camera catches the fact that the moment is a special one for her. Annie has eyes for me. Here she is about to be pulled for a sled ride through the snow by the one little boy at the Chalet for whom she is the school's most special little girl. On the sled behind Annie sits an older girl named Marie. Marie's arms are wrapped around Annie in a loving embrace, her expression full of gentleness, love, and affection.

I stand off to the left in this picture holding the rope, ready to pull Annie through the snow. I look at the camera with an unsettled and somewhat troubled expression, as though unsure of my ground. The two girls easily express their affection, Annie hugging Minou, and Marie hugging Annie. I want into this circle. I have large ambitions of earning my way into it by giving Annie the sled ride of her life. The sled, though, turns out to be a lot harder to pull than I imagined. By the time I've pulled Annie as far as the school's narrow gate, a distance of about 20 yards, I'm all done in.

Marie had started a girls' club whose members were herself, Annie, and another younger girl. Not only did the girls' club have two of my very favorite people in it, but the girls had a to-die-for clubhouse built up in a tree. I wanted in in the worst way, and I began to pester Marie to be allowed into the club. Marie pointed out to me that I couldn't very well be a member of the girls' club in light of the fact that I was a boy. I was undeterred. I was not about to let so marginal a consideration as gender keep me out of the girls' club, and so I kept up my relentless assault on membership.

Marie did not give in that easily. There was, she pointed out, a second, all-but-insuperable hurdle. The girls had invented a secret password. No one could gain entry into their club unless she knew the password. I pestered Marie so long and hard trying to guess the password that she got tired of it. To get rid of me she delegated the task of monitoring my guesses to Annie. Annie gave me so many hints that I soon cracked the code. And so it was that I became an honorary girl. The club, clubhouse, and its members were every wonderful thing I had ever imagined.

One afternoon soon after I gained admission into the club Annie slipped into my cubicle, suggesting that if I were to drop my pants and show her what made little boys different from little girls, she would drop her pants and show me what made little girls different from little boys. It was the kind of bold and wonderful initiative I would never have had the courage to suggest myself, and so it took me a moment to take it in. Unlike Annie, I was acutely aware that if Mlle. Alice caught us in the act the consequences would be unimaginably awful—the rack, if not the guillotine. Annie's pretty, excited, and eager face, however, soon overcame my fears and doubts. The appeal of it being too wonderful to resist, I soon proved myself worthy of Annie's adventurous suggestion. Sharing the experience of that wonderful and exciting moment of discovery, the mysterious difference between us, and the curiosity and attraction that drew us together, created a special bond between us, something that only Annie and I could or would ever know about.

I was a very little boy in those days, far away from home. I missed the love, affection, and caring I received from Mom and Dad, my special relationship with Hassan, and everything that had made Egypt feel safe and secure for me. For someone as shy as me to be singled out as the special friend of this pretty, warm, and lively little girl was more than good luck. It was the warming light of a benevolent providence.

CHAPTER 12

Grandpère

ONE morning, when I was seven years old, my Tante Jacqueline Dior suddenly appeared at the door of the Chalet de Caux, announcing that she had come to take me back to Paris to live with the beloved Grandpère I had first met a little over two years before.

Grandpère was waiting for me at the gate of his house at 202 Avenue Victor Hugo in the Paris suburb of Clamart. I was a pretty forlorn character by the time I arrived at Grandpère's home. He immediately saw that I needed industrial quantities of tender, loving, care, and proceeded to administer them. He instituted a set of routines and rituals to get us through the day; it was absolutely essential that I be there and participate in all these events; otherwise life simply could not go on.

My first task after getting up in the morning was to blow out the match Grandpère used to light the gas stove. The second was to help Grandpère grind the morning coffee in an old-fashioned Peugeot coffee grinder. He would clasp the grinder between his knees; my task was to get the job started. At the age of seven I was good for about eight to ten turns of the crank. Grandpère would take over for ten to fifteen, and I would take over for the next five to eight, and so on until the coffee was all ground.

Every day when school let out at the Cours Maillard I would run to the school gate where Grandpère, an elegant old-world figure in his three piece suit, gold watch and chain, vintage Fedora, and fashionable walking cane, would be waiting for me. We would go for long walks together, or rather strolls, as Grandpère sauntered along at a leisurely pace, swinging his cane at a jaunty angle, tipping his hat to each woman that he passed with a polite "Bonjour, Madame." He knew all the best nooks and crannies in Clamart, including a magical municipal park at the top of Avenue Victor Hugo whose streams ran under arching bridges. He would sit quietly on a bench while I ran around and played, coming back frequently to make sure that Grandpère was still there waiting for me. He always was.

Two or three times a week Grandpère would check his gold watch against the large clock over the Clamart train station. He would stop a hundred yards or so short of the station, feigning that the street off to the right was the shortest way home, and squint in the direction of the clock.

"Je n'y vois pas claire, mon petit. Qu'elle heure est-il?" ("I can't see clearly, my little one. What time is it?")

"Il est trois-heures vingt, Grandpère," ("It's 3:20, Grandpère.")

"T'est bien sur?" ("Are you very sure?")

"Oui, Grandpère." Grandpère would then set his watch, and we would be off.

Once home again Grandpère would often entertain me with near-professional pantomime, dancing, and singing he'd learned during his youth, when he was a handsome "boulvardier" striding the fashionable boulevards of Paris, or spending evenings at the Moulin Rouge in Montmartre where he watched acts later made famous by the painter Toulouse-Lautrec.

Sooner or later Grandpère would declare:

"Je suis fatigué, mon petit" ("I'm tired, my little one") and retire to his study. I would climb up to the attic where my mother's and her brother's schoolbooks had all been saved. I would plunge into Mom's two volume *Histoire de France* (History of France) *Histoire Sainte* (a child's illustrated history of the Old and New Testaments told as one continuous story), biographies of my French heroes, Vercingetorix who fought against Cesar to keep Gaul free from Roman rule; Jeanne D'Arc and Bertrand DuGuesclin, heroes in France's victory over England in the Hundred Years War. I soon became a minor encyclopedia on French history.

A crisis loomed on the horizon as the school year neared its end. Academically speaking the Chalet de Caux had been far from excellent.

When I entered the Cours Maillard I was well behind my classmates. While I strove valiantly to catch up, by graduation date the pack was still far ahead of me. The Cours Maillard was owned by an old and kindly couple who strove mightily to recognize all of their students for their particular gifts. My case, however, stretched the benevolence of the Maillards to the limit. Rather than humiliate me however, they devised a special prize so that I too could walk up to the dais and receive it. The graduation program, however, papered over the sad truth.

"Special Prize, the student not having attended the full school year."

Grandpère had prepared for this debacle with the most creative of corrective solutions. On returning home I discovered that he had arranged the chairs in his living room in the style of a show at the Moulin Rouge. As master of ceremonies he strode onto center-stage, hushing up the large (imaginary) crowd, pantomiming all the scenes and all the figures in it.

"Messieurs, Mesdames" he announced with a flourish. "Welcome to the real awarding of prizes." Grandpère leaned heavily on the word "real." "We will begin with first place in Mathematics, the prize going to . . ."

Here Grandpère paused to open a mock envelope, pulling the inset card out of its envelope, squinting at it to make out the name of the recipient.

". . . Tony Gaenslen."

Grandpère now pantomimed the gasps of astonishment rippling through the crowd at this signal achievement. ("Can you believe it? Tony Gaenslen?) Grandpère then handed me my prize which, when I unwrapped it, turned out to be the first volume in a two volume set of the *Fables* of La Fontaine, the French Aesop.

Grandpère now hushed down the still murmuring crowd.

"Silence, please, messieurs et mesdames. Next, first place in French Composition goes to . . ."

As Grandpère once again opened the non-existent envelope and squinted at the inset car, a look of disbelief spread across his face

"Also Tony Gaenslen!"

The astonishment of the crowd at this momentous news (all pantomimed by Grandpère) was beyond all bounds. "Can you imagine that? First prize in both French Composition and Arithmetic to Tony

Gaenslen?" The prize, when opened, revealed itself to be the second volume of the *Fables* of La Fontaine.

There was method to Grandpère's madness, though. He used the *Fables* to teach me the life lessons that he thought I most needed to learn. The one he stressed most frequently, and with the greatest emphasis, was that I should learn to think for myself, and not be swayed by other people's opinions.

CHAPTER 13

Denny Orton

WHEN the bottom dropped out of the Egyptian oil business the summer I turned eight, Dad had to scrounge for new work in the depressed oil business. He eventually settled on a job with a regional oil company called Carter Oil, relocating our family to Council Grove, a small town on the Kansas plains. Springing up as a settlement along the Santa Fe trail in the 1850's, the town had grown and prospered with the fortunes of the trail for a few decades before the railroad ran through it on its way to greater destinations. Thereafter Council Grove had settled into the life of a typical small farming community, its population numbering no more than 2,000. Two blocks of old-fashioned Western storefronts formed the heart of its downtown, Main Street ran through its center, dividing the town into north and south sections. The Neosho River, running just east of the business section, divided into east and west.

Dad's salary hit rock bottom, and we were poor. Picking Mom and me up in Kansas City, he drove us to our new home, a tar-paper shack some six miles northeast of town. The shack was mounted on stilts, four rough wooden steps leading up to its front porch to its front door. On the right side of the rickety porch stood a hand-pump mounted over a rainwater cistern, the shack's one source of running inside water. Although the water wasn't potable it could be used for washing dishes, except in drought times such as Kansas was then experiencing. Dad hand-pumped all our water from a well 30 feet distant, carrying it into the house in buckets.

Our outhouse, a two-holed affair standing some 40 feet from the house, worked just fine in good weather, but when relentless winter winds blew in off the plains, getting to it wasn't much fun. From time to time snow blew in through the cracks, covering the seats. One morning Mom woke up to discover that during the night wind had blown the outhouse over.

Inside the front door stood the shack's cookstove, which Dad filled with kerosene a couple times a week. If you were in no particular hurry, the stove eventually heated everything that was put on it. Its primary use was as Mom's stove, but it was also our source of hot water for the once-a-week baths we took on Saturdays. Dad lifted a galvanized iron bathtub off its hook on the kitchen wall, set it on the floor, filled the stove with kerosene, and heated up a bucket of water. That one went for my bath. While I was bathing Dad heated a second bucket of water. When I had finished he poured the second bucket into the tub, and Mom climbed in for her bath. While she was bathing Dad heated a third bucket, adding it to Mom's and my bathwater for his own bath.

An ice-box stood in another corner of the kitchen. Dad fetched a large block of ice in Council Grove every three or four days, breaking it with an ice pick then broke into pieces small enough to fit inside. Mom loaded our most perishable items, such as butter, milk, and eggs, directly onto the fresh ice.

Dad generally got home from work after dark. Every evening I would stand by the window watching the headlights of passing cars until one of them turned into the dirt track leading to our shack. My Dad was home again.

• • •

After Mom came close to dying from appendicitis in the shack we moved into Council Grove to a house whose advantages included outer walls with siding to keep the winter winds at bay, indoor running hot and cold water, and an indoor toilet. True, the floors sagged, and the free-standing oil heater in the living room once backfired, covering everything in the house with a fine layer of oil-soot—and setting me on fire. Dad put me out before any permanent damage was done, but the burns were exceedingly painful. In later years I came to refer to these two homes as our "downscale shack" and our "upscale shack." How Dad could think of isolating Mom in the downscale shack to save $10 a month still stuns me.

• • •

Denny Orton became my best friend in Council Grove. He was about a year older than me, and a steady, loyal, fellow adventurer.

To grownups, who know everything and understand nothing, Council Grove was a small, dusty farming community and shopping center whose dynamic frontier days lay far behind it. Denny and I looked at Council Grove through different eyes. In our imaginations its Main Street was still an important destination on the bustling Santa Fe trail, the last outpost of civilization perched on the edge of the endless plains. For us the Last Chance Store, its long-closed doors notwithstanding, still provided vital foodstuffs to westward-bound adventurers such as ourselves, bursting with imaginary supplies of peanut butter and jelly sandwiches, fresh hot chocolate, and Baby Ruth candy bars for emergency rations.

There was a great deal in Council Grove that fed our imaginations. On the east side of town stood the grove of trees for which the town was named, a stand under which representatives of the Osage Nation had met with white settlers, signing a treaty granting westward-bound pioneers safe passage through tribal lands. Not far from the grove stood the Post Office Tree in which early settlers had deposited and picked up mail. On a rise overlooking the river just south of town stood a monument marking the burial spot where a Spanish missionary had been killed in 1560 while trying to convert the Indians. All these sites and many more were the settings for our adventures.

A shadow hung over our friendship, though; I was Catholic and Denny was Protestant. The Ortons, like most of the Protestant majority in town, descended from of pioneer homesteaders settling the land during the years of the Santa Fe trail and "Bloody Kansas," the bloody race between "Free State" and "Slave State" settlers to bring Kansas into the Union on their side. The Catholic minority in town descended from the Irish who built the railroad.

The wars of religion were alive and well when Denny and I were friends in Council Grove. Billy Van Fossen headed up the Protestant gang for boys around my age. His Catholic counterpart, Mike O'Malley, was the son of the town butcher. Both of them were fighters to be reckoned with.

Billy was a couple of years older than me, in fifth grade while I was in third. Whenever he and I were on the playground together at Garfield Public School and he could catch me away from teachers and other kids, he never failed to pounce on me and pummel me. He never got far before an alert teacher would spot the fray and put an end to it.

One of Billy's younger brothers, Joey, was in my class. He was the only boy my age I didn't like fighting with, because he smelled so bad. While Billy met the challenges of his poverty-stricken home life by finding what was tough, mean, and aggressive in his nature, Joey was cut from an altogether different cloth. He was shy and sensitive. Even at age 8 there was something pathetic about him. We kids all liked Joey and felt sorry for him, working him into the games we played together on the playground. Still, it was hard to get close to him. None of us ever invited him home to play.

For a time Joey was drawn to me in particular, inviting me to come home and play with him at his house. I tried desperately to work my way out of this invitation, largely because I feared running into Billy and getting beaten up. Since it meant so much to Joey I set my fears aside and followed him home. On our way to their house we did indeed cross paths with Billy. When he saw that I was playing with his pathetic younger brother though Billy, for the first time ever, he let me be.

The Van Fossens were, notoriously, the poorest family in town. They lived in a shack that made ours look like a palace. It consisted of two dirt-floor rooms, the larger one doubling as bedroom and living room. The smaller room, equipped with a sink, a single cold water faucet, and a rickety kerosene stove, served as the kitchen. Mr. and Mrs. Van Fossen and their four daughters all slept together in a large ramshackle bed. The other four children, all boys, slept on pallets laid on boards resting on the dirt floor.

The shack's most striking feature was a giant Socony-Vacuum sign covering its north wall, shielding it from howling winter winds. Joey told me that the sign had cost his father the princely sum of $35. Painted in red on the sign was a giant Pegasus, the mythical winged horse. Joey was inordinately proud of that sign. The main reason he had invited me home was so he could show it off. Other families may have had indoor plumbing, floorboards that kept out the cold, roofs that didn't leak, airtight walls and windows, hot and cold running water. But their homes weren't graced with anything half as glorious as the Van Fossens' winged Pegasus.

• • •

The small Catholic community in Council Grove worshipped at St. Rose of Lima Roman Catholic Church, a lovely small church built solidly of white limestone blocks, its inside decor simulating a marble sanctuary and altar. I found the church beautiful and liked going there.

When we moved to Council Grove I was overdue to receive my first holy communion. Mom made the necessary arrangements, and Father Divers performed the ceremony. Returning to my pew after receiving communion, I experienced a strange, warming presence, immensely comforting, bringing with it a sovereign sense of peace and security. That feeling lasted for about 15 minutes before slowly fading away.

• • •

Other than seeing them at Mass on Sundays, I rarely saw other Catholic children in Council Grove. Catholic and Protestant boys in town kept to themselves. Denny Orton and I, though were an exception. We were best friends, and hung out together.

At the end of our first year together at Garfield Public School, Mom persuaded Dad to transfer me to St. Rose of Lima Parochial School, where the sisters maintained higher academic standards. Dad would normally have resisted Catholic education to the bitter end. Even he had to admit I had learned very little at Garfield, though, so he agreed to the transfer.

My first run-in with Mike O'Malley, leader of the Catholic gang for boys my age, took place right after school on my very first day at St. Rose of Lima. For a 9-year-old boy, Mike was tough as nails, and he made it clear that as long as I attended St. Rose's I would have to become a member of his gang. Mike didn't have to spell out the consequences if I refused. My loyalty to Denny as my best friend made me deeply reluctant to join, but I didn't see that I had a lot of choice. As I stood there contemplating my options, I also realized that I wanted to be friends with these boys and not be the odd man out. And so, with deeply mixed feelings, I agreed to let Mike tattoo an anchor on the back of my hand (with an ink pen), signifying membership in his gang.

Later, at home, I felt deeply ashamed of what I had done. I scrubbed the anchor off and went off to play with Denny. The following day, though, the reality of my situation hit fully home. I did not have the fortitude to stand alone against the Catholic boys for the entire school year. Mike inked in the anchor a second time, and this time I let it stay.

Thereafter I saw a lot less of Denny than I had before. During my year at St. Rose of Lima I mostly played with the Catholic boys. Today, more than 60 years later, I still have feelings of regret for not having been a more loyal friend to Denny.

• • •

It did not take long for my place in the hierarchy of Mike's gang to get established, and established it was in the timeless tradition of little boys in small communities. We settled it with our fists.

It was during recess at St. Rose of Lima A couple weeks into the school year we were all playing baseball on the playground during recess and Mike claimed it was his turn at bat. I thought it was mine. Mike strode to the plate and took his place. This was not the sort of thing I was in the habit of letting pass. Since Mike batted right-handed and I left-handed, I went to the plate and took my place on the opposite side. We both swung at the pitches, and Mike connected on the second or third pitch. Instead of running toward first base, he went after me.

Mike O'Malley was a very short boy, the shortest member of his gang. Because of his size he had been regularly picked on and beaten up by bigger boys. His father, the town butcher, evened the field by teaching Mike how to box. Mike was thus the only boy my age in Council Grove to have mastered this manly art, and master it he had. No one in town could stand up to Mike when the fists were up.

Mike proceeded to take me apart systematically. Since he had chosen the weapon of combat, I had no choice but to follow suit. Boxing was an art about which I knew nothing. All of the fighting I did with other boys my age involved a sort of free-form wrestling in which the strongest, ablest, and most determined boy ended up on top.

Mike knew how to duck and feint. My punches might have knocked him into the middle of next week had only one of them connected, but Mike ducked under these wild swings and pummeled my stomach and chest with a tattoo of punches while my fists swung helplessly over his head. Out of the corner of my eye I could see Father Divers standing in the classroom, watching the whole proceeding. Father Divers was far too wise a man to think of stopping the fight. He knew that if he did Mike would lie in wait for me after school and hand me the drubbing of my life.

I was enraged by the pummeling I was getting, roaring and crying as I tried to lay a hand on Mike, but all in vain. The fight did not last long. I was soon reduced to a mass of helpless blubber, my status in Mike's gang now irrevocably established. Mike stood firmly at the pinnacle of his gang.

Mike, notably, had not thrown any blows at my nose or face. The rules of engagement in Council Grove were well established. That little boys fight was a well-accepted fact of life. What was not accepted was that these fights should result in any meaningful injury. Had Mike punched me on the nose and made it bleed, Father Divers would have been on top of him in a minute, and the outcome of the fight would have been very different. Mike would have gotten a good scolding, lost face, and suffered a much worse fate after Father Divers reported the fight to Mike's dad and mom.

Father Divers in fact did not lose any time after the fight to go to both my house and the O'Malley's house, telling our mothers all about it. He made it clear to both that Mike had not seriously hurt me but had stayed within the established conventions for fights of this kind. When I got home after school that afternoon Mom greeted me:

"Father Divers was here a little while ago and told me you got into a fight at school today with Mike O'Malley. He said you took your beating like a man."

Mom said those last words with a distinct ring of pride in her voice.

Since it was neither her practice nor Dad's to lavish praise on me, Mom's evident pride hit a resonant chord. I hitched up the belt of my self-esteem a couple notches and walked about with a bit of a swagger.

• • •

Several months before the end of that school year Dad had found exploration work in the jungles of Venezuela. He left for South America, and Mom and I would follow him about six weeks after school was over. As soon as school let out for the summer, I took my membership in Mike O'Malley's gang to be dissolved and went straight over to Denny Orton's house. I never saw the gang members again. Denny and I knew our time together would be short, so we spent every hour we could together.

One day, after Denny and I had circled by the Last Chance Store, the monument to the Spanish missionary, and other Council Grove hot spots, we headed back to my house. Rather than go the long way over the Main Street bridge, we took a shortcut over the Neosho River trestle. We were in Billy Van Fossen's territory, but we didn't think much about until we were actually on the bridge. Suddenly, Billy and three members of his gang spotted us. Denny and I ran as fast as we could, trying to reach the east bank of the Neosho before they caught us. Billy and his gang members, however, were two years older than we were and a good deal faster. They caught up with us just past the middle of the bridge. Billy's gang divided in half, Billy and one other boy going after Denny. Billy's top lieutenant, a boy named Allan, together with another boy, went after me. I fought both boys off, trying to get off the bridge before anything really bad happened. I made it, turning and running as fast as I could toward home. But Allan and the other boy easily outran me, twisting my arm behind my back and roughing me up in other ways.

In my rage I began cursing both boys out, using every bad word I had ever heard Dad or anyone else use. To my surprise, after my first string of oaths, Allan called the other boy off. As everyone knows, if you can get a Catholic boy to say "Goddamn" he will go straight to hell when he dies, roasting forever in eternal flames. Having just consigned my soul to hell, Allan didn't see any point in hurting my body, so he let me go.

Denny wasn't so lucky. He was a renegade Protestant whom Billy had saved him for himself. He hung Denny over the Neosho River trestle, dangling him high above the water below and dragging him along the railing to drive splinters into his armpits. By the time Billy got through with him Denny had been pretty well worked over.

Denny cried for a while as we made our way home together and got cleaned up. Taking the trestle shortcut was a mistake we would never make again. Denny didn't let the incident interfere with our friendship, though, and we continued to play with each other every day until the day came for me to leave Council Grove.

* * *

On our last day together Denny made the rounds of his paper route, collecting every overdue penny that was due him, until he had amassed the princely sum of one dollar and 25 cents. He then treated me to the feast of our lives at a soda fountain on Main Street. In those days an ice-cream cone went for a nickel, hot dogs and hamburgers for 15 cents. Denny and I stuffed ourselves with hot dogs, root-beer floats, ice-cream, and candy until we couldn't hold another bite.

Our meal over, we walked outside and stood facing each other on the sidewalk. By the look in his eyes I could see how much this goodbye was costing Denny. After a short pause he held out his hand, and we shook for the last time.

"So long, Tony," Denny said simply.

"So long, Denny, I said.

Denny turned and walked one block west on Main Street, rounding the corner and turning north on Mission. A Plainsman to the end, Denny never looked back.

And so disappeared forever from my sight Denny Orton, the truest friend of my youth. Denny was made of finer stuff than I was. I knew it then, and I know it now.

* * *

All my life I hoped that one day Denny's and my paths would cross and that we would see each other once again.

In November, 2011, 60 years after Denny and I had said goodbye, I came to Kansas City on a Thanksgiving break. With Council Grove only 120 miles to the west, I rented a car in hopes of tracking Denny down. Arriving in town around noon, I was both delighted and relieved to discover that Council Grove looked very much as it had when Denny and I played together there as kids. My wife Annie and I made our way to the Saddlerock Café, crossing paths with a cowboy in a ten-gallon hat, boots, and spurs coming out on our way in.

Standing up in the café after lunch, I spoke up and said:

"I know it's a long shot, but 60 years ago I was best friends with a boy from Council Grove, Denny Orton. Has anyone here heard of him?"

"Sure, I have." The speaker, a heavy-set middle aged man in farming overalls, explained, "Denny and Bonnie don't live in Council Grove any more, though. They're in Strong City, 40 miles south of here."

Annie and I didn't have the time to track Denny down in Strong City; on leaving the Saddlerock, though, I gave my contact information to our waitress, Vicki.

Three days later Denny and Bonnie Orton walked into the Saddlerock. Someone told him, "Denny. A tall guy from out of town was in here the other day saying you were best friends 60 years ago. Any idea who that might be?"

It took Denny no more than a moment or two to collect himself.

"Sixty years ago? That's got to be Tony Gaenslen. Did he leave his phone number?" Vicki wasn't in, and no one else had the information.

Later that day, back in Strong City, Denny dug through a box of old papers. He couldn't remember how to spell my last name, but he had kept a letter I had sent him as a Yale senior, 48 years before. He turned it over to Bonnie, who gave it to her boss to track me down online. At home a couple of days later, Denny picked up his phone:

"Denny," I said, "This is Tony Gaenslen."

"Well I'll be darned," Denny said.

"Denny," I said. "You're one of the finest people I've ever known. I want you to know that."

"I feel the same way," Denny said. "You're the best friend I ever had."

Denny and I picked up our friendship where we had left it off 60 years before, talking long and eagerly on the phone. I called him every week, enjoying each conversation more than the last.

"I'll be coming back to Kansas City next Thanksgiving, Denny" I said. "I'll come to Strong City, and we'll get together."

"Try not to wait so long," Denny answered.

Six weeks later, though, the phone rang. It was Denny's granddaughter Heather.

"Grandpa died last night," she said. "He was so happy the two of you got together again. He talked about you all the time."

Some months later I made it out to Strong City; all of Denny's children, with their spouses and children, came over to Bonnie's house to meet me. I treated them all to a chicken dinner at a favorite local "chicken shack."

"I'd like to visit Denny's grave," I told Bonnie, and so we drove to where Denny had been born. All the Ortons were buried there, and I laid a bouquet of flowers on Denny's grave. Leaving the site, Bonnie kissed the top of Denny's headstone.

"He was my life," she said simply. "He was my life."

CHAPTER 14

Venezuela

MOM and I sailed for Venezuela in mid-summer of 1951. Dad was there to greet us, beyond happy to see Mom and me again, as our ship docked at Puerto Cabello. We drove for over an hour on the small, windy road that connected that port city, with its hot tropical climate, to the perpetual spring of Caracas, Venezuela's capital. The lush mountain scenery made breathtaking contrast with the dry flat plains of Kansas.

As we rose over the crest of the last Andean pass into the valley of Caracas, it spread out below us like a magical green wonderland bounded north and south by towering mountains. In 1951 much of the valley was still lush countryside, with the Caracas River wending through the heart of the valley, and with trees and tall grasses lining its banks and the adjoining fields. Within a few years the entire valley would be paved over, small picturesque villages giving way to high rises and expressways. But the Caracas I knew was a paradise.

Mom plunged whole-heartedly into learning the language, history, and customs of her new country, teaching them to me as well. Unlike most American mothers, she saw to it that I immediately made Venezuelan friends, inviting boys my age over to the house and getting me invited to theirs. Within a very short time I learned to speak fluent Spanish with no hint of an accent.

• • •

The English-speaking school in Caracas was called Campo Allegre, which means "Happy Field" in Spanish. Our teachers, for the most part young American women questing for adventure and husbands in an exotic land taught us less out of dedication to the cause of educating expatriate children, and more because it was their meal ticket financing a year or two of South American adventure.

Miss Grandover, who taught fifth grade, lost her temper more often than Dad, and almost as spectacularly. Whenever she got riled, which was often, she stamped her foot hard on the tile-covered cement floor. It was a wonder that Miss Grandover, who wore high heels, didn't injure her foot with all that stomping. I learned remarkably little in her class.

Going to school, I had learned by now, was mostly a waste of time. It was like eating pigs' feet, which Dad liked but I hated. Dad made me eat them anyway, telling me that doing things I disliked built my character.

The same philosophy, it was clear, applied to going to school. Although it did me precious little good, the fact that I hated it no doubt built my character. Since, in my personal opinion, my character was being built enough in other ways, I took to doing the absolute minimum of work needed to get a passing grade. I spent as little time on schoolwork, in and out of the classroom, as I could.

• • •

Since Dad was in the field seven weeks out of eight, I saw very little of him when we lived in Venezuela. He did find time, though, to bring me out into the field on adventures that few 10-year-old boys had ever had. On one occasion Dad took me into a section of western Venezuela inhabited by Indians who were fighting to keep their ancestral lands. To get to our destination, an exploration oil well being drilled deep in Indian territory, we first drove a full day around Lake Maracaibo, leaving civilization far behind. The following morning, rising early, we motored by river launch several hours up river, then drove to the oil rig in an armored Jeep. Thick mesh wiring over its windows protected the Jeep's passengers from the arrows occasionally shot by Indians hidden in the thick jungle underbrush. I was disappointed, at the end of the trip, not to have been shot at even once.

Another time Dad took my friend Tony Cook and me into a remote jungle area in a region where the Indians still lived their traditional lifestyle. Since their settlement was a good distance from where we would be camping, and they were said to be peaceful, Dad thought we would be in no great danger.

At dusk, as Dad was cooking supper for us over his Coleman stove, 15 Indians strode into the glade. Their leader wore an old pair of dirty khaki pants. The others, naked except for loincloths, all carried bows and arrows. The leader spoke with Dad in halting Spanish for three or four minutes, then led his party back into the jungle cover from which they had come.

"It's too dark to drive away on these twisting jungle tracks," Dad said. "We'll have to spend the night here. I'm sure these Indians are peaceful. They've come far from their village, probably on a hunting party of some sort. They want nothing more from us than to leave them alone. If I'd known we'd be intruding on them, I'd have brought you out here another time."

Not wholly reassured, I stuck Dad's geologic hammer into the ground under my jungle hammock so I could reach it in a hurry in case of Indian attack. Tony, for his part, leaned his .22 rifle against a tree next to his hammock.

I'd been asleep for a couple hours when I was awakened by a quick succession of "twanging" sounds. An instant later I found myself in a free fall, landing suddenly on the dull end of my hammer. I let out a loud, pain-stricken *yowlp*! A suddenly awakened Tony Cook lunged for his rifle, flipping his jungle hammock over and tangling himself tightly in it. Dad jumped quickly out of his hammock, shone his flashlight on the tangled mess that was Tony and me, and extricated both us. Other than my sore back, no harm had been done. A close look revealed that the strings on my hammock had been largely rotten, and the twanging sound I had heard was simply the strings giving way.

The following morning, pushing deeper into the jungle, the three of us came across a man who could well have passed for Robinson Crusoe's twin brother. He was naked from the waist up, wearing only a pair of dirty, torn khaki pants and a homemade fur hat of the kind you see in illustrations of Daniel Defoe's famous novel. In his hands he carried a 19th-century muzzle-loading percussion-cap musket.

While we were talking to him in Spanish, a toucan suddenly flew onto the top of a nearby tree. Shouldering his musket, Robinson Crusoe took aim, pulled the trigger, and *click* . . . . the hammer fell harmlessly on the percussion cap. He cocked the musket, took aim a second time, pulled the trigger, and click. The third time he adjusted the percussion cap on its nipple, pulled the trigger, and . . BANG . . . the percussion cap and main charge went off simultaneously. A small cloud of smoke blasted from the percussion cap, blackening Robinson Crusoe's face. A larger cloud of black smoke blasted out the muzzle. The toucan flapped heavily away, altogether unhurt.

"That man is employed by a wealthy landowner who probably lives in Caracas," Dad told us later. "He's basically squatting this land on behalf of the landowner, who has staked out thousands of acres of Indian territory. He's waiting for the Indians to be driven off, bribing his connections in Caracas to grant him title to the land once the Indians are gone."

"I saw another case like this once before," Dad went on. "A band of Indians attacked and killed two squatters of a wealthy ranchero. The squatters are paid a pittance. The rancheros, members of wealthy families with connections in Caracas, end up making millions. In this particular case the ranchero had fenced in his 'claim' with barbed wire. Soldiers from the 'guardia civil,' going in after the attack, found a piece of cloth torn from a Franciscan missionary's cassock hanging over a section of barbed wire. The Franciscans, or at least some of their missionaries, had taken an active hand in helping the Indians hang on to their tribal lands. The ranchero went after the missionaries, but the Franciscans too had connections in Caracas and were able to talk their way out of it.

"Our Robinson Crusoe," Dad added, "is cut from the same cloth. He's a pawn in a high-stakes land grab."

• • •

Dad also gave me extensive courses on the geological history of Venezuela in particular, and the earth in general, both of which had unfolded, so Dad taught me, over hundreds of millions and even billions of years. The history was there to be read in the rocks, and Dad taught me a lot about reading it, not only teaching me but also asking me to reach my own conclusions about the formations he would show me. He was intent on developing my own capacities for critical thinking, and when my insights were good, Dad's praise was warm and unqualified.

Dad himself, when he thought about geology and such subjects as the massive scale of the universe, the phenomenon of life, the extinction of species, continental drift, and Darwinism, was an original and independent thinker. Although he never used the term himself, the key to his method for approaching difficult problems was to identify what I came to think of as the fulcrum fact or facts: those that explain the entire phenomenon and through which all its disparate and seemingly scattered elements fall into place. He was emphatically an empirical and synthesizing thinker, but his approach was refreshingly and inspiringly imaginative and creative. Thus, when his line of reasoning led him to conclusions at odds with prevailing scientific, religious, or other orthodoxies, he did not hesitate to rely on his own opinion and break with prevailing views.

About the time I turned 14 I came onto Dad's screen as a full-fledged man, and the nature of our relationship shifted dramatically. He discussed all manner of things openly with me, from his personal life to problems involving geology, relationships with his colleagues at work, and evolutionary theory. In many ways he became my best friend.

• • •

I eventually paid a steep price for my miserable study habits and the mediocre quality of the schools I had attended. Dad and Mom quite clearly saw that something had to be done. Mom prevailed on Dad to look into a school in Caracas run by Christian brothers, which had an excellent academic reputation. We all went to the school together, where I was interviewed by Brother Juan. My Spanish was good enough to get me through the interview, but it had gaps. Brother Juan told us bluntly, "The Christian Brothers' Academy is not for your son. Our curriculum is taught in Spanish, and while Tony's Spanish is very good, he would need extra study to develop the vocabulary and grammar skills for participation at the seventh grade level in this school. Academically his skills are uneven. His knowledge of history and literature are impressive, but in math, science, and other subjects he is very weak. His report cards from Campo Allegre, moreover, work against him. Even if he does apply himself here, good study habits are not developed overnight. He might never catch up. That would not be good for us, and not good for him. I'm sorry."

I strongly regretted Brother Juan's decision. I had come to love almost everything about Venezuela, its incomparably beautiful land, its climate, its lush jungles, its towering mountains, its architecture, its history and culture. Above all I loved the people, from middle-class Venezuelans who were my father's colleagues and my mother's friends to the peasants who lived in the countryside towns we visited during Dad's trips into the field, or who worked with him in his exploration camps.

With the Christian Brothers Academy closed to me, we headed back to the States to look for an academically challenging school for me. I knew that I would miss Venezuela, but I did not begin to guess how much.

CHAPTER 15

The Education of a Shanty Irishman

THE quest for a better education began with a summer vacation in the states. Mom favored a Catholic school, but Dad was strongly opposed and wanted to explore Quaker-run schools. "Some of the finest people I've ever known have been Quakers," he explained to me. Mom would have no part of it. "I don't want Quakers influencing Tony with their strange religion," she said. With Dad crossing all Catholic schools off the list, and Mom all Quaker schools, the options narrowed considerably.

Dad hit on the idea of visiting his cousin Eleanor, married to John Randolph Tucker Alford III, a descendant of the aristocratic Randolph family of Virginia. Uncle Randolph and Aunt Eleanor lived on an estate named Dawn on the Miles in an impressive white-columned mansion which overlooked the Miles River on Maryland's aristocratic Eastern Shore of Maryland; the mansion was surrounded by 99 acres of fields and woods. One of Robert E. Lee's sons had been Uncle Randolph's godfather and had given him a silver baptismal goblet when he was born. Uncle Randolph preserved that goblet in a niche of his mansion with a reverence reminiscent of the Holy Grail.

Since Uncle Randolph liked to pontificate and Aunt Eleanor was quiet and retiring, we spent a good deal of time that day listening to Uncle Randolph's views on a broad range of subjects. Dad, who had long been fascinated with aristocratic families, was highly impressed. Mom took an immediate strong dislike to Uncle Randolph, but she was gracious and polite while we were there, keeping her views to herself.

Uncle Randolph gave Dad and Mom expansive advice about tending to my education. He sang the praises of the Calvert School, a correspondence-based teaching system through which I would be able to get a certified education by mail. Uncle Randolph's children all attended Calvert Country Day School in nearby Easton. Both Dad and Mom had heard favorable reports about the Calvert system from other sources and were impressed.

Shortly before we left, Uncle Randolph astounded us all by inviting me to spend the academic year at Dawn on the Miles with him, Aunt Eleanor, and their children, Jocelyn, Linda, and Randy, so I could attend the Calvert School in Easton. Uncle Randolph made the offer extremely appealing: I would be able to roam his 99-acre estate, and his foreman, Hamilton Winchester, would take me hunting in the fall. Dad thanked him in the warmest possible terms. Mom said nothing.

That evening in our hotel room, Mom and Dad had the worst argument I had ever seen. Dad was nigh euphoric about Uncle Randolph's offer, while Mom had found him pretentious, overstuffed, jealous, and petty. She profoundly distrusted and disliked Uncle Randolph and wanted to keep me away from him.

Dad thoroughly lost his temper. My mother rarely cried; only twice in my life did I ever see her sob, and this was one of those occasions. She pleaded with Dad not to send me to Uncle Randolph's, but Dad's mind was made up. And so I moved to Dawn of the Miles.

• • •

Seventh grade at Calvert Country Day was taught by Mrs. Morris, a fine teacher who made schoolwork fun, challenging, and interesting. For the first time since the Cours Maillard at Grandpère's, I actually began to apply myself in school. I soon made friends with a number of boys and began to be invited to their homes.

These invitations were the cause of my first rift with Uncle Randolph. It turned out that his main motivation in inviting me to spend a year in his home involved his daughter Jocelyn, who was my age. She was a serious, quiet, shy, and unhappy girl. Her one friend in school, Margie, as serious, quiet, and shy as herself, had recently come out of her shell and made new friends; she and Jocelyn now rarely saw each other. Uncle Randolph had expected me to fill the social gap in Jocelyn's life. Although I liked her well enough, we never became good friends.

My first run-in with Uncle Randolph was not long in coming. His son John Randolph Tucker Alford IV (Randy) had taken a strong liking to me, and we played often when we got home from school. Randy and I were out on the estate near the shack of Hamilton "Ham" Winchester, the estate foreman. Ham's ax lay on the ground, and I decided to show off for Randy by splitting some firewood. Ham's wife spotted me and yelled at me to stop, which I did. She reported me to Aunt Eleanor and Uncle Randolph, who promptly grounded me.

I accepted the punishment without complaint, expecting it to be lifted after a week or two, but it never was. For the next eight months, through the school year, I was restricted to the mansion and its surrounding yard while Jocelyn, Randy, and their sister Laura had the run of Uncle Randolph's 99 acre estate.

• • •

When I first started at Calvert Country Day, my grades reflected my poor study habits. Uncle Randolph, reviewing our monthly report cards, took pleasure in commenting on my bad grades in front of all us children, dwelling on how ashamed I must be about my poor performance. Dad and Mom had never shamed me over my bad grades. They knew I was exceptionally well-read and well-informed and could discuss a wide range of subjects intelligently. Nor had they believed that the key to curing me of bad study habits was to shame me into getting excellent grades at mediocre schools. They understood that the key was to find good schools that could challenge me. When I finally became motivated to work harder in school it had nothing to do with Uncle Randolph's attempts to shame me, but because I liked Mrs. Morris, enjoyed the subject matter, and quite naturally wanted to do well in her class.

My indifference to grades got on Uncle Randolph's nerves. Jocelyn worked extremely hard to excel on her report card, and was rewarded with the highest grades in Mrs. Morris' class. That fact, however, won her few friends and did not make her happy. It rankled Uncle Randolph that a ne'er-do-well like me should make good friends and be happy, and he decided to do something about it. Thus, one day after school, Uncle Randolph invited Jocelyn and me into his study. We had been studying world history for the last week and so, he said, it was time for a general review.

"I want to help you both with your homework" he announced. "We're going to review the history assignments you've been doing. I'm going to give you the date of a historical event. I want you to tell me the event to which the date refers. Whichever one of you knows the answer should just say it out loud."

Jocelyn and I both said we understood, and the quizzing began.

Uncle Tucker: "732"

Tony: "Charles the Hammer defeats the Saracens at the Battle of Tours, turning back the tide of Islamic influence in France and Europe."

Uncle Tucker: "800"

Tony: "Charlemagne has himself crowned Emperor by the Pope in Rome, reviving the Holy Roman Empire."

Uncle Tucker: "1452"

Tony: "Fall of Constantinople, bringing an end to the Byzantine, or Eastern, half of the Roman Empire."

Uncle Tucker: "1517"

Tony: "Martin Luther nails his 95 theses to the door of the Cathedral in Wittenberg, thereby starting the Protestant revolution."

On and on this went, question after question. I pounced on each answer before Jocelyn could begin to collect her wits, until Uncle Randolph couldn't take it anymore:

"SAY SOMETHING. SAY ANYTHING. JUST SAY IT BEFORE HE DOES!!" he roared at Jocelyn, who burst into tears and ran out of the room. Uncle Randolph, it was now clear, had not been the least interested in helping Jocelyn and me with our homework. He had wanted rather for Jocelyn to humiliate me with her superior knowledge. Uncle Randolph had badly misread the situation. I have a natural passion for and interest in history and, thanks in large part to Mom and Grandpère, I was very well-read in European and American history. I was gifted, moreover, with a steel-trap memory for historical dates and events.

The consequences of this incident were not long in coming. Until then I had had a comfortable room on the second floor of the mansion with the other members of the family. Not long after this incident I was moved to a much smaller attic room, where I stayed for the rest of the academic year.

About this time Uncle Randolph treated me to a lengthy discourse on the distinction between Shanty Irish and Lace-Curtain Irish that went something like this:

"Did you know, Tony, that there are just two kinds of Irishmen: Shanty Irish and Lace-Curtain Irish. Back in Ireland the Irish are all shanty dwellers. That's why we call them Shanty Irish. When they come to this country, though, some of them manage to scrape some money together to fancy up their shanties by tacking lace curtains around the windows. But whether they've got lace curtains on their windows or not, they don't fool anybody. Lace curtain or not, at bottom they're all Shanty Irish."

These remarks stung. Uncle Randolph knew that just three years before Dad, Mom, and I had been living in a shack on the Kansas plains, which gave his tale an aura of authenticity. "Uncle Randolph's too dumb to know the difference between Irish Catholics and French Catholics," I told myself. It helped, but not a lot.

About this time Uncle Randolph also took to calling me a Yankee. The eastern shore of Maryland in the early 1950s was still solidly Old South. The grandfather of one of my good friends at school, Tommy Holliday, had been an aide-de-camp to Robert E. Lee during the Civil War. Proudly displayed in the ante-room of the Holliday home was one of the certificates that Lee, at the end of the war, had signed for all his aide-de camps. Hanging next to the certificate was period engraving of Lee, and next to both a perpetual light illuminating this Robert E. Lee "shrine." Such displays were a common feature of many homes in the area.

Being called a Yankee stung. At my age a sense of place and belonging were important, and I was acutely aware that I couldn't say I was really *from* anywhere in particular. I couldn't truthfully claim to be *from* Granville or Normandy on Mom's side, or *from* Wisconsin on Dad's. I could, however, truthfully and proudly say that I had been *born* in San Antonio. I was a Texan.

It was not a purely superficial identity. Dad and Mom had fondness for and many affinities with the Southern way of life, and I identified with these. Influenced by my friends at Calvert Country Day I came to see Robert E. Lee as a noble character. He became, and remained, my greatest hero until I was close to 20 years old.

Identifying myself as a Texan brought with it two supreme satisfactions. In the first place it gave the lie to Uncle Randolph's assertion that I was a Yankee. Better yet, I was a manly South-*Westerner* from Texas like my Dad, a hard-riding, gun-toting plainsman bearing no resemblance of any kind to that effete, plantation-owning South-*Easterner* Uncle Randolph.

CHAPTER 16

In the Kitchen with Mary

CUTTING my foot on an oyster shell precipitated the final break with Uncle Randolph. Since my cousins were out playing on Uncle Randolph's 99 acres, leaving me to play alone, I had bought a small electric-powered boat early the spring, sailing it in a shallow cove on the Miles River. One day, stepping on a buried oyster shell, I cut my foot badly. Bleeding profusely, I headed up the lawn toward the mansion, wondering who I could turn to help me staunch the flow of blood. Uncle Randolph was out of the question; I neither liked nor trusted him.

Aunt Eleanor tried to soften Uncle Randolph's harshness toward me as best she could, and I liked her well enough, but not enough to turn to her in my moment of distress. The only other person present in the mansion at that time of day was Mary, the "colored" cook. Intuitively I knew that Mary was the one person at Dawn on the Miles I could trust, and so I headed toward the kitchen.

Mary put a piece of newspaper on the floor which quickly was soaked with my blood. She stopped the flow, cleaned my foot, and bandaged it. While she was doing all this I started talking with her and discovered that I liked her.

Every afternoon thereafter, on my return from school, I took to visiting my new-found friend Mary. Until then I had seen very little of her, since all her work was done in the kitchen. The only time I did see her was at breakfast and dinner every day. Whenever Aunt Eleanor rang a little bell on the dining room table, Mary emerged from the kitchen in her uniform holding the next course, serving each one of us by turn, children included. She stood slightly behind us, one hand behind her back, the other hand extended holding the dish forward so we could help ourselves. Before Mary helped me with my injured foot I had rarely spoken to her at all.

I enjoyed my visits with Mary a lot, and looked forward to them. She was always kind and friendly with me, but reserved. I think she had a naturally reserved temperament. She was, moreover, cautious about our burgeoning friendship.

One weekend, while talking in the kitchen with Mary, I came up with a brilliant idea.

"Mary," I said. "I've got an idea. Why don't you take me to the movies?"

"I can't take you to the movies, honey," Mary answered.

"Why not?"

"I'm colored, honey. They don't let colored folk into the movies."

"Mary!" I exclaimed in genuine distress. "That's not fair."

"I don't think it's fair either, honey. But that's just the way it is."

"You shouldn't let them do that to you," I said. "You should go to the movies anyway."

"I can't, honey," Mary answered. "They just wouldn't let me."

I took in this astounding information and gave it some careful thought. Another bright idea then popped into my head.

"I've got it, Mary," I said. "I'll take you to the movies. They'll let you in if you're with me."

"No they won't, honey," Mary said. "It just wouldn't work."

I was sure that if I told the men down at the movie house to let Mary into the theater they would do so, particularly since I would be going in with her. I thought Mary lacked nerve, and was disappointed in her.

• • •

Uncle Tucker chaffed at the time I was spending with Mary and sent Aunt Eleanor to straighten me out. "Tony," she said, "You've got to stop spending so much time in the kitchen with Mary. It would reflect badly on the family if anyone saw you there with her."

Like so many things that I heard from the adult world, this statement did not make a lot of sense. Uncle Tucker and Aunt Eleanor had few friends and correspondingly few visitors. Of the few who did come to visit not one, so far as I knew, had ever stopped in the kitchen to pay their respects to Mary. The chances that I would be seen there, thereby bringing disrepute to family, appeared to lie on the far side of remote. I therefore disregarded Uncle Randolph's instruction and spent just as much time in the kitchen as I had before. My refusal to obey his order took a heavy toll on Uncle Randolph's state of mind. He resolved to get rid of me once and for all, lying in wait for the right opportunity.

• • •

The stratagem he hit upon was to have Aunt Eleanor take me to a child psychologist. Aunt Eleanor explained to me that Uncle Tucker thought I was jumpy and that it would be helpful to have a child psychologist help me with my problem.

I was perfectly willing to go. For the most part I was an exceedingly polite and cooperative kid in the presence of adults. In this case, I tried to be helpful by consciously putting the "jumpy" side of my personality in evidence so the child psychologist could see it. We spoke together, played games, and after an hour or so Aunt Eleanor and I left and went home.

Uncle Tucker then wrote a letter to my parents describing the visit to the child psychologist. The psychologist, Uncle Tucker told Dad and Mom, had found me to be emotionally disturbed. Accordingly, he wrote, he could no longer keep me at Dawn on the Miles. He told my parents to send him a check for my airfare home. As soon as he received it, he said, he would put me on the first plane back to Venezuela.

Mom was close to hysterical when she got the letter. The next day, she flew from Venezuela to Baltimore.

I was playing in the front yard when Mom got out of a cab in front of the estate. She gave me a quick once-over to make sure I wasn't the victim of physical abuse, and then walked directly into the mansion. She told Uncle Tucker and Aunt Eleanor that she was leaving immediately, taking me with her. She would come back later, she said, to give them a piece of her mind and collect my belongings. Twenty minutes later Mom and I left Dawn on the Miles in the still-waiting cab.

I never returned to Dawn on the Miles. Mom and I stayed a night or two in the Tidewater Inn in Easton, an elegant old hotel, and then moved into two rooms in a rambling old guest house. Graduation was another six weeks away. Mom and I stayed there for the duration.

A day or so after getting into Easton, Mom made an appointment to see the child psychologist. The woman had seen me no more than a week or two before and remembered me well. She told Mom I was a perfectly normal, healthy, intelligent, and well-adjusted 12-year-old boy. She chalked up the "jumpiness" which had so vexed Uncle Tucker to the perfectly typical eagerness and enthusiasm of boys my age. She had said all of this in the report she had given Uncle Randolph. She had an extra copy and gave it to Mom. In a word, Uncle Randolph had falsified the psychologist's report in order to get rid of me.

The matter, unfortunately, did not end there. Uncle Randolph feared the reaction of Aunt Eleanor's Milwaukee relatives if Mom and Dad were to tell them what had transpired. Aunt Eleanor belonged to the most socially prominent branch of the Gaenslen family in Milwaukee. Her father, my great-uncle Dr. Frederick Gaenslen, had been a famous and successful orthopedic doctor, universally known and beloved in Milwaukee and even nationally.

It was a high-stakes game, and Uncle Randolph went on the offensive. He described Mom's trip to the Eastern Shore as the overreaction of a hysterical French woman. He ascribed my predilection for socializing with the colored help to my mother's unhealthy influence. Uncle Randolph's line of attack was well-honed to win the support of our Milwaukee relatives, and Mom's French origins and strong French accent worked heavily against her. In the end all the members of the extended Gaenslen family in Milwaukee sided with Uncle Randolph and Aunt Eleanor against Mom, with the exception of my father's youngest sister, my beloved Aunt Polly.

Mom remained scarred by what had happened. While she never criticized me directly for anything I had done, the Maryland incident marked the beginning of a lasting change in our relationship. In her eyes, and despite all the despicable things Uncle Randolph had done, she could not deny that I, a guest in his home, had transgressed the social barrier that lay at the heart of Southern aristocratic society. In the Old South of that time, no tradition was more sacred than the one that separated black from white.

By spending so much time in the kitchen with Mary, and by disregarding Uncle Randolph's and Aunt Eleanor's instructions to stop doing so, I had crossed that boundary. Mom could understand, indeed sympathize with, Aunt Eleanor's explanation that by persisting in spending time in the kitchen with Mary, and by refusing to change my ways, I had seriously embarrassed the family.

The truth is, in subtle but unmistakable ways, the year at Dawn on the Miles had deeply and irrevocably changed me. Until that time I had been what the French call *bien elevé* or "well brought up." While adventurous and mischievous when on my own, I had invariably been polite, respectful, and obedient with adults.

After that year my obedience was uncertain. It deeply offended me that Mary couldn't go to the movies with me simply because she was black. And I had no intention of betraying my friendship with Mary by staying away from the kitchen or of avoiding her simply because she was a "colored" servant and Uncle Randolph had told me to do so.

What I had done had repercussions with my mother also. When I was smaller Mom had often referred to me as her "little Jesus." "You were such a good little boy," she would say. My days as Mom's little Jesus were coming to an end. In its place "Where did I go wrong with you?" became her constant refrain. I was going my own way, doing things she didn't understand and couldn't approve of. It had always mattered to her that I make a good impression on her friends. Now I was beginning to act in ways that seriously embarrassed her.

CHAPTER 17

An Old Money School

ARISTOCRATS caught Dad's imagination. They were people who acquired fortunes and passed them down from generation to generation, a skill he admired and dreamed of imitating. His fascination, moreover, had a more pragmatic side. Aristocrats saw to it that their children got the best education money could buy. Two years into his new-found prosperity working in Venezuela, Dad was making enough—barely—to pay the bills at the kind of prestigious schools to which aristocrats sent their children. When Uncle Randolph and the Southern aristocracy turned out to be a bust, Dad was neither discouraged nor deterred. Rather, he shifted his focus from the Virginia-Eastern Shore aristocracy to New England.

Thus it was that Dad and Mom sent me to the Academy, a prestigious, centuries-old New England private boarding school just outside Boston whose registry of graduates included such famous Bostonian blue-blood families as Cabots, Lowells, Lodges, and the like. It also boasted a healthy number of representative from such other famous American families as Vanderbilt, Rockefeller, Roosevelt, Mellon, and Kennedy.

The Academy was an "old-money" school. Its families whose dynasties began accumulating their fortunes in the seventeenth century ranked higher in the Boston Social Register than those who became rich in the eighteenth. Those who began in the eighteenth ranked higher than those in the nineteenth, and so on. Dad's money, on the other hand, was so new the ink on it had not yet fully dried. In the eyes of many at the Academy we were Shanty Irishmen just off the boat, still making payments on the few shreds of lace we had managed to tack onto the windows of our shack.

This was brought home to me shortly after I came to the school. One of my classmates invited me home for a weekend, not realizing that his parents did not welcome Catholics. When I asked to be taken to Mass on Sunday morning, his father replied, "The last time I went to the Catholic Church was when I took my Irish maid."

* * *

The wealthy and powerful sent their children to the Academy to occupy positions of privilege and responsibility in the world. My warm, affectionate house master, Mr. Torney, educated me on this point succinctly and tellingly:

"Gaenslen," he said, "always remember: 'RHIP—RHIR. Rank Has Its Privileges—Rank Has Its Responsibilities.'"

The Academy boasted a flunky system in which all lower-class students were "flunkies" to upper-class students, who could order them around. The supposed beauty of the system was that with seniority came rank and the opportunity to exercise it responsibly. It was also subject to rank abuse, a reality I came into painful contact with a couple of weeks after my arrival at the Academy. An upper classman named Stockton had been hazing me, and I shouted loud enough to draw our floor master, Mr. Pocock, to the fray. He issued a punishment slip to Stockton, and Stockton never forgot it. For the next couple of years he made it his business to push me to the brink of raw misery. He made a practice of bringing one or two other boys with him into my room, knocking my stuff off the shelves, and pushing me around.

"Are you fighting mad, Gaenslen?" he would ask, sweeping more of my stuff onto the floor. "Not mad yet? Maybe this will help," he would say, giving me a hard push.

"What's wrong with you, Gaenslen? Get mad!" he would order. Had I lost it and gone after him, he and his mates would have pounded my head through the floor-boards.

Dad wore a black mustache in the picture of him I kept on my shelf. "Heil Hitler!" Stockton and his claque kept shouting out whenever he saw me. They took to supplementing this with a selection of choice epithets such as "You dirty Jap," "Slant Eyes," "You little Nip," and "you little yellow bastard."

Before coming to the Academy I had always liked and gotten along well with the other kids in school. Now I became fearful and shy.

* * *

Another form of abuse at the Academy was a practice I called "pack hazing." For a while a boy named Peter Kane was the school's favored target for the so-called "pink belly" treatment. Walking through the campus you would suddenly come across a pack of boys yelling and shouting. In the middle of it all would be Peter, thrown on his back, his shirt pulled open, his belly exposed, being rubbed hard with a stiff hairbrush. By the time the sport was over, his belly would have been scrubbed into a bright shade of pink.

Another underclassman, Victor Miller, exuding entirely too much self-confidence and self-satisfaction for a flunky, paid a steep price for it one day as he was making his rounds as house "yeller." The yeller's job was to leap into action the moment the daily wake-up bell rang in the dormitory at 7:00 a.m. and run through all four floors of the dormitory at five-minute intervals yelling "five past," "ten past," and so on.

Yelling could prove hazardous to your health. Such was Victor's fate. A pack of upperclassmen pounced on him on one of his rounds, stripping him naked and holding him under the hot water faucet in the shower. Since a single central steam-driven system provided hot water to all the buildings on campus, water came out of these faucets red hot. By the time the boys got through with Victor he was well cooked. His crying caught my attention. Sticking my head out the opening of my cubicle, I watched Victor, stark naked and red as a lobster, tears streaming down his cheeks, shuffling back to his cubicle at the end of his yelling run.

I learned my lesson well, which is to remain absolutely impassive in the face of hazing or bullying. Expressing feelings, pleading for mercy, showing fear or weakness, or getting angry arouses a veritable hazing frenzy. After I figured this out I was rarely targeted, with one memorable exception which took place in my senior year.

* * *

A boy who had moved through all the stages of flunky-hood finally rose, in his last year of school, to the top of the system, becoming at long last a "First Classman." Each year's First Class chose its own distinctive emblem for the class blazer. Only by First Classmen wore a class blazer, their mark of distinction, their badge of authority.

Responsibility came with this emblem of high rank. Each First Classman took his turn as head of a table in the dining room, maintaining order, serving the food as it came in from the kitchen, supervising distribution of extra portions of food or desserts, formally announcing the end of the meal. Until he did so, everyone remained sitting in his place.

Most boys got through the job with a reasonable display of authority and flair. Some boys, however, simply didn't have it in them to ride herd over a restless bunch of "underclassmen. They instead became the targets of what I called "reverse hazing."

The reverse hazer was always a boy with a sharp wit, a smart mouth, and a keen instinct for the vulnerable spots in his victim's psychological makeup. In the dining room for my residential house most of the targets for reverse hazers came from a subgroup in the school widely known as "the Vultures."

The first, and last, time a Vulture named Ezra took his seat as table head a reverse hazer named Kissel, who had shrewdly and mercilessly mastered the power realities of the boarding school life, read Ezra's vulnerable psyche like a book; he proceeded to tear the pages out one by one. Each time Kissel sliced into him verbally Ezra, utterly unable to defend himself or exercise the authority of his office, sank lower and lower into his chair, his head bending closer to his chest. By the time the meal was over Kissel had sliced him to ribbons. Too damaged by the experience, Ezra never again sat as table head.

When my turn came up, a reverse hazer by the name of Hitzig made it his business to go after me. He was the designated server at my table, charged with responsibility for bringing large trays of food in from the kitchen for me to serve to the other boys. Hitzig, however, had shrewdly spotted a "deer in the headlights" quality in me that made me an ideal target. He lost no time in going after me, scoring high, he was sure, with his classmates. Instead of putting the tray in front of me where I could start serving it, he threw slices of meat down the table directly onto the other boys' plates.

"Cut that out, Hitzig," I said.

"You're a wimp," Hitzig said, throwing a couple more slices down the table.

"I mean it, Hitzig," I said.

"You do? What are you going to do about it?" asked Hitzig, throwing another slice or two down the table.

"Hitzig," I all but pleaded. "Cut it out."

"You sorry little nerd," Hitzig said. By now he had thrown slices of meat to all but one or two of the other boys' plates.

Quite suddenly another voice at the table made itself heard;

"Cut that out Hitzig, you dirty Jew."

Hitzig stopped dead in his tracks. The speaker, Tim Mellon, was the scion of one of the wealthiest families in America, the Mellon name being associated with such institutions as the Mellon Bank and Gulf Oil Company. Tim was a year younger than me. That he, as an underclassman, should intervene to save the skin of an upper classman came as a stunning surprise to everyone at the table, not least of whom Hitzig and myself.

Hitzig stood in dazed silence, turning to the boy sitting next to Mellon's in hopes of getting some sign of support. Instead, the boy seconded Tim.

"That's right, Hitzig" he said.

Each boy in turn now took up the refrain, repeating "That's right, Hitzig." It went all the way around the table until it came back at last to me. I hesitated no more than a moment; Tim had, quite literally, just saved my emotional and psychological life, and so I chimed in:

"That's right, Hitzig."

Hitzig sat down, stunned. He was raw inside, deciding to get even by having another go at me the following day. Tim Mellon, he knew, couldn't save me a second time. This time, Hitzig vowed, he wouldn't stop until he'd reduced me to a pile of emotional rubble.

• • •

Sam Taylor, our House Monitor, came over to see me right after the meal.

"Tony," he said. "You've got to maintain order at your table. If Hitzig starts up again assign him to sorting rusty nuts and bolts in the basement of Wolcott House on Saturday morning. Hit him as hard as you have to as often as you have to, and I'll back you up, whatever you do."

A bright light lit up inside me. Until that moment I had failed to fully grasp the shift in power realities brought on by First Class status. I was now the authority figure at my table, vested with the rank, authority, and power to maintain order and decorum.

I turned the full implications of this stunning turn of events over and over in my mind until I had fully internalized them. Further, I prepared myself mentally for my next encounter with Hitzig, anticipating his moves and readying myself to take him down no matter what he came up with.

The next night Hitzig did indeed go after me a second time. Instead of sitting in his designated seat next to me, he stood at the far end of the table thereby constituting himself as its new center of power, and as far from Tim Mellon as he could get. He began taunting me, working the boys at his end of the table, laughing and joking with them at my expense.

"Sit down, Hitzig" I ordered.

"Think you know how to make me?" Hitzig responded.

"That's half an hour on Saturday morning sorting nuts and bolts in the basement, Hitzig," I said.

"You sorry little wimp," Hitzig said. "Running for help when you can't stand up for yourself?"

"That's an hour, Hitzig," I said.

"You little nerd," Hitzig replied.

"Shut up and sit down before I count to three, Hitzig. If you're having trouble understanding what that means, I'll hit you with another half-hour on the nuts and bolts detail, and we'll give it another try. Believe me, you will have learned how to count to three before I'm through with you."

Hitzig stood in stunned silence for a moment or two and then sat down. He was well and thoroughly beaten, and he knew it.

Thus it was that thanks to Tim Mellon I learned the most valuable lesson I was to learn in my five-year stay at the Academy, discovering the existence of an unsuspected and radically different me. Once the predatory survival instincts of this second self were aroused and I awoke to its hidden powers, there was enough iron in my soul to go after the likes of Hitzig, break them down, and enjoy myself in the process.

CHAPTER 18

A.O. Smith

THE flunky system and reverse hazing do not tell the whole story of my life at the Academy—far from it. I was lucky enough to have a teacher there who decisively changed the course of my life.

Beyond the shadow of a doubt, A.O. Smith was the most eccentric teacher at the school. He kept his shoulders hunched and walked with a kind of peculiar shuffle, his hands stuffed into the outer pockets of his jacket. Since he gesticulated a lot when he lectured, with his hands still stuffed into his pockets, his jacket flapped about a good deal as he walked around the classroom.

A.O. did not like bullshit. Whenever he felt that a boy's remarks in class had wandered too far off the point, he would lift his right hand out of his jacket pocket, make horns out of his thumb and little finger, and give a little staccato laugh (eh-eh-eh-eh-eh) punctuated at the end with the word "Bull." Although A.O. came across as odd and could be very direct, he was the soul of kindness. His frequent use of the word "bull" never hurt. It was his trademark, and we boys soon went around making horns out of our thumbs and little fingers and going "eh-eh-eh-eh-eh Bull" every time we got the chance to let a classmate know he was wandering off the track.

A.O. taught the Honors English class in Third Class (sophomore year). He became my academic Buddha, leading me out of the darkness of academic indifference. Thanks to him I discovered not only that I was good at something, but that I had a passion for doing it.

It all came about because of A.O.'s core principle in teaching us to read and write about English literature. He leaned repeatedly on the phrase that summed up his entire philosophy of teaching: "Feel it, gentlemen. Feel it." A.O. insisted that below the explicit rational meaning of words lay their deeper meaning, and that you couldn't understand the full meaning of a text until you engaged your feeling functions no less than your rational functions. When a particularly beautiful or meaningful passage was read in class, A.O. would pause to draw the entire class's attention to it.

"Did you feel that, gentlemen? I mean, did you *really* feel it? Shakespeare is trying to tell us something here. Do you get it? Do you really get it?"

For the first time I knew why I was in school. I was going after the deeper meaning, the felt quality of the stuff I was reading. It was a moment of immense self-discovery, the beginning of a journey into discovering the deeper layers not only of the world around me but of my true self as well.

It was A.O. who taught me that the real and essential me is not the analytical thinker but the storyteller, the romantic, the sensitive poet and mystic. A.O. awoke the artistic side of my being. I began to look at nature and devour literature with new eyes and new ears.

A.O. saw talents in me I could not see for myself. When he could not push me into putting them to use, he took the initiative himself. The Academy had a literary magazine, but I never imagined anything I had written was good enough to submit. On a couple of occasions A.O. suggested that I submit one of the pieces I had written in his class to the magazine. When I proved too insecure to risk rejection, he took the piece to the magazine himself, and they printed it. After A.O. broke the ice for me, I later submitted a number of pieces to the magazine, all of which were published.

He touched me so deeply that long before my year in A.O.'s class was over I knew what I wanted to do with my life: I wanted to be a writer. When I went home for Christmas vacation in Venezuela that year, I told my parents all about A.O. and my desire of becoming a writer. Dad and Mom lost no time letting me know exactly how they felt about it: "We're not investing all this money in your education so you can starve in an attic." Dad told me. They resented the Academy for exposing me to an odd-ball like A.O. Smith; Mom took to referring to A.O. as "B.O. Smith."

Although I did not, in the end, become a writer, I did find an outlet for the love of writing first awakened in me by A.O. Smith in the practice of law. I was never happier as a lawyer than the moment I could shut my office door, tell my secretary to hold all calls, take out a pad of paper, and devote hours on end to pouring all my creative talents into writing briefs.

CHAPTER 19

"Those Venezuelans Should All Be Shot"

ON May 8, 1958, riots broke out in Caracas when Vice President Richard Nixon paid a state visit to Venezuela. Relations between the United States and Latin American countries had sunk to their lowest point in years. Protests had broken out not long before when the United States awarded the Legion of Honor to Venezuela's dictator, Marcos Perez-Jimenez. A brutal anti-communist, Perez Jimenez's secret police ruthlessly tracked down, imprisoned, and tortured opponents of his regime. In January, 1958 he was ousted by a military coup. Less than four months later Nixon planned a state visit to Venezuela. Although he was warned by both the Venezuelan government and the American Embassy in Caracas not to make the trip, Nixon went ahead with his state visit anyway.

As his motorcade moved through the streets of Caracas, Nixon's car was set upon by an angry mob. The car got dented and its windows smashed. Venezuelan soldiers were called in to rescue the beleaguered Vice President. Nixon, getting out of Venezuela ahead of schedule early the next morning, was greeted by a cheering crowd on his return to Washington.

A day or so after his return, as I was walking across the Academy campus, I came across a bunch of students discussing these events. One of them, a First Class student named Nelson Abeel declared belligerently:

"Those Venezuelans. They should all be shot."

These Academy students knew nothing about conditions in Venezuela; their conversation angered me and I decided to do something about it. I asked my House Master Mr. Torney to arrange for me to address the school's morning assembly on the subject of current events in Venezuela. He agreed, and a couple days later I was on.

The school day began for the Academy's three upper classes, about 150 boys in all, with morning assembly in Wigglesworth Hall. We all sang a hymn chosen from the Academy Hymnal, and the day's announcements were made. Student announcements were almost always made by school monitors and team or club captains regarding special events, extra practices, and the like. No announcements were ever made by nerds or flunkies. When the master presiding over morning assembly announced that Tony Gaenslen had an announcement, a titter of amusement rippled through the hall. Nothing deterred, I strode to the front of the room, stepped up to the dais, and turned to face my schoolmates.

"I'm here to talk to you about recent events in Venezuela," I said. "I'm doing this because one of our classmates recently stated, and I quote: 'Those Venezuelans should all be shot.' Well, those Venezuelans should not be shot, and I'm here to tell you why.

"My Dad works for Creole Petroleum Corporation, the largest oil company in Venezuela, a subsidiary of Esso, the largest oil company in the world. I live in a compound owned by Creole. Our compound is surrounded by a tall cyclone fence topped with strands of barbed wire. Two guards stand at the gate of our compound 24 hours a day. No one comes in without an okay from the guard.

"Not long ago I saw a boy living in the barrio just the other side of our compound clinging to the cyclone fence separating his world from mine, staring longingly in. Our compound must have appeared a paradise to him. It's lush with flowers, trees, vegetation, paved streets, comfortable air-conditioned houses, and neatly tended lawns. Our club has a swimming pool, tennis courts, and a clubhouse where I hang out with my friends. It's a great place, but until recently Venezuelans were not allowed to be members.

"He was dressed in rags, living in a barrio of tin-roofed shacks baking in the sun. The streets in the barrio are unpaved, dry, dusty. There are no flowers and no trees. The contrast between our two worlds could not be greater, and yet Venezuela is his home. I'm a guest in his country.

Something about him sticks in my mind, and I can't get it out. I don't think I'll ever forget him. And yet, if we're going to talk about shooting Venezuelans, I suppose we might as well begin by shooting him.

"But I don't want to talk about shooting him. I think that's a dumb thing to say. I'd rather talk about getting to know him and getting to be friends with him and other Venezuelans."

I talked for another seven or eight minutes, drawing attention to the poverty and hardship in which many ordinary Venezuelans lived. My anger stemmed from the way a lot of Americans, including company men who I knew personally through Dad's work, liked to throw their weight around without ever getting to know Venezuelan people, their country, or their culture. The president of Creole Petroleum had spent 30 years in the country without ever bothering to learn Spanish. The top company man in Maracaibo, Shorty Hedlund, who I knew personally, was a short, squat Texan who, as far as his knowledge of Venezuela and Venezuelans went, had never left West Texas.

My parents belonged to a significant population of ordinary Americans who behaved exactly the opposite from these examples. Both Dad and Mom learned Spanish. Dad expressed the same admiration for the Venezuelan workers in his exploration camps as he had for roughnecks in the Texas oil fields early in his career. He introduced me to these men when he brought me out to his field camps. They were real people to him and became so to me. Mom, for her part, learned Spanish well enough to become an adjunct professor of French literature at the Universidad de Zulia in Maracaibo.

I don't remember exactly what kind of reception I expected to receive when I finished speaking, but I certainly wasn't prepared for what I got. It came close to a standing ovation. My message itself was well received by the great majority of the boys. Beyond that, no boy at the Academy had ever done what I just had. Boys who were the big men on campus came over to say that they admired my courage. Even my house master, Mr. Torney, took me aside to say, "Well done, old man."

• • •

What happened that day was almost as much a surprise to me as it was to all of my classmates and the teachers at the Academy. Who was that boy who shot out of his chair that morning, striding confidently to the front of the assembly to challenge long-held points of view? It certainly wasn't me, at least not the me that I, and they, were familiar with. That me is fundamentally shy and quiet. He dislikes arguments and avoids controversy. He thinks a lot, but for the most part he keeps his thoughts and opinions to himself, sharing them, if at all, with only a few of his closest friends. He is never happier than when he can retreat into his own den or room to read, think, or write. In later years, I would baptize this side of myself with the name Antoine, the dreamer and mystic.

Nothing like the character who stood up that May morning in Wigglesworth Hall had ever showed up in my life before. He was supremely self-confident. He relished the thought of taking center stage on a controversial stand, sure of his ground and his ability to defend it. He had his point of view and his opinions and was determined to see them prevail, come what may. While readily roused into action in situations of injustice and cruelty, he was otherwise nigh impossible to prod into action. I dubbed this side of my identity Tex.

The confrontation with Hitzig and the talk in Wigglesworth Hall rounded out my education at the Academy beautifully. Mr. Torney had been prescient. Acquiring Rank wasn't all that bad. If you put your mind to it you could use the advantages of a privileged education to do good and make the lives of other people better.

CHAPTER 20

Anti-Semitism

EVERY few years, Mom and I would go to France for the summer to see our extended family. They were joyous trips, and what I treasured most was seeing my Grandpère.

Grandpère told me a lot about his life, and as I got older it became important to him that I should know something deeper about him. Thus it was that when I was a teenager, Grandpère told me about the part he had played in the Dreyfus Affair.

The Dreyfus Affair was a scandal that tore French society apart around the turn of the twentieth century. The central figure in the scandal was Alfred Dreyfus, the youngest son of a wealthy Jewish manufacturer. Dreyfus had been 11 years old when German armies invaded his home in the French province of Alsace, annexing it into the German Empire. Rather than live under German rule, the strongly patriotic Dreyfus family moved to Paris. Wanting to defend France should it ever be invaded by Germany again, Alfred decided on a military career. After graduating with honors from the prestigious Ecole Superieure de Guerre, he was posted to the French Army's General Staff.

Shortly after he joined the General Staff, the French Army's counter-intelligence section learned that military secrets were being passed to the Germans by a highly placed spy, most likely in the General Staff. Suspicion immediately fell on Dreyfus, the only Jew on the General Staff. He was immediately arrested and charged with treason. In early 1895 he was summarily convicted in a secret court martial, publicly stripped of his army rank, and sentenced to life imprisonment on Devil's Island in French Guiana.

In 1896, however, the new chief of French military intelligence, Lt. Colonel Picquart, reported that he had found evidence that Dreyfus had been framed. The French General Staff moved quickly to suppress this evidence and silenced Lt. Colonel Picquart by transferring him to the southern desert of Tunisia. It later arrested him and brought him up on false charges. The General Staff simultaneously mounted a sham trial to exonerate the real culprit, the spy and traitor Major Esterhazy, who was unanimously acquitted by a military court based on sham evidence after the second day of trial.

The Dreyfus Affair, though, refused to die quietly. It leapt into national and international attention when, in 1898, the influential author Emile Zola published an open letter addressed to the president of the French Republic accusing the government and General Staff of anti-Semitic motivation in their conduct of the Dreyfus Affair.

The situation split every level of French society along religious and political lines, pitting the small minority of pro-Dreyfus activists against those who thought Dreyfus was guilty. Large anti-semitic riots broke out throughout France. The small minority of Dreyfus supporters refused to be suppressed and persevered for years against great odds until 1906, when Dreyfus was exonerated.

• • •

Grandpère was 22 years old and a young lawyer just two years out of law school when Zola published his letter. He familiarized himself thoroughly with the facts of the case and became convinced of Dreyfus's innocence. Almost his entire family, devoutly Catholic and politically conservative, had lined up on the anti-Dreyfus side of the controversy. Only Grandpère himself and his uncle Paul Caurette stood up for Dreyfus.

Grandpère was the only person in my family who ever spoke to me about the problem of anti-Semitism. Years later, it dawned on me how much it had meant to Grandpère to have a grandson who, he knew, would one day be able to fully appreciate not only the significance of the Dreyfus Affair itself but also what it had meant to him, as a young man, to have stood up and been counted in a cause that the French author Anatole France would later call "a moment in the conscience of humankind."

• • •

A year later, on our annual visit to the Gaenslen family in Milwaukee, I would encounter the problem of anti-Semitism in a very different way.

My paternal grandfather, Richard Gaenslen, entered this world an unwanted child, and spent his difficult childhood keenly aware of his parents' resentment over his very existence. His harsh childhood produced a harsh edge in him that was terrible and frightening when he lost his temper. I was quite young when I learned to recognize a cold, hard look that often came into Grandpa's eyes. I called it his "killer eye."

Sitting in his large armchair in the living room of his house in Milwaukee, Grandpa smoked expensive Upmann cigars imported from Cuba. He chewed Peerless tobacco, a brand fiery enough to raise the dead, his cuspidor at the ready on the floor next to his armchair.

Grandpa's stories pulsated with abundant energy and excitement. He had an instinct for vivid details, a wonderful sense of timing, and an elephantine memory. He told stories with such zest and energy that you were carried along on the flow of his words. When he described his rambunctious childhood in Old Milwaukee or told of his hunting exploits and adventures in the wild, I loved to listen to him.

By the time I was 10 or 12, I had learned to try to steer Grandpa's conversation in the direction of these kinds of stories. I watched his eyes as I did this. If I was successful, we were in for a wonderful visit. Often, though, I would see the killer look steal into his eyes. Then he would launch into diatribes detailing his many antipathies, prejudices, and hatreds. When things took this turn, I knew the evening was doomed.

Grandpa usually began by tearing into all of my grandmother's relatives. He listed their various shortcomings and faults with vivid contempt, concluding this part of the evening's discourse by telling his children:

"Of all your mother's relatives, I like myself the best."

With his in-laws disposed of, Grandpa would launch into the next of his favorite targets: kikes, niggers, Micks, dagos, wops, Polacks, and other members of what he called "the lesser breeds." When I was very young, most of what Grandpa said did not make much of an impression on me. When I reached my teen years though, the things he said began to truly bother me

"God made the niggers dumb, but he made them happy," I recall him saying. He had gone on a golfing trip somewhere in the South and had a black caddy. Grandpa mocked all the "Yassuh" and "Nossuhs" his caddy had come out with, and the extravagant way in which he had laughed at Grandpa's jokes.

Grandpa's most relentless and intense antipathy was reserved for the Jews. When he got cranked up he leaned forward into his subject with all his powerful physical frame. His face would redden, and when he concluded an anecdote with an expletive, it could make you jump even if you were in the north bedroom at the other end of his house. "They're all shysters," he would bellow. "Everybody wouldn't hate them if they hadn't done something to deserve it."

Things took a decisive turn for me when we visited Milwaukee in the summer of my 14th year. Grandpa had a penchant for bathroom stories. On this occasion he described the Turkish toilet that served the eight tenants on the third floor of his office building on East Wisconsin. Turkish toilets are simply holes in the floor of the bathroom; Grandpa described in some detail how you had to squat to use one.

He then went on to describe the large, hard turds left by one of the tenants on his floor. These did not flush down, often clogging the Turkish toilet. Grandpa went on to say that they were left by the sole Jewish tenant on his floor. Grandpa took it upon himself to put a lock on the bathroom door, giving a key to all the Aryan tenants, effectively locking out the Jewish tenant. Grandpa concluded this story with the grand generalization:

"That's the Jews for you. They eat cheap and shit bricks."

Unlike previous stories he told me, I couldn't get this one out of my mind. The image of the Jewish tenant going to the bathroom and finding it locked kept pushing its way up into my mind; I couldn't help imagining what he felt when he discovered that his neighbors had ganged up on him to shut him out. How did he feel when he had to walk up to the fourth floor to use the bathroom there? Did he fear that the Aryan tenants on that floor might lock him out of that one too?

I decided that Grandpa had a major screw loose on the subject of the Jews, and decided to ask Dad what got Grandpa so worked up about it.

"With the Jews," Dad said, "you can never be sure where their loyalties lie. You never know whether they are true Americans or whether they are more loyal to the State of Israel or to being Jewish."

I took this statement under advisement. Since I didn't know any Jews personally, I had no way of knowing how pro-Jewish they might, or might not, be. Grandpa, however, often went on and on about the superiority of all things German. Jews, I concluded, couldn't possibly be more pro-Jewish than Grandpa was pro-German, and in any event it wasn't a sufficient reason to lock a man out of the bathroom. Since Dad's explanation didn't satisfy me I sought out my Uncle Richard, a Pastor of his Lutheran Church.

"Uncle Richard," I asked, "what is it about the Jews that gets Grandpa so worked up?"

"The Jews killed Jesus," Uncle Richard replied. "They're responsible for the death of Jesus Christ."

It was the first time I had ever heard anyone say this, and I thought Uncle Richard had cooked it up himself. I also thought it was just about the dumbest thing I had ever heard. It made about as much sense as saying that after the Civil War the American people had assassinated Abraham Lincoln. Of course some American people had murdered Lincoln, but it would have been ridiculous to suggest that the American people as a whole were guilty for his death.

My family's case against the Jews collapsed with Uncle Richard's remark; their stories simply didn't hang together. I resolved that one day I would try to meet some Jews, and get to know them as human beings.

CHAPTER 21

Cold Harbor

DURING my years at the Academy, Robert E. Lee remained my hero. In my senior year, I read a four-volume history of Lee's life and wrote a paper for history class arguing that Lee was the greatest general to emerge from the Civil War and a man of the highest moral and ethical character. My paper did acknowledge the corrupting influence of slavery, and I also wrote about the degenerating influence of the institution of slavery on the character of the Virginia aristocracy. Despite this, I argued that Lee should be counted one of the great Virginians, along with Washington, Jefferson, Madison, and Monroe. I got an A on the paper.

During spring vacation of my senior year I decided to go on a bicycle pilgrimage to Virginia to visit the sites of Lee's greatest victories. With my friend Joe Bradley, we visited the sites of all of Lee's famous battles, leaving out only Antietam and Gettysburg because they were too far out of our way. It was my first taste of Southern life since I had left Uncle Randloph's mansion five years before.

• • •

I must have been around 10 years old when I noticed that black people never ate at any of the restaurants we went to and indeed were rarely seen anywhere we went. Puzzled, I asked Mom about it.

"They have their place," she had replied, "and we have ours."

I accepted Mom's explanation as reasonable. We preferred to go our way, and they preferred to go theirs. The Southern way of life simply institutionalized an innate preference.

In the mid-1950s, though, black people began to emerge from "their" places and to show up in some of "our" places. My first experience of this was when Dad took us out to lunch at one of Milwaukee's better restaurants. After we sat down, a black family walked in and sat down at a table near us. Although Wisconsin law did not discriminate against black people in eating establishments, none of us had ever witnessed this before. When our waitress came to take our order, Dad said to her: "You'd think those people wouldn't eat in a restaurant where they know they're not wanted."

I felt really bad about what Dad had said and looked at the family at the nearby table. There were four of them, a father, a mother, and two children about my age. I thought they looked very much like us and hoped they had not heard Dad. I also knew precisely the solution to the problem of black people eating in restaurants where they weren't wanted: white people needed to get over it and start liking it.

None of this made me question my identification as a Southerner, however. I still shared my parents' attraction to the South and the respect and affection they felt for their Southern friends. This identification had the additional virtue of distinguishing me from Yankees and the Yankee environment I experienced at the Academy. I wasn't any of the things the Academy stood for. I was a Texan and a Southerner.

• • •

My senior-year pilgrimage to the sites of Lee's great victories brought with it unexpected adventures. One evening, about an hour before sunset, we rode our bikes to a small country store deep in rural Virginia.

"They found the bodies," the storekeeper announced cheerfully.

"The bodies?" Joe and I queried.

"Yes. That family of four from Annapolis that disappeared about a month ago. This morning they found two of the bodies in the brush about a mile and a half down the road." She pointed the direction in which Joe and I were riding.

Joe and I talked over this exciting development while we ate peanut butter and apple butter sandwiches.

"It'll be dark in about an hour," I said. "The safest thing for us is to camp as far into the woods as we can get, where the murderer will never find us."

"Are you crazy?" Joe asked. "If the murderer finds us, we'll be goners for sure. There'll be no one around to help us. We should camp right next to the road."

"Joe," I said. "You're crazy. The side of the road is where the murderer is likeliest to spot us. If he does, we're finished. One car passes by on this road every 15 minutes, and it's only six o'clock. By midnight there won't be one car an hour. It's the worst of all possible places."

Unable to agree on a plan, Joe and I glumly got back on our bikes, hoping the heavens would miraculously drop a solution into our laps. After about a mile, they did. We came across an abandoned church and graveyard.

"That abandoned church is our ticket," I said. "We'll ride along for another mile or two to throw the murderer off the track. After dark we'll come back here, break the church door open, and hide until morning." Joe agreed it was a brilliant plan.

After dark Joe and I rode back, sneaking through the tall grass and past the eerily leaning headstones to the door of the church which, fortunately, was easily broken into. I took a step inside and . . . CRUNCH . . . Shining my flashlight on the floor, Joe and I saw the corpses of at least a hundred dead birds littered about. My flashlight soon revealed the reason. The circular window above the entrance door was broken. Birds could fly in, but once in the church they couldn't find their way out.

Luckily the birds had all died long ago, so there was no smell of decaying flesh. I found an old broom in a corner and swept away dead birds to make a place for Joe's and my sleeping bags. I took my sheaf-knife out, sticking it in the floor within ready reach. If the murderer breached our sanctuary, I would have one last desperate chance to do him in before he gunned us down. We turned our flashlight off, lying anxiously in the dark, listening to the sounds outside.

We'd been lying there for about ten minutes when the sound of a branch breaking in the graveyard made us both jump six inches in sheer terror.

"JOE," I whispered hoarsely, "DID YOU HEAR THAT?"

"YEAH," said Joe.

"DO YOU THINK IT'S THE MURDERER?" I whispered.

"I DON'T KNOW," said Joe.

We waited breathlessly together in the dark.

If it was the murderer, he decided to come no further, and Joe and I finally fell into a restless sleep. We awoke at the crack of dawn, jumped on our bikes, and set a new bicycle speed record to Fredericksburg. We didn't feel fully safe again until the following day when, after a night spent in a garage in Fredericksburg, we rode swiftly south again toward the Civil War battlefields around Richmond.

* * *

The high point of the trip for me had been our visit to Chancellorsville battlefield, the site of Lee's "perfect battle." Lee's crushing victory at Chancellorsville prepared the way for his second, and last, attempt to invade the North. Two months later, at Gettysburg, Union forces prevailed, turning the tide of the Civil War.

Toward the end of our trip, Joe and I visited Cold Harbor battlefield. In one of the bloodiest and most lopsided battles of the Civil War, Grant's men had charged heavily defended Confederate ramparts, suffering heavy casualties. I ran from the Union trenches across the open field Grant's men had crossed toward the Confederate fortifications. I was 17 years old and in excellent physical shape, and it was an exhausting run. Confederate gunfire into the exposed Union troops took a terrible toll. Though Cold Harbor counts as one of Lee's victories, I took no pleasure in it.

Leaving the battlefield around noon, Joe and I rode on toward Richmond looking for a bite to eat. We soon came to a roadside shack with signs advertising hamburgers, hot dogs, and Coke. We parked our bikes at the rear. As I made my way to the customers' window I noticed the word "Colored" over it. Changing course, I made my way around to the side of the shack where I found a window bearing the legend "White." The owner, a heavyset white woman, greeted us effusively.

"How'ya boys doin'?" she asked. "Where ya comin' from on those bicycles?"

"We go to school in the Boston area," I said, "but I'm originally from Texas. We've been visiting the battlefield sites of Lee's great victories."

"General Lee was all over this country," she replied. "Beat a lot of Yankees. In the end, though, there was too damn many of 'em."

Joe and I each ordered a couple of hot dogs. We chatted pleasantly with the woman as she cooked, treating us to generous doses of Southern hospitality.

"Y'all hurry on back," she said, pushing the dogs in our direction. We thanked her, paid for them, and sat on a bench a few yards away to enjoy our meal.

Suddenly I heard loud, angry sounds coming from inside the shack. The owner was shouting at customers on the "Colored" side of her establishment. I made my way around the corner to see what was happening and found two black sharecroppers, their clothing like rags, their heads bent against the torrent of words like sailors bent against the headwinds of a gale. In exchange for the same hot dogs that Joe and I were eating, and in place of the heavy doses of syrupy Southern hospitality the owner had ladled out with our hot dogs, these sharecroppers were being treated to generous measures of abuse and contempt.

In that instant I realized that I had just been an active participant in a vile conspiracy to deprive these men of their human dignity. I felt profoundly ashamed of myself. To compensate for my feelings of guilt, and to break some of the burden of contempt heaped on these men, I went over to speak a few friendly words. My presence, though, clearly made them uncomfortable. I left after a sentence or two, returning to the bench and finishing my lunch.

The battle of Cold Harbor had just claimed another casualty. Me. It killed off my identification with Lee and the Old South. When the Greensboro, North Carolina, sit-in-movement leaped into national prominence some ten months later, I knew which side I was on.

CHAPTER 22

"A Lawyer Like Grandpère"

SUMMER finally came at the end of my senior year at the Academy, bringing with it my final release from that school. A couple of boys that I knew would be cruising in their family yachts in such exotic waters as the Mediterranean. Since my parents did not own a rowboat, let alone a yacht, my summer would not involve a maritime adventure. Far better, they gave me a month's vacation in Spain followed by two months in France.

Grandpère was 83 years old that summer. Although he walked more slowly, he still made a striking figure in his three-piece suit, gold watch and chain, fashionable cane, and elegant fedora. We recreated the rituals we had followed ten years earlier when, at age 7, I had lived in his house while my mother recuperated from her bout with tuberculosis. We talked, did our daily shopping for food together, and played cards.

• • •

A few days after arriving in France, my cousin Francine, 15 years older than me and more like a big sister than a cousin, took me into Paris for a day of sightseeing and visiting. As we strolled along the Trocadero, the Eiffel Tower in my line of sight, she asked me:

"Tony, since you're going to college in the fall, have you decided what you want to do when you graduate?"

"I haven't thought about it at all," I said. "I don't have any idea what I want to do."

This was not actually true. With A.O. Smith's warm compliments about my gifts as a writer under my belt, I had thought I might like to become a high school or college teacher, doing my writing on the side.

But my parent's uncompromising opposition had, in the end, persuaded me. I was far from certain that I had anything to say that the world would be eager to hear, or that I had a true vocation for writing. Had my convictions had been stronger, I might have taken my parents on. But they weren't, so I put my shaky ambitions for becoming a writer on the back burner.

I had no fallback position, though, and Francine's question jarred me out of my reverie. I was still thinking about it, wondering what I might say, when she cut in with a piece of advice: "Why don't you become a lawyer like your grandfather?"

A lawyer like Grandpère? Of course! That was it! Why hadn't I thought of it myself? In that instant the decision was made and my course in life set. I would become a lawyer like Grandpère, using my legal skills to fight for the things I believed in. I never looked back.

Me sitting on Mom's lap, Midland, Texas, spring 1942 (I'm about 6 months old). Mom was raised by servants, and had no idea how to go about hugging a baby, probably contributing to her remote look. France is under German occupation; Dad swells with pride at the triumph of German arms.

Pearley Bee, my "colored" nanny in Midland, Texas, 1943.

Hassan, our Sudanese house servant in Egypt and my caretaker. I loved Hassan—note how happy I am holding his hand.

Mom and me at the Sphinx. I'm six or seven.

Dad, Mom, and me in the Egyptian desert—Dad in his field clothes. I'm six or seven.

Catherine and me holding hands on Grandpère's porch. I am, I think, 6 years old—I've had a crush on Catherine since age 5, reciprocated. Dad and Mom gave Catherine a gyroscope top as a present, which I broke showing Catherine how it worked. Dad beat the holy hell out of me. Catherine hid under the dining room table, and remained afraid of my father for the rest of her life. None of the Diors had ever seen anything like this before.

A picture taken about half an hour later, on the same porch. Dad looks at the camera with Teutonic intensity. My fists are clenched. Grandpère puts two protective hands on my shoulders, looking away from the camera.

Cesar Chavez, Jerry Cohen, and me after testifying in the California legislature for the California Agricultural Relations Bill that I had drafted.

Cesar Chavez holding my children Max and Elisabeth. I'm next to them, holding a little playmate of Elisabeth's.

Me standing next to a poster-size picture of Christian at the Christian Dior museum in Granville.

PART 3

THAT HARD, DUSTY ROAD

CHAPTER 23

An Unemployable Jailbird

MY interview with the attorney from Milbank, Tweed, Hadley, and McCloy appeared to be going well. He was friendly and seemed interested in my record, glancing frequently down at the file on his desk. In a few months I would be graduating from the Cornell University Law School, having accumulated a record good enough to land a job with a top firm like Milbank Tweed.

Midway through our allotted half-hour, though, my interviewer said he needed to take a bathroom break and walked out of the room. I jumped up and ran around the desk to look at the file he had been consulting so frequently. There, prominently displayed, was an article from the Cornell Law School newspaper describing the year I had spent in the Civil Rights movement, with a detailed description of my time in the Leflore County Prison. Returning from the bathroom, the lawyer wrapped up the interview, thanked me for coming in, wished me well, and told me I would be hearing from the firm very soon. He was as good as his word. My rejection letter came within the week.

As the fall interview season at Cornell drew to a close, my letters of rejection from high-profile New York firms made clear that my time in jail had trumped my academic record. Until that time, I had thought only of becoming a lawyer like Grandpère, and I had naïvely assumed that work bridging both my French and my American heritages—work that involved my presence in both New York and Paris, for example—was the way to fulfill that dream. Now I had some serious doubts, not only about whether I'd ever land such a job, but about whether I even wanted one. I had no talent for business and even less enthusiasm for large international corporations and their legal problems.

Lacking a better idea, I decided to pound the streets of New York right after graduation the following summer. A month or two after receiving my rejection letter from Milbank Tweed, though, I bumped into Professor Lewis Morse while searching for a book in the library stacks.

"How are things going, Tony?" he asked. "Did you get any offers from any of the New York firms?"

"As a matter of fact, I didn't," I said. "I've pretty well struck out."

"Have you ever thought of taking a job in Washington?" Professor Morse asked. "I know that the prestige jobs are concentrated in New York, but there's plenty of work in Washington for a good student like yourself. Besides, Washington is a lot more livable as a city than New York. I have some friends in Washington. Would you like me to contact them on your behalf?"

I was stunned. Professor Morse, a lieutenant colonel in the Army reserve, had a reputation for being politically conservative. I would have thought him the least likely law professor at Cornell to take an interest in the job search of a Civil Rights activist with a jail record. As it turned out, he was the only one to do so. I told him I was grateful for his help.

Professor Morse got back to me a few days later. He had contacted three Cornell Law School graduates with whom he had kept in touch over the years. One was an African American federal judge, the second a well-placed official in the Export–Import Bank, and the third an attorney working at the Civil Rights Division of the Department of Justice.

I immediately jumped at the prospect of an interview at the Civil Rights Division of the Department of Justice, so I put that interview at the top of my list. A job clerking for a federal judge would be a wonderful opportunity, so I signed on for that interview too. As a fallback I told Professor Morse I would also like to interview at the Export–Import Bank.

Professor Morse soon made appointments for me with all three. Since he knew of my interest in social justice, he also mentioned that his friend at the Civil Rights Division regularly chatted over his back fence with a neighbor who worked at the National Labor Relations Board (NLRB). Professor Morse asked me if I had any interest in interviewing there.

Working for the NLRB hadn't occurred to me before, but now, hungry for work, I was grateful for this unexpected opportunity.

My first interview, at the Department of Justice, seemed to go extremely well. The lawyer interviewing me was so impressed that he put in a personal call to John Doar, assistant attorney general for the Civil Rights Division, and Doar agreed to talk to me. I was elated. Doar's was a famous name. I knew that he had protected Freedom Riders in Montgomery, Alabama, faced off against Ross Barnett when that governor of Mississippi had blocked the door of the University of Mississippi to James Meredith, its first black student, and had calmed an angry mob in Greenwood, Mississippi, when Civil Rights leader Medgar Evers was murdered outside his home.

My interview with Doar, though, went badly. He made it absolutely clear that my client would be the United States government, not Civil Rights workers or the African Americans who would be involved in any cases I might work on. The government, Doar emphasized, might make decisions with which I would be in profound disagreement. He stressed that my loyalty would have to be to the government, no matter how I felt personally. His remarks took me by surprise. I tried my best to make my declaration of loyalty to the government credible, but I left Doar's office far from confident that he was convinced.

The interview with the federal judge fell through when he was unexpectedly called out of town. The official at the Export–Import Bank, it turned out, had agreed to give me an interview only as a personal favor to Professor Morse's friend and had no interest in me of any kind.

The neighbor who worked at the NLRB, though, turned out to be an extremely kind man. Remembering his own time as a first-time job seeker, he went to considerable lengths to make sure I had good interviews. He lined up a personal interview for me with one of the five labor-law "judges" (called Board "Members") who preside over cases at the NLRB, and with a number of other top attorneys in the agency.

As I was leaving the agency I felt a sudden and urgent need to find the men's room.

"It's right there," the kindly neighbor said, pointing to a door a few feet away.

"By the way," he added, pointing to a door directly across the hall, "this is Arthur Leff's office. He's the Chief Counsel to the Chairman of the NLRB. I'll see if Arthur is in and if he would be interested in talking to you."

When I came out of the bathroom, he told me that Arthur was indeed in and had agreed to talk to me. I walked into Arthur's office and sat down.

Arthur Leff was at that time about 60 years old. He had a strong, kindly face and quickly made me feel at ease. He didn't seem to have any real interest in a job interview in the formal sense of the word, though, wanting rather to chat about what I had done to get myself thrown in jail.

After I answered his questions, he switched the subject to the only other line on my résumé that seemed to interest him: tennis. I had been on the second tennis team at the Academy, and so I told Arthur that I was a decent, but by no means great, tennis player. We kicked that subject around for about ten minutes. Arthur then looked at his watch and told me that he needed to leave. I stood up, walked out, and that was that.

Returning to Ithaca, I eagerly visited my mailbox every day, my hopes pinned on getting an offer from the Civil Rights Division. Failing that, I was hoping for a favorable letter from one of the NLRB members who interviewed me.

None of these letters ever arrived. About ten days later, though, I did receive a letter postmarked from Washington. Its return address showed that it came from Arthur Leff, and it contained the only job offer I was to receive that season. In it Arthur offered me a position as attorney-advisor to the Chairman of the National Labor Relations Board. In my wildest dreams I had never dared to hope for such an outcome.

And so it was through the kindness of strangers, and an opportune trip to the men's room, that this sometime jailbird landed a job at the pinnacle of the field in which he would practice law for the next 42 years.

CHAPTER 24

Pygmalion in Management

DURING the time that I worked at the NLRB an article appeared in the *Harvard Law Review* entitled "Pygmalion in Management." The article describes a certain kind of teacher, supervisor, or mentor who sculpts ordinary, insecure, young protégés into highly skilled and supremely confident practitioners. The article's title was inspired by George Bernard Shaw's play *Pygmalion*, which was adapted years later into the Broadway musical *My Fair Lady*. In it a phoneticist named Henry Higgins trains a cockney girl, Eliza Doolittle, to rise into the ranks of the social elite by learning to speak upper-class English. Arthur became my Henry Higgins; every success I achieved in later life practicing law I owe to Arthur Leff.

Within a few months of my arrival at the NLRB I found myself disagreeing with the judgment of lawyers who were my supervisors, some of whom had decades of seniority. In each case, puzzled by what seemed to me evident, I sought Arthur's opinion. In every one of these cases Arthur agreed with me, running interference with the lawyers or supervisors involved to change the outcome of the case to the one that he and I agreed was correct.

The first time I presented a case to the chairman himself came several months later. The case presented some difficult issues and was hotly debated by the chairman, Arthur, and the senior attorney who had supervised me. I was drawn into the discussion, defending my point of view and the result I thought was the correct one. After the discussion ended, as Arthur and I were walking back to his office, he turned to me and said, "I want to thank you for that."

"Thank me for what?"

"For the way you handled yourself in there. I've been criticized for hiring you. You just made me look good."

• • •

As I got to know him better, I realized that I had misread Arthur at our initial interview. Like so many other Americans of his time, he had suffered grievous economic hardship during the Great Depression. He was also Jewish, and intensifying the suffering of those dark times was the rampant anti-Semitism and terrifying extermination of six million Jews in Hitler's death camps. Gentiles who had risked their lives to hide, protect, or help Jews escape the Holocaust owned a place deep in Arthur's heart. I hadn't saved any Jews, but I had put my life on the line for people who had suffered oppression, beatings, and lynchings and were fighting for justice and freedom. Arthur knew I was qualified for the job, and he also knew he would take heat for hiring a Freedom Rider who had done time in jail. He didn't care.

Arthur loved young people. He had hired a number of truly talented young lawyers for the chairman's staff. Besides getting top-quality work out of us, he loved nothing better than coming down from his office on the sixth floor to chat with us and joke around in our offices on the fifth floor. All of us considered our work with Arthur and Frank McCulloch, the chairman, to be a privilege. For the first time in a very long time I was entirely happy in my surroundings.

• • •

One day, when I had been with the NLRB a little under a year, I heard Arthur's voice shouting from an office down the hall belonging to Bernie Goldberg, one of the senior supervisors on the chairman's staff and one of its most gifted legal thinkers. Bernie was profoundly deaf.

Arthur often came down to Bernie's office to get input on difficult cases. On this occasion I could hear Arthur shouting:

"BOREN CHERTKOV IS LEAVING THE BOARD TO TAKE A JOB ON CAPITOL HILL. I'M RECOMMENDING TONY GAENSLEN FOR HIS JOB. WHAT DO YOU THINK?"

I was stunned. Arthur was talking about one of the most responsible jobs on the chairman's staff. Cases at the NLRB were divided into two categories: so-called “C” cases that involved unfair labor practices and “R” cases that involved questions of union representation. The chairman assigned one member of his staff to review all the “R” cases that came across his desk. After reviewing the facts and the case law, that person wrote a one- to two-page memo analyzing the issues and recommending a decision. The “R” case specialist saw more of the chairman than almost any other member of his staff. The job brought with it a new title—“Special Advisor to the Chairman”—and a raise in salary. I was both elated and terrified.

* * *

On Memorial Day in 1937, 24 years before Frank W. McCulloch became chairman of the NLRB, he had been present at the Republic Steel massacre in Chicago. Republic Steel was on strike at the time. A crowd of hundreds of union members, their families, and sympathizers were marching across an open prairie toward the steel mill in a show of support. When they were met by a line of Chicago policemen blocking their path, the lead protesters argued for their right to continue onward. The police opened fired into the crowd and clubbed the strikers. When the dust cleared, ten people lay dead on the field. No policeman was ever prosecuted; the press mostly characterized the demonstration as a Communist riot.

Frank McCulloch was in the crowd that day. The Republic Steel Massacre, as it became known, had the same effect on him as the fire hoses and dogs in Alabama had on me a generation later. He devoted the rest of his life to protecting and advancing the rights of working people. When John F. Kennedy became President, he named Frank McCulloch chairman of the NLRB.

My new assignment meant that I read and made recommendations on every “R” case coming before the NLRB, discussing the cases in personal sessions with Arthur and the chairman before the five board members met to formally deliberate and vote on them. I sat in on the board meetings where these cases were discussed, following the best lawyers in the agency as they reasoned their way through my cases.

McCulloch was always ready to explore innovative solutions, making my job of recommending new approaches to old problems exciting. It was heady stuff for a young attorney just out of law school to be given the assignment of thinking up creative approaches to cases affecting national labor policy. I was often in well over my head, but I always felt that McCulloch gave my views serious consideration, whether he adopted them or not.

One of the cases I reviewed for him involved the wiring of aircraft manufactured by Ling-Temco-Vought, at the time one of the largest U.S. conglomerates in the electronics, airspace, steel manufacturing, airline, and pharmaceutical industries. A panel of three board members had voted for a particular outcome. In most such cases the full board routinely confirmed the decision of the panel, but when I read the panel's decision, I questioned whether it had reached the right result. It took me several days to work my way through the complicated wiring systems in the aircraft before I could fully understand the legal issues. Once I did, though, I concluded that the panel had reached the wrong result and said so in my memo to the chairman.

Arthur and I met with the chairman for no more than 30 minutes before the board meeting. In those 30 minutes McCulloch gained a complete grasp of the facts it had taken me days to master. He and Arthur both agreed with my line of reasoning. When we entered the board's deliberation room, he announced his opposition to the panel decision and launched into a discussion of Ling-Temco-Vought aircraft as though he had spent years of his life wiring the things. The vote went five in favor, none against, the chairman's view.

• • •

On a few occasions I disagreed openly with the chairman, usually on questions involving policy rather than issues of legal reasoning. I would state my position as clearly and forcefully as I could and let the matter rest. When McCulloch stuck to his guns (which he almost always did), I appreciated that he always listened to what I had to say attentively and respectfully.

On one occasion, though, I presented a real challenge to his principled tolerance of challenging and unpopular views. A coalition of peace-churches and organizations opposing the Vietnam War had requested an audience with the Secretary of the Army at the Pentagon. They asked me to be part of the delegation; since the meeting took place during working hours, I signed out on leave-time from the NLRB to do so. The Secretary of the Army received us cordially and heard us out. I articulated our anti-war position as clearly and forcefully as I could. My tone was respectful even if the message I was delivering was strongly critical of U.S. policy in Vietnam.

McCulloch was a hawk on the Vietnam issue. The following morning, when I came into his office to present the cases of the day he remarked:

"I understand the interests of the National Labor Relations Board were well represented at the Pentagon yesterday."

It was clear that he had not been delighted to receive a phone call from the FBI advising him that one of his senior advisors had advocated a peace-activist position before the Secretary of the Army. McCulloch had no doubt been put in an embarrassing position, which he did not appreciate. To his great credit, though, he did not criticize me outright for my stance, and he never mentioned it again.

* * *

Arthur was always on the lookout for some way of giving me extra assignments that added to the scope of my experience. I thought he did it as much to boost my self-esteem as because he needed me for the job. The most dramatic instance was when Arthur assigned me to represent the chairman at a subpanel meeting. Subpanels were usually made up of senior supervisors from each of three board members' staffs. Each supervisor cast a vote on behalf of his board member on the proposed outcome in a case under consideration. Based on their vote and the reasoning supporting it, the attorney assigned to the case would then write up a proposed decision. In most cases the subpanel's decision ended up being adopted first by the panel and then by the full board.

On this occasion Arthur sent me to represent the chairman at a subpanel meeting and to vote on his behalf. It was a signal honor. The other two attorneys present were senior staff members and in their 40s. I had been on the chairman's staff less than two full years, was 27 years old, and looked young for my age.

When I walked into the room, the chairman's big, empty chair stood at the head of the table. The two attorneys from the other staffs sat in chairs on either side of the table. As the chairman's representative, I was supposed to sit in that chair and call the meeting to order. I was so intimidated, though, that I couldn't bring myself to do so. Instead I sat down along one side of the table next to one of the other attorneys. Since I couldn't muster the nerve to call the meeting to order either I said nothing, sitting there in silence. After about ten minutes one of the other attorneys said:

"No one is here for chairman."

"I'm here for the chairman," I managed to say.

Both attorneys turned to give me a look of blank astonishment. After a moment or two one of them said:

"Well, alright. Let's call the meeting to order. I've reviewed the facts in this case. In my opinion outcome [A] is the right disposition."

"I read the case the same way," said the other attorney. "My vote is for outcome [A].

Horrors. The worst of possible nightmares was unfolding before me. I had read the facts and the law carefully, reaching the conclusion that the correct disposition in the case was outcome [B]. Now I found myself disagreeing with two senior attorneys who had, between them, a couple decades more experience than me. I sat there for close to a minute, going over all my options in my mind. These were senior attorneys, after all, with a lot of experience. The better part of valor, I thought, might be to go along with them and not cause waves on my very first subpanel assignment.

As I sat there, though, pondering this alternative, I simply couldn't bring myself to do it. I had reasoned my way through the case and had done, I felt, a thorough job. I had been confident I had reached the right result. If I backed down now simply out of fear or intimidation I would take the first step on a slippery slope that could turn out to be endless. My confidence in myself and my reasoning powers were the only reliable assets I had. At all costs, I realized, my integrity had to remain intact.

"I dissent," I said. "I think the right disposition in this case is outcome [B]."

"All right," said one of the other attorneys. "Mr. Arbuckle [the staff attorney assigned to the case], write up disposition [A] as the majority decision. You [he designated me] write up your dissent, and we'll circulate the case."

All three of us trooped back to our respective offices, I to prepare a dissenting memorandum on behalf of the chairman, outlining my reasoning and the considerations leading me to believe the result I recommended was the right one.

A few days later the subpanel decision was circulated to all five board members' staffs. The cover memorandum recited that a majority had reached outcome [A], with the chairman's representative, Gaenslen, dissenting. I felt a thrill of pride when I saw it. Two of my heroes on the Supreme Court, Justices Douglas and Black, had in years past often dissented together on cases involving Civil Rights issues. Now, after many years in the legal wilderness, their views were being adopted by the majority. I, in my imagination at least, had now joined their distinguished company.

In the end, the chairman agreed with me. Not wanting to embarrass the senior attorneys who had worked on the case, he did not bring it up for deliberation by the full board. Rather, he went to see each of the other board members privately and persuaded them to adopt his point of view.

It was an incredibly important life lesson. I had stood by my convictions in the face of people vastly more experienced than I. Despite the fact that I had been too shy to claim the chairman's presiding chair, I had nevertheless been vindicated. After this experience I stood a little taller, and when I looked my opponents in the eye I no longer blinked.

By the time I left the chairman's service I had stood in the presence of some of the best labor lawyers in the country. A good many of these men were smarter than I was in the conventional ways in which lawyers are smart. They were quicker than I was at sorting through complicated fact patterns and performing the deductive and inductive reasoning steps that lie at the heart of legal argumentation. I could do all these things well, but more slowly and laboriously than they.

When I reviewed a case, though, I took serious account of facts and patterns of behavior that other lawyers generally overlooked. What appeared to them to be the imponderable elements in a case were the very things to which I gave particular attention. Where they were quick, I was deep. Arthur had first seen, and the chairman later confirmed, this quality in me. Blessed with Arthur and the chairman as my mentors, I never again doubted my ability to hold my own with the best and brightest lawyers in my field in the country.

CHAPTER 25

The International Brotherhood of Teamsters

FRANK McCulloch's job as chairman of NLRB came onto the chopping block after the election of 1968, when Richard Nixon was elected president of the United States.

I was in the position of an aging "bright young man" in Washington, an eager, ambitious professional who had landed in a company town when its management was in the hands of his political party. Now that management had switched sides, aging "bright young men" whose allegiances lay on the Democratic side of the political ledger were a surplus commodity. Most left Washington to find jobs elsewhere.

Arthur once again came to the rescue. He told me that the International Brotherhood of Teamsters was looking for a new Associate House Counsel, that they had a reputation for hiring the best labor lawyers in the country, that they paid top-dollar salaries, and that he would back me for the job. With no other options in sight, I took it.

The president of the Teamsters Union when I went to work there was Frank Fitzsimmons. Everyone in Washington labor circles knew that Fitz owed his top position at the Teamsters to his good friend Jimmy Hoffa, his predecessor in that office. It was Hoffa, with his many ties to organized crime, who had built the Teamsters from a small union into the largest and most powerful labor organization in the country. When Hoffa was convicted on charges of jury tampering, conspiracy, and fraud, and sentenced to 13 years in jail, he maneuvered Fitz into his high position with the understanding that Fitz would warm his chair until, through legal appeals and political clout, Hoffa got himself out of prison and resumed his position as president.

I soon learned through my interactions with Fitz that dealing with him was not an enlightening experience. Since he was highly inarticulate, it was often hard to understanding exactly what he was saying or what he wanted. He had, everyone knew, essentially been an errand-boy in Hoffa's rise to power, making coffee and holding chairs for other Teamsters officials. Fitz's one qualification in his meteoric rise to the top job in the Teamsters hierarchy had been his utter and unquestioning loyalty to Hoffa.

Fitz soon discovered that he liked Hoffa's large, comfortable chair, deciding to keep it for himself. He turned out to be a good deal shrewder than anyone had imagined, maneuvering all of Hoffa's allies out of their positions of power in the union. Fitz also won the allegiance of Teamsters rank-and-file workers through his unsuspected skill in contract negotiation, winning larger wage packages for them than even Jimmy Hoffa.

Fitz was nevertheless stuck between a rock and a hard place. The Teamster rank and file, with whom Hoffa was still massively popular, expected Fitz to use his political clout to get Hoffa out of jail. If he didn't, his betrayal of his old friend would undermine his power base with the Teamsters membership. If he succeeded, Hoffa would push him out of his chair, and Fitz would return to his old job as Jimmy Hoffa's errand boy.

Fitz's problem was solved by his new friend, Richard Nixon, President of the United States. Nixon enjoyed Fitz's company, inviting him frequently to the White House and flights on Air Force One. Nixon soon came up a plan to solve Fitz's problem. Nixon would commute Hoffa's sentence to time served, but attach a rider to the order of commutation preventing Hoffa from occupying the Teamsters' presidency for another nine years.

I was sitting at my desk the day Hoffa was released. By early afternoon a copy of the order of commutation had landed on my desk, and I was reading the language that barred Hoffa from resuming the Teamsters' presidency. White House attorney John Dean would later testify that it was he who had drafted the clause. My task was to analyze Dean's language to make sure it would stand up when Hoffa challenged it in court. I was relieved to report that I thought it would. I would not have looked forward to telling Fitz that, in my professional opinion, he was out of a job.

In return for this signal favor to his good friend Fitz, Nixon asked Fitz for just two things in return. First, he wanted the Teamsters' endorsement in his run for re-election in 1974. Fitz delivered. Nixon got both the endorsement and something on the order of a million dollars in campaign funds.

The second favor was Fitz's help in destroying Cesar Chavez's United Farm Workers (UFW) union. In 1970, thanks to its nationwide boycott of grapes, the UFW had won contracts covering all of the Delano, California, grape industry. California agribusiness interest had long formed a major part of Nixon's power base, and the growers wanted Nixon's help in driving the UFW from the fields. Nixon asked Fitz to throw the Teamsters' weight into the fight; Fitz delivered on this count, too.

Hoffa, however, did not give up on his dream of recovering the Teamsters' presidency. He fought determinedly to get it back through court challenges and on every other available front. In the afternoon of July 30, 1975, Hoffa went to meet Tony (Tony Pro) Provenzano, the "Caporegime," or captain, of the Genovese crime family of New York City, at a restaurant outside Detroit. Tony Pro had been one of Hoffa's top lieutenants during his rise to power, and the two men had remained good friends as long as Hoffa remained in jail. Once Hoffa got out of jail, though, they had a falling out. Tony Pro became Fitz's friend and political ally.

When Hoffa did not return home that evening, his wife notified the police. Hoffa was never seen again, nor was his body ever found after extensive searches and investigations. Although Fitz had a clear motive for wanting Hoffa out of the way, and despite the fact that Hoffa was scheduled to meet with Tony Pro the day he disappeared, nothing was ever pinned on either of them.

It was sometimes said that Frank Fitzsimmons had no sense of humor. The charge is certainly unfair, as the following anecdote well illustrates. At the Teamster convention that followed Hoffa's disappearance, Fitz addressed the gathered assembly:

"Jimmy Hoffa! Jimmy Hoffa! Everybody's asking me what happened to Jimmy Hoffa! Why are they asking me? Why, I don't have any better idea of what happened to Jimmy Hoffa than anybody in this room." Tony Pro, who was widely reputed to have been the one who fingered Jimmy, was in the room, and an appreciative murmur of laughter rippled through the crowd.

• • •

What Arthur had told me about the Teamsters lawyers who represented local unions and regional associations from around the country turned out to be true. They were men of integrity, highly intelligent and competent senior partners in their respective law firms. I enjoyed working with and getting to know these out-of-town lawyers at conferences held periodically at Teamsters headquarters. It was by far the best part of my job.

But my employer was not local unions, regional associations, or the lawyers representing them. As associate house counsel, my client was International Brotherhood of Teamsters itself; I was responsible to it and not to Teamster locals and regional organizations. It was jarring, for example, to be told that I could stop working on a case involving a challenge to the leadership of a Teamsters local in Florida because the challenger had just been gunned down in front of the union office.

One day, sitting at my large desk at Teamster headquarters, looking out my window at the Capitol, I asked myself this question:

"Do you really want to spend the rest of your life helping people who already have lots of power and money acquire even more, or do you want to help people who desperately need these things, and without you might never get top-of-the-line legal representation?"

The answer to that question was obvious, but before I could decide what to do or when to do it, my boss called me into his office:

"Tony," he said, "I think it would be a good idea if you started looking for other work." He gave me no specific reason at the time, but Teamsters' general counsel, David Previant, later told Arthur Leff that I was too liberal for them.

I immediately got on the phone, calling everyone I knew. One call went to my old friends Blase and Theresa Bonpane, both of whom had been Maryknoll missionaries in Guatemala. They had both been expelled from the country for working too closely with Guatemalan peasants targeted by the Guatemalan government.

"What are you and Theresa doing now?" I asked Blase.

"We're both working for Cesar Chavez," Blase said. "Theresa and I are organizers with the United Farm Workers Union."

Blase put in a good word for me with union's general counsel, Jerry Cohen. A couple days later Jerry called, inviting me to come out to California. I did, and we hit it off. He offered me a job on the spot, working with him at the UFW headquarters at La Paz, a compound located in the Tehachapi Mountains 30 miles outside of Bakersfield.

"It would be a good thing, though, if you could meet Cesar before signing on." Jerry added. "He's organizing in Arizona. If you can fly there to meet him on your way back to Washington I'd suggest that you do so."

A couple days later I stood outside the UFW headquarters in Superior, Arizona, waiting for Chavez to return from a day in the field. Sometime around six o'clock, hot, tired, and dusty, Cesar came into sight. Walking with him were a number of co-workers on the Arizona campaign. The scene is etched indelibly in my memory as the day I first met him.

As he would for as long as I knew him, Chavez spent the rest of the evening talking to the farm workers who lined up to tell him their concerns, large or small, union related or purely personal. He was their leader, their advisor, their big brother, their father confessor. Jerry had called ahead to tell Cesar about me. When I introduced myself to him, Cesar told me he would meet with me after the last farm worker had left. I waited until the union hall emptied around 11:00 p.m. Chavez then told me he was tired, inviting me to visit him the following morning at the house where he was staying.

The following morning, Chavez asked me wide-ranging and probing questions about my personal background, the time I had spent in the Civil Rights movement, and my work with the NLRB and the Teamsters. The UFW and the Teamsters were at that time in open warfare with each other; I was switching sides just as Fitzsimmons was beginning to launch an all-out assault on Chavez's union. Cesar was eager to know anything I could tell him that might be helpful. While I knew a good deal about the inner workings of the Teamsters headquarters in Washington, I knew very little about the Western Conference of Teamsters in California and its constituent unions.

After about an hour Cesar stood up to say goodbye. It had been, we both knew, a great encounter. Chavez was giving me the opportunity to work on the cutting edge of a labor movement dedicated to bettering conditions for migrant workers, the most exploited and vulnerable labor force in America. I could not have designed a job for which I was better suited by my training and professional experience, nor one that was closer to my heart. For his part Cesar was getting a labor lawyer seasoned by years of experience in areas of the law that would prove to be of great importance to "La Causa."

CHAPTER 26

Cesar Chavez

TWO months after my meetings with Cesar and Jerry, I drove with my wife and our two children up to the security gate of Nuestra Señora Reina de La Paz, national headquarters of the United Farm Workers (UFW). We found ourselves in a 180-acre compound nestled at 3,000 feet in the Tehachapi Mountains east of Bakersfield.

La Paz had served as a tuberculosis sanitarium before becoming UFW headquarters. The compound consisted of a large, abandoned hospital building, about a half dozen small houses, and a number of smaller buildings in various stages of disrepair. It also boasted sewage treatment and boiler heating plants, both in need of constant repair.

The administration building, a large one-story whitewashed wooden building, occupied the center of the compound. Cesar's large office stood at the north end of the building's central corridor. Sparsely furnished, it had a plain, uncluttered desk, four or five chairs, and bookshelves on the walls laden with a wide variety of books, including the complete set of Gandhi's collected works. Jerry Cohen and I shared an office midway down the hall from Cesar's.

When I had talked with Cesar in Arizona, he had told me the UFW would soon be acquiring a number of house trailers for staff, including one for our family. In the meantime we would be housed in the abandoned sanitarium. Pulling our U-Haul trailer up to the door, we unloaded our belongings into two tiny rooms with peeling paint flaking off the walls, a tiny hand basin sink doubling for kitchen and hand washing use. We trudged a good way down the hall to the bathroom and shower.

We survived almost three months in these cramped quarters before I stumbled across a large empty room on the lowest floor of the sanitarium. We appropriated it at once. More months dragged by without any sight of the promised trailers. One day, though, La Paz's septic system backed up. Since the room that served as our home was on the lowest level in the building, it was soon layered with an inch of sewage. Seizing the occasion, I turned disaster into opportunity. Charging up to Cesar's office, I made an emotional case:

"Cesar! Get us out of this crap and into one of the promised trailers, and do it as close to now as humanly possible."

Cesar moved the item to the top of his notoriously backed-up "to do" list. Within a couple of weeks six of the long-delayed trailers appeared on the La Paz grounds. We moved into new digs lavish in comparison to their humble predecessors.

• • •

I spent a lot of time with Jerry Cohen and Cesar Chavez during my two years at La Paz. Since Jerry and I shared the same office, and since we drove to many California locations together, we talked a lot. I sat in on, or heard Jerry's end of, legal and strategic conversations of a kind I had not been familiar with before. He was a creative and hard-hitting advocate for a cause he believed in. On more than one occasion I watched the hands of opposing attorneys or government officials begin to shake when Jerry walked into the room. When Jerry went into Cesar's office to talk over legal strategy, I often went in with him, and from time to time Jerry and I saw Cesar on legal projects of my own. In the rugged legal environment in which our battles were fought, a strong home-court advantage invariably tilted the playing field against us. Cesar and Jerry's free-wheeling legal tactics went a long way toward leveling it.

Cesar had an outstanding mind. Because he listened so intently, Cesar generally understood the people who surrounded him more deeply and completely than they understood him. He entered into their personalities, knowing them and collaborating with them to an extent that was almost symbiotic. At the same time he remained the perpetual organizer; he was always on the job, always advancing the interests of "La Causa" as he understood and interpreted them. His many friendships were largely determined by loyalty and commitment to "La Causa."

Jerry had been serving as UFW's general counsel for five years. After graduating from law school at U.C. Berkeley, he had gone to work for California Rural Legal Assistance (CRLA). One day, on his time off, he joined a UFW boycott picket line at a nearby supermarket. A few days later he received a memo at work advising him that CRLA was neutral in the dispute between UFW and the grape growers and that his picketing had violated that policy. As Jerry saw it, the UFW was doing far more for migrant workers than the politically cautious CRLA. When Cesar and Jerry met each other not long afterwards, Jerry went to work for Cesar.

Although the entirety of Jerry's prior legal experience had been his few months at CRLA, Cesar could not have found anyone better qualified to serve as UFW's general counsel. Jerry was a big man with a quick grin and a big laugh. He generally managed to look disheveled, even when he donned a suit and tie to go to court. His sense of humor ran to the irreverent. In the midst of a hot legal fight he liked to quip that while his brains were Jewish his ass was Irish. The tone was mischievous, but the implication was clear: he was not a man to be messed with.

Jerry had the born instincts of a consummate legal fighter. He also had an astonishingly quick mind that could grasp complicated facts and legal theories and cut the ground out from under legal opponents in oral arguments. Jerry did so by proposing, in rapid-fire succession, alternate approaches to the facts and theory of a case. He could jump from scenario to scenario so quickly that the best and brightest of opposing counsel were dazed and disoriented.

When Jerry went to work for Cesar, he had told him that he was inexperienced in the kinds of law they would be facing in building the union. Cesar had replied, "Then we'll learn together."

• • •

Because of our isolated location in the Tehachapi Mountains, Cesar spent a good deal of time being driven from place to place in his underpowered yellow Plymouth station wagon. He always sat in the passenger seat, his son-in-law and bodyguard Richard driving, his two German Shepherd guard dogs Huelga and Boycott riding in the back. Jerry and I were frequent passengers as he was driven to locations hours away.

Cesar was great company. He was a great listener and a light-hearted conversationalist, enjoying company and banter. He was also astonishingly well read, a self-educated man who talked easily on a wide range of subjects. He was so well informed on so many subjects that it was hard to remember that his formal education had ended in the eighth grade.

As an organizer Cesar spent inordinate amounts of time tracking down, listening to, talking to, creating personal relationships with, and finally recruiting the people who ultimately joined his movement. One day, as we passed through a small town in the Central Valley, Cesar said to me:

"I was in this town for a month before anyone would talk to me. Then one day I spotted two workers sitting down on the banks of that river over there [he pointed]. I ran into that grocery store, bought a sandwich, and ran to sit down next to them. They became my first two union members here."

Cesar built his national movement through literally countless one-on-one conversations like these. At the end of long, hot days in the field, Cesar invariably returned to the union office and, while eating dinner out of a carry-out box, met with long lines of local people waiting to see him. He talked to them about whatever was on their minds, hearing them out and giving advice. In this way he won people over to his cause and to himself.

When I met him in 1972, Cesar had been keeping up this routine for some 20 years. He would stay until the last person waiting in line had been heard, often quite late at night, sometime nearing midnight. I was usually exhausted when we finally climbed into his car for the long drive back to La Paz. The next day, I would haul my carcass out of bed and drag it to the office by 8:30 or 9:00, at which time Cesar had been hard at work at his desk for two or three hours.

• • •

From time to time Cesar would talk about his early life. He had been 12 years old when he watched bulldozers smash down the posts and fences of the 100-acre farm in Arizona where he had spent his childhood. His grandfather, Cesario Chavez, had homesteaded the land some 30 years before; it was a scene repeated all over the heartland of America during those Dustbowl and Depression years. Tens of thousands of small farm families unable to pay their taxes or meet their mortgages lost their land to absentee landlords, lawyers, and agribusiness interests who acquired the property for a fraction of its worth, consolidating the homesteaders' small farms into large tracts of land adaptable to large-scale farming.

In the case of the Chavez family, the Anglo president of the local bank, who owned the land adjoining theirs, paid off their back taxes and took title. With their homestead gone, Librado and Juana Chavez loaded their five children into their 1927 Studebaker, joining the flow of displaced families streaming into California.

In the years that followed, the Chavez family lived in shacks, barns, tents, spare rooms, and labor camps. At times they went hungry; Cesar joined his family to search for wild mustard greens to have something to eat. In Oxnard during their first year in California, they lived in the muddy back yard of a friend of Juana's. Their home was made up of two tents at right angles with a wood stove between; their belongings were often wet or damp from rain and fog. Wherever they lived, though, Juana saw to it that her children went to school. They worked in the fields on weekends and during the summer.

When they first began to learn the ways of California agriculture, the Chavez family often had to settle for the worst jobs. The workers were frequently insulted and shamed in front of their families. Women were harassed sexually, touched and asked for favors. Since growers did not provide bathroom facilities in the fields, women shielded each other for the little privacy they could get.

The jobs themselves were filled by labor contractors and other middlemen who regularly cheated workers. Contractors found scarce jobs for attractive young women in exchange for sexual favors and replaced them as soon as they came across other young women who ignited their fickle fancy. They withheld wages due for work already done. They undercounted the amount of produce the workers harvested, underpaid them, and overcharged them for food, transportation, and lodging. They fired workers the day before pay day, refusing to pay them for the work already done. A not-uncommon sight was farm workers camped in front of a labor contractor's door on Sundays, refusing to leave until they received the wages due them.

Often the work was backbreaking in both its physical pain and oppressiveness. The most infamous labor practice in the California fields was the short-handled hoe. With its 18-inch handle, it forced workers to work all day stooped close to the ground. If a worker stood up to relieve the strain on his back he would immediately be spotted; the supervisor would yell at him to get back to work. By the end of the day workers' back pain could be sufficiently intense that they found it hard to stand up. Cesar recalled his time working with the short-handled hoe as a kind of crucifixion; it injured his back permanently, leaving him subject to life-long chronic back pain.

For the first time in their lives the Chavez family experienced discrimination and prejudice. Stores refused to serve them. They were seated in segregated sections of restaurants and movie theaters. They worked in towns controlled by white growers, bankers, and lawyers; housing was separated by the railroad tracks, with whites on living on the "right side" and Mexicans living on the "wrong" side.

The Chavez family gradually learned the ropes of surviving in the migrant world. They learned to find the jobs that paid the best wages and avoid those that caused the most pain or degradation. They developed circuits; each family member had favored crops and crops they avoided. But however well they learned to work the system, the oversupply of cheap labor allowed growers to treat migrants as a surplus commodity, paying them survival wages and, when they were no longer needed, deporting them to Mexico or otherwise discarding them at will.

Cesar often said that he was not a true migrant, one who had been born into the migrant stream. He never forgot the shocking difference between the life he had known on his family's homestead in Arizona, surrounded by a community of friends and relatives all working their own plot of land, and the desperate conditions of workers on corporate-owned farms in California.

CHAPTER 27

I Think I'll Keep 'Em in Jail

SOON after arriving at La Paz I signed up for a cram course in California law to prepare for the state's bar exam, notoriously one of the most difficult in the country. Since the nearest cram course was taught in Los Angeles, I stayed with friends there during the week and spent weekends at La Paz with my family.

As the exam approached I began to fear that if I crammed one more fact into my brain, it might explode. Late in the afternoon the day before the exam, I decided to stuff one last subject in before throwing in the towel. The last subject I forced myself to memorize in this way involved the law of lateral and subjacent support, which involves questions of liability when one party, digging a foundation for a new building, causes the neighbor's building to collapse into it. There were three different levels of liability depending on the depth of the hole. Additionally, I had to memorize three different versions of the law: the rule followed by a majority of the states, the rule followed by a minority of the states, and the California rule, which differed from both of those. By the time I staggered out of the library, my head was bent low by the weight of several hundred pounds of legal lore.

Wouldn't you know it, the following day the real property law question on the bar exam involved the law of lateral and subjacent support. I got the fat part of the bat on that one and sent the ball flying high over the outfield fence. Admitted to the State Bar of California, I was off and running.

Right after being sworn in I called Jerry Cohen to tell him I was ready for action.

"We're in the middle of an organizing drive in the lower Imperial Valley," Jerry told me. "Cesar's cousin Manuel Chavez is in charge, and he's just been arrested. Go down there and see what you can do." Manuel had been arrested in a small town a few miles outside Calexico on the Mexican border. He was out on bail, awaiting trial.

Manuel Chavez's name was well known, if not notorious, in California in those days. He was more like a brother to Cesar than a cousin, as he had been raised by Cesar's parents. When Cesar started the UFW, he persuaded Manuel, then working in San Diego as a car salesman and making $2,000 a month, to quit his job and move to Delano to help start up his new union.

Manuel was engaging and liked to walk on the wild side. He was the consummate wheeler-dealer, the man to put through a deal when you needed a deal cut. He had not always been able to keep on the right side of the law and had spent time in jail on a series of minor and not-so-minor criminal charges. Cesar loved Manuel dearly though, missing him and staying up late at night to write him letters when he was in prison. Cesar took Manuel to task from time to time, sometimes becoming seriously angry with him, but he never lost his affection for his cousin. To Cesar nothing counted more than family.

When I arrived in town on the day of the trial I found the courtroom, a mini-Roman Coliseum, packed with farmers, farm hands, and other rural folk, all eager to see Manuel thrown into the lions' den.

It was hard to say who was more terrified: me, the judge, or the prosecuting attorney. I had never appeared in a courtroom before, let alone as counsel in a criminal defense case. I had not the slightest idea of how to proceed. Fortunately, the judge was also quaking in his boots. If he nailed Manuel with the kind of heavy sentence that his rural constituency expected from him, he would likely be facing newspaper reporters and a massed line of UFW pickets the next morning. But if Manuel was convicted after a jury trial and the judge was too easy in the sentencing stage, he might face the prospect of being lynched by his hometown crowd. The assistant district attorney prosecuting the case was a young lawyer excited to be in the presence of the famous Manuel Chavez.

In the best of legal traditions, we cut a deal. Manuel pleaded guilty and was let off with a modest fine and no jail time. To the satisfaction of the hometown crowd, Manuel was found guilty. To Manuel's satisfaction, he walked free after paying the fine. To the D.A.'s satisfaction, he left the courtroom with a number of Cesar Chavez anecdotes to share with the other attorneys back at the office. To the judge's satisfaction, he did not have to confront the press, UFW pickets, or dissatisfied townspeople. To my satisfaction, I hadn't made an utter fool of myself in my first trial in an open courtroom.

* * *

Over the next few years I would try a number of cases in rural California "justice courts," defending migrant workers before judges and juries. "Justice" is an approximate term to describe what went on in many of these courts. As Judge Smith, who presided over the Lost Hills court, once explained to me:

"Ah gits these criminals in here, and the onliest reason any of 'em gits off is 'cause of their constitutional rights."

Lost Hills, some 40 miles northwest of Bakersfield on the outer boundaries of California's agricultural heartland, counted some 2,000 souls when I did my trial work there. Judge Smith was what one might loosely characterize as a "hanging judge," though since he had jurisdiction only over misdemeanor cases, hanging was not on his list of punitive options. California rural justices in those days did not have to be lawyers, and Judge Smith had never darkened the door of any law school. When he wasn't busy dispensing justice, he drove the Lost Hills school bus.

Since he was limited to misdemeanor cases, Judge Smith did not have authority to block or limit union picketing or strike activities. But he tended to sock people convicted in his court to maximum sentences, so he was a force to be reckoned with. A picket line incident for which another rural judge might sentence a defendant to two to four weeks in jail could get a six-month sentence in his court.

Getting my clients out of jail while awaiting their trials was not easy matter in Lost Hills. Judge Smith liked to keep defendants in jail from the time they were arrested to the time they came up for trial. Although California did have a law providing for release of defendants "on their own recognizance," Judge Smith had never released a single defendant under its provisions. I decided to work over the judge's mind on this issue in an effort to get some of my migrant clients out of jail while awaiting trial.

"Judge Smith," I said, "The California legislature passed this 'own recognizance' law, and it contains four criteria for release. Wouldn't you think that the legislature, in passing this law, must have contemplated that there would be at least some people who met all four criteria, and that those people would deserve to be released?"

Judge Smith wrestled with my logic for a few moments before rendering his decision.

"You've got a point there, counsel," he said. "But I think I'll keep 'em in jail just the same."

• • •

Almost all of my trials in Lost Hills and elsewhere involved allegations of petty picket line violence. Picket lines can be messy places, and when tempers got hot, it was easy to nail all the blame on the migrant picketers. Since the police had a tendency to exaggerate the criminal conduct of defendants, my aim was always to expose inconsistencies in their testimony, thus throwing doubt on their veracity.

Winning verdicts from juries in a setting like this was a very tall order. I settled instead for giving my all to deadlocking the jury. Scrutinizing the faces of the jurors, I looked for those who might show some shard of sympathy for my migrant clients. When I identified a minimum of two such faces, I would work them until I sensed I had won them over. In one such case in Lost Hills, when I had a Mennonite woman and an African-American woman on my jury, I aimed my entire pitch at them. When I saw them going off together for the lunch break, their heads nodding and full of friendly smiles, I felt confident that I was home free.

I prepared myself carefully and shrewdly for these cases. I always referred to my migrant defendants as "my clients" to give the jury the impression that, only slightly less impoverished than they, I depended on the likes of them to pay my bills and support my family. Pushing this ploy a little farther, for my court appearances I always wore a blue jacket with pants of a slightly different shade of blue. I wanted the jury to get the impression that I was too poor to afford a suit but was trying to cover over that fact with my ill-matched wardrobe.

All this subterfuge was an absolute necessity in Judge Smith's court. I couldn't have lived with my conscience if I hadn't done everything in my power to keep the good judge from sentencing my defendants to jail.

"They're too soft on these here criminals," Judge Smith once explained to me. "If it was up to me, I'd turn the heat on in the summer and the air conditioning on in winter."

Luckily, Judge Smith never got the chance to sentence anyone I represented in his court. I deadlocked all his juries, and the Kern County district attorney, with more important things on his mind, always dismissed the charges in misdemeanor cases when the jury had been deadlocked.

I hadn't always been so lucky in other courts, particularly in the early days when I was learning the ropes of criminal trial practice. After one migrant worker I had defended was sentenced to three months in jail, I suddenly thought of a fairly obvious line of defense that I had completely overlooked. I was devastated. My client, seeing my stricken face, asked me what was wrong.

"I'm so sorry," I said. "I think I might have won your case if I'd handled it differently. It just didn't occur to me until now."

"Don't be troubled," she said. "You did your best."

"I just wasn't thinking," I said. "I'm so sorry."

"Don't feel bad," she said. "The jail is in Indio, and I have much family there. They will visit me often. I'll be out of jail in time for Christmas."

I could still see the concern for me in her face as the guards came to take her away.

• • •

About a year after a particularly satisfying trial in Lost Hills in which I deadlocked a jury, I attended the annual UFW convention in Fresno. A man sitting in a seat a few rows behind mine suddenly began to shout and wave excitedly at me. I vaguely recognized him as a migrant worker I had seen somewhere before. Clambering over all of the rows of chairs separating us he threw his arms around me. It turned out that his elderly father had been one of my defendants in Judge Smith's court, and by deadlocking the jury I had kept his father out of jail. He was beyond grateful.

CHAPTER 28

Basilio Chavez

ONE morning during grape harvesting season the phone rang in our office, and Jerry picked it up. Basilio Chavez, the UFW Ranch Committee president at Gallo Winery's vineyards, was calling to report that the well supplying Gallo's farm workers with drinking water had tested positive for coliform, the bacteria that may indicate the presence of feces or sewage waste. Basilio asked for help filing a grievance. Jerry sent me up to Modesto to see what could be done.

Gallo's workers lived in company housing: a long single-story, cement-block compound divided into single family units. I met Basilio in his unit, where he lived in cramped quarters with his wife and five children. Although the units were small and plainly furnished, they were clean, dry, and a good deal better than other camps I had seen.

Cracked or unsealed wells can allow unfiltered coliform to flow freely into drinking water, so the grievance we wrote requested, among other things, that Gallo inspect and rebuild the well if necessary.

After helping Basilio fill out the grievance form I headed up the valley on another assignment. Ten days later, to my surprise, Basilio called me to say that Gallo had rejected the grievance. The company had taken the position that there was no indication that the coliform in its well was the disease-carrying kind, and it refused to rebuild the well.

Basilio had pushed the UFW's position, tempers had flared, and discussions deadlocked. A day or so later Gallo told the workers that if they didn't want to drink its water, they didn't have to live in its rent-free housing either. A few days after that, the company bulldozed the camp. The workers, driven off Gallo's property, now had to find housing of their own.

Not long afterward Basilio was laid off. I drove back to Modesto a couple times to try to help him. I stayed with him in his new home, a ramshackle old house that was larger than his quarters at Gallo but more run down. Rain came through a hole in the roof as we ate supper, dripping water onto our plates.

Each day Basilio got up early to drive his gas-guzzling pickup truck over dusty valley roads looking for new work, and not having much luck. Gas prices had spiked dramatically that summer, and Basilio's sporadic earnings went out the exhaust pipe as he drove from ranch to ranch. Basilio's wife explained their predicament to me this way:

"El dinero del pobre no rinde."

Roughly translated, this mean "The poor man's money brings him no return"—no sooner does a poor man get his hands on a little money than it slips away through his fingers.

I drove around for a couple of days with Basilio, discussing our legal options, which were minimal, and checking out potential work locations. We took my car to save him gas. As we talked, Basilio said things I have never forgotten.

"Do you think it is just, Señor Antonio," he asked as we drove through Gallo's 10,000 acre Modesto ranch, "that the rich man should have so much land and the poor man none?" I had no answer.

On another occasion he described his life's dream:

"We have come to El Norte, my family and I, to work hard and save money. One day, we will return to Mexico. We will have saved enough money to buy a rancho, and we will have horses for our children."

When Basilio used the word "rancho," he did not have the King Ranch in mind. Two or three acres, surrounded by a corral, would have been rancho enough for him.

As the harvest season neared its end, though, all of Basilio's savings had been largely eaten up. The last time I saw him Basilio told me that he and his family could no longer hold on; they would be returning to Mexico in a few days.. Saying goodbye to each other for the last time, he said to me:

"Señor Antonio, for now you have dedicated your life to helping the campesino. But the time will come when you will return to your own people. You are well educated. You have a good profession. You will make good money. And one day you will buy a rancho, and have horses for your children."

Basilio Chavez was a poor man. In saying goodbye to me, though, he gave me his most precious treasure: his life's dream.

CHAPTER 29

The Hole

AS I stood there watching them, beginning around 2:00 a.m., the oldest and most infirm of the migrant workers who would labor that day in the hot fields of the lower Imperial Valley began their daily trek from their homes in Mexicali, just south of the border, into Calexico on the north. It was early November 1972, not long after I had started working with Chavez and the UFW. The migrants passing by me that day trooped by for hours, an unending stream passing through the glaring lights of the border station on their way to *El Hoyo* ("The Hole"), an immense parking lot on the California side where hundreds of "coyotes" (contractors) were waiting for them, ready to bid for the price of their labor.

Seventy years earlier, what is now called the Imperial Valley had been dry land occupying the southwest quadrant of the Colorado Desert. The 20 miles of sand dunes bounding its eastern edge had made it impenetrable to westward-bound settlers in the 1800s, and with an average July temperature of 107 degrees, it is one of the hottest places in the United States. The Mexicans who were already there when the first Anglo settlers arrived called it the Valley of the Dead.

The transformation of this valley into an integral part of California's agricultural heartland began with the construction of the Hoover Dam in 1931. It would take nine years, and the construction of three other publicly financed dams, to finally tame the Colorado River.

Beginning in 1940, the water dammed up in Hoover Lake was channeled the length of the newly constructed All-American Canal, winding through 80 miles of desert into the Valley of the Dead. For the first time, too, the U.S. government allowed its heavily subsidized irrigation water to be used on farms larger than 160 acres. Two years later, when the Bracero Program made large supplies of cheap Mexican labor available, the future of the aptly renamed Imperial Valley was assured. It would become one of the three great valleys making up the heart of California's $3 billion-a-year agribusiness empire.

The people first streaming across the border that morning in 1972 were the truest of what Cesar Chavez had described as the "true workers" working the migrant trail. Speaking of them, Cesar had said:

"This worker is not recognized because he is white, brown, or black but is recognized because his back aches with the tortures of farm work and his shoulders are stooped with the weight of injustice."

Because of their age and infirmities, their work commanded the lowest price in El Hoyo. As they went from bus to bus in their quest for work, each "coyote" sized them up. In the end these workers had to settle for the oldest buses in the worst condition traveling the longest distances to the ranches paying the lowest wages under the worst working conditions. These buses were the first to leave El Hoyo on their four-hour one-way trips to reach distant fields as dawn's first light broke, just in time for the day's work to begin. These workers received no pay for the four hours of painful jolting they endured in order to begin their ten-hour work day under the broiling sun, nor for the four hours of jolting on their return home on the Mexicali run.

These were the workers most likely to endure the indignities of squatting in the fields to relieve themselves or to seek relief from the broiling sun by sharing one cup of lukewarm water with 20 other workers. They bent low to the ground in back-breaking pain, working their short-handled hoes or dragging 100-pound bags laden with produce. Coyotes commonly withheld wages until the end of the week, skimming off hours and sometime days, firing anyone who complained.

Added to the sufferings these workers endured, the buses they took were in the worst mechanical condition, most likely to break down and leave them stranded for hours by the side of the road or to have worn brakes that might fail. Some years before my visit to El Hoyo, one of the drivers careened his bus into an irrigation ditch, drowning some 20 migrants in the process. The driver had been working back-to-back 20-hour days. Exhaustion caught up with him, and he had lost control.

As the hours went by that November morning, the workers I saw crossing over the border became younger and younger. They rode on better buses for shorter distances to work on better ranches under better conditions for more money. An hour or so before dawn, the aristocrats of labor began to cross the border. These were the men still young and fit enough to earn good money working fast in the hardest crops, such as lettuce. They looked and dressed differently as they walked past me with a certain swagger in their step. They had money in their pockets at the week's end, taking their girls out to the bars and nightclubs clustered in Mexicali's crowded streets. Life, for now at least, was good.

It was hard not to admire the ruthless efficiency of this most relentless of all free-market economies. The Hole, in the eyes of those who profit so abundantly from its efficiencies, is a level playing field. Consider the case of Miguel and his wife Esperanza, 36-year-old farm laborers with six children passing in front of me on their way to the Hole that morning. Stripped of all legal fictions, the true parties in interest negotiating with Miguel and Esperanza are, in the case of agribusiness corporations, anonymous absentee shareholders who may be worth millions, if not billions, of dollars and may come from any and every part of the world. In my day Tenneco, a multinational with petroleum as well as agricultural holdings, was just such a corporation.

The individual human being with whom Miguel and Esperanza faced off that day was the "coyote," or labor contractor, acting as agent for the corporation. The corporation itself, by virtue of Supreme Court decisions, is deemed a "person" within the meaning of the law. Hence, in contemplation of law, Miguel and Esperanza bargained face to face, person to person, with transnational corporations like Tenneco. The efficiencies of The Hole as a labor mart thus assured investors from around the world that the wages of the likes of Miguel and Esperanza would be driven as close to the frontier that separates subsistence from destitution as a free market system would allow. With their aging bodies their one capital asset, an asset depreciating in value with each passing year of hard labor in the fields, and excluded from the protections of the National Labor Relations Act or any other labor law covering farm or migrant workers, Miguel and Esperanza had no one to rely on but themselves.

CHAPTER 30

Winds of Change

CESAR had long been reluctant to include farm workers in any comprehensive labor law. His reasons are easy to understand. He had achieved his stunning victories winning contracts with major California growers through nationwide consumer boycotts. Cesar's "La Causa" had won the support of people both here and abroad, and in the process Cesar's name had become a household word. It was the consumer boycott that had brought California agribusiness to the bargaining table, winning stunning victories for Cesar and his union during the 1970 growing season. Cesar justly feared that any California state labor law modeled on the National Labor Relations Act, which prohibited secondary boycotts, would almost certainly eliminate or limit this most powerful of the UFW's economic weapons.

Winds of change had begun to blow, however, after Chavez and the UFW won their table grape contracts in 1970. Parties on every side of the struggle, and from all sides of the political spectrum, began to look at farm labor legislation through new eyes, asking themselves what might be in it for them. With the passage of time, the prospects that legislation of some kind would be enacted were becoming more and more likely. The only question was how favorable (or unfavorable) the law would be to migrant workers.

Those winds of change rose to gale force in 1973, when negotiations to renew the UFW's Delano contracts broke down. During those years Frank Fitzsimmons had made good on his pledge to Richard Nixon for help in bringing down the UFW. Teamster Union locals were at the ready, prepared to sign "sweetheart" contracts with the Delano growers the moment negotiations to renew their UFW contracts fell through.

It did not take long for all hell to break loose in California agriculture. For the rest of 1973 and all of the 1974 growing season, thousands of workers struck not only in the table grape industry but in many other crops as well. The Delano growers were hit by a nationwide boycott of table grapes to boot.

The Teamsters soon became a public relations nightmare for the growers as well. Teamster heavies roamed the dusty roads of the Coachella Valley on flatbed trucks, looking for a fight. Pictures of Teamster goons beating up strikers half their size on the picket lines did not play well in the national press.

For its part the UFW desperately needed money with which to pay benefits to thousands of striking workers. It turned for help to George Meany, President of the AFL-CIO.[1] Meany was willing to help the UFW with a strike fund grant of $1.6 million, but only on the condition that Chavez propose farm labor legislation bringing farm laborers under the coverage of an agricultural labor relations act.[2] The bottom line was simple: the union needed Meany's strike benefits, and to get them it would have to commit itself to legislation.

Given my background at the NLRB, Cesar and Jerry delegated to me the task of writing a bill to submit to the California legislature. Jerry and I met with Cesar in his office to work out its terms, and I crafted a bill to incorporate every provision that Cesar, Jerry, and I could think of that would favor the cause of migrant workers.

We submitted our bill to the California legislature, co-authored by Assemblymen John Burton and Richard Allatore as A.B. (Assembly Bill) 3370. At its first hearing, Cesar, Jerry, and I testified in its favor. The hearing room and surrounding hallways were jam-packed with highly motivated and noisily supportive farm workers.[3] It was a heady moment.

But our bill immediately faced unexpected challenges from our supposedly "liberal" allies.[4] Two prominent assemblymen, Berman and Wood, had created what they described as an "ideal labor law" in consultation with a prominent labor law expert, a professor at U.C. Davis

Law School.[5] Their bill would have traded away the union's right to strike and boycott in exchange for union organizers' right of access to workers in the field. Another Democrat also introduced amendments removing the union's right to boycott and cutting back its right to strike.

Our supposed friends and allies were falling all over themselves to save us from ourselves. According to them our bill had no chance of being passed. Their "ideal labor law," so they said, was a statesmanlike product designed to win bipartisan support, unlike the partisan bill for which we were fighting with tunnel-like vision.

Not long after we had drafted and submitted our bill, Jerry Cohen, another UFW lawyer named Sandy Nathan, and I met with Leo McCarthy, Speaker of the California Assembly:

"I want to be honest with you," Leo lectured. "You guys are emotional, irresponsible, irrational, rigid, dogmatic, arrogant. We don't want a bill that has your fingerprints on it."

Jerry leaned over to Leo as though to say something confidentially, and Leo leaned in to hear it:

"It's liberals, Leo," Jerry said. "They're wishy-washy. They make me sick. I want to puke. Here. Right now."

Jerry broke into hearty laughter as he said this, cutting the ground out from Leo, who had intended to put us in our place with his sweeping slam. But our confrontation with him put us on notice of just how hard we would have to fight to get an acceptable bill through the legislature.

* * *

The fight to get A.B. 3370 enacted into law came to a head in August 1974 when I got a call from Jerry telling me to drop everything and join him in Sacramento. We needed to make a final push to get our bill voted out of committee and onto the floor of the California Assembly. Jerry told me that the votes in the committee were two in favor of our bill, five against. The bill would be voted on in three days, and we had to get three legislators to shift their votes. It looked to me like a mission impossible. I was wrong. I had seen Jerry fight in court but never before in a legislative setting. Once Jerry's blood was up and the stakes were high, there was no stopping him.

Three days later, when A.B. 3370 came up for vote in committee, five of the committee members voted in favor of our bill, and two against.

A.B. 3370 then moved onto the floor of the California Assembly, where we generated enough momentum to win a favorable vote.

The next stop was the Republican-controlled California Senate where, facing strong opposition from agribusiness, it was defeated.

The fight over A.B. 3370 had given Cesar a lot to think about. Long before it came to a final vote, Cesar had already begun to plan his strategy for a new and vastly more ambitious and visionary legislative campaign.

---

1. Bardacke, p. 434
2. Meany wanted Chavez to work out a jurisdictional agreement with the Teamsters, thus ending the strife and divisions within the house of labor. However neither Meany, Chavez, nor anyone else had any good suggestion on how to get the Teamsters to so agree, and nothing came of it.
3. Levy, supra, p. 8.
4. Levy, p. 9,
5. Professor Buckminster Levy, p. 10

CHAPTER 31

The Sting

CESAR was a shrewd and subtle strategist, able to ride the shifting winds of political change with consummate skill, and a genius at turning defeat into victory. Our experience in Sacramento made it clear that no farm labor bill with his "fingerprints" on it would survive the California legislative process. A politician of major status with no ties to Cesar or the UFW would have to carry our bill. We knew that such a political figure would do so only on one condition. At the end of the day he would have to stride onto central stage in the great drama of California agricultural politics as the statesman who finally succeeded in bringing peace to a troubled land. Where everyone else had failed, he alone would have hammered out a workable compromise between two perennially intractable parties, Cesar Chavez and his motley crew of agitated migrants and overheated idealistic volunteers on the one hand, and California's keystone economic block, its agribusiness industry, on the other.

It was possible, Cesar was now thinking, that just such a seismic shift in the political landscape might be in the offing. Ronald Reagan, a sworn enemy of organized labor and no friend of the UFW, was nearing the end of his term as governor. Jerry Brown, Secretary of State and son of the popular and progressive former governor Pat Brown, was leading in the polls in his run for the governorship. While Brown was an unknown quantity, he had done favors for the UFW in the past and just might, Cesar thought, prove to be a valuable ally in the UFW's struggle to get legislation it could live with.

To meet all these challenges Cesar devised a bold strategy. We would draft and submit to the legislature what were in substance two very different bills, combining their provisions in the form of one single bill for the purpose of getting our essential provisions through the California legislature intact.

The first was the real bill that contained our true bottom-line position. But Cesar's authorship of this bill would have to be masked, so he had me draft a second bill that was in effect a decoy. It would be publicly associated with his name and would have his fingerprints all over it. The decoy would contain a host of truly radical provisions.

In the battle to get the real bill through the legislature, Cesar would "reluctantly" compromise away the decoy clauses of our bill, denouncing the politicians who were "forcing" him to abandon its "crucial" provisions, hoping all the while to preserve the essential elements of the real bill.

Sandy Nathan, a UFW lawyer who read and commented on my drafts, made creative and useful suggestions, and would later participate in negotiations, dubbed our two bills our "way-out bill" and our "way-way-out bill." The "way-out bill" which was already quite radical, was our true bottom line. The wildly more radical "way-way-out bill" was our false bottom. If Cesar's game plan was to work, he would have to appear extremely radical at the beginning of our campaign. He would need all the negotiating room he could get as we worked our way progressively down, reluctantly compromising away provisions from the "way-way-out bill" until, with howls of protest, we would submit to the coercion of having our "way-out bill" enacted into law.

I drafted all of this language into a single bill. In a private copy that I gave to Cesar and Jerry, and that was designed for negotiating purposes only, I put distinctive brackets around each of the "way-out" and "way-way-out" provisions. This would give us maximum maneuverability in the superheated environment in which high-stakes negotiations take place.

At the time all this was going on, a highly successful movie starring Paul Newman and Robert Redford was in theaters all around the country. Called *The Sting*, it tells the story of two small-time grifters who con "the mark," a mob boss, out of a $500,000 bet placed in a bogus horse-race scam. Cesar was writing the script for his own version of *The Sting*. In Cesar's script, in the first instance "the mark" would be California growers, their agribusiness associates, and the politicians beholden to them. In the second instance "the mark" would be the liberal politicians so eager to rescue us from ourselves by compromising away essential elements of our bill. If our plan worked, liberal politicians like Leo McCarthy would never see a bill marred by Cesar's fingerprints. We would have wiped our "way-out bill" clean of every trace of them long before Leo got his hands on it.

It was a very long shot. Ranged against us would be the most powerful power block in California, its agribusiness lobby. Other parties too had interests differing strongly from the UFW's. Unions that had to live under the NLRA's prohibition on boycotts could not be counted on to support an exemption for the UFW. Liberal politicians would continue to work hard for the prestige of forging compromise legislation between the UFW and agribusiness.

Cesar had no great faith that even under the best of circumstances the California legislature would enact the "way-out" bill into law or, if it did, that any governor of California would sign it. He was therefore courageous and inventive enough to plan a strategy in the likely event that our bill would be rejected in the 1975 legislative session. He would use that defeat as a springboard to carry our case to the people of California in 1976 through a statewide referendum campaign. In the 1976 referendum we would drop all of the decoy provisions and present only the true bottom-line provisions of the 1975 bill.

Cesar's deep confidence in the people of California convinced him that they would support us even if their politicians did not. If he was right, and the referendum were successful, our bill would become part of the California constitution, insulated from subsequent amendment. It was in order to draft just such legislation that Cesar called Jerry asking that he and I join him in his car one afternoon.

Cesar had a first-rate legal mind. Jerry was as remarkable in his own way as Cesar, quick, shrewd, aggressive, able to see a problem from many different angles, supremely gifted at outmaneuvering his opponents, keeping them off balance, luring them down the primrose path. Cesar and Jerry worked together symbiotically, playing off of each other's ideas. They were brothers under the skin, in deep harmony with each other not only as to the goals to be achieved but as to the tactics to pursue in achieving them.

My own presence in Cesar's car that day was so improbable as to strain credulity. Since I had spent two years in Washington, D.C., as the representation case specialist for Frank McCulloch, Chairman of the National Labor Relations Board, and his Chief Counsel Arthur Leff, I knew as much about that field as any lawyer in the country. It was for this reason that Cesar had asked me along for the ride that day, not only to work with him and Jerry to craft a proposed law but to do so while drafting language modeled as closely as possible on the National Labor Relations Act. While our bill would be substantively progressive, its form would appear as conventional as I could make it.

CHAPTER 32

A Secret Meeting

THE first piece in Cesar's grand plan fell into place two months after our ride together, when Jerry Brown was elected Governor of California in November 1974. Brown's election signaled that a new day had dawned for the farm workers' union and its friends. Brown had joined in farm worker protests before his election and was one of the few major California political figures to have endorsed the UFW-sponsored A.B. 3370 in 1974. Now, in his inaugural address, he spoke eloquently about their needs: "The time has come," he said, "to pay unemployment benefits to farm workers and to extend the rule of law to them, including secret ballot elections."

The second piece fell into place a few months after that, on March 15, 1975, when Brown hosted a meeting at his house in Los Angeles to discuss farm worker legislation. Cesar and Jerry Cohen came to explain and promote the UFW's positions. Present from the governor's staff was his Secretary of Agriculture Rose Bird, the member of his cabinet charged with responsibility for drafting farm labor legislation. With her as her labor law expert was Herman Levy, a law professor at Santa Clara University. Levy had worked for a number of years at the National Labor Relations Board in Washington, D.C. on special assignments and was broadly knowledgeable about the history of the NLRB and the National Labor Relations Act. He would be doing the actual drafting of Brown's proposed California Agricultural Labor Relations Act. LeRoy Chatfield, a key personal aide to Brown who had previously long been a close assistant to Cesar, was also present.

Sharp differences soon emerged between Rose Bird and Herman Levy on one hand and Jerry Cohen and Cesar on the other. Tempers flared, and heated words were exchanged.

Jerry Brown said very little while the two sides battled. He listened silently, taking it all in, assessing both sides of the deep disagreements. And then quite suddenly, he spoke up for the first time:

"Let's take a walk, Cesar."

Jerry Cohen and LeRoy Chatfield exchanged glances. Both knew that Cesar did not trust politicians and did not like to be trapped in one-on-one meetings with them. This time though, Cesar agreed. The two men went off for a private meeting together.

* * *

It was a crucial moment in California, if not American, labor history. Governor Jerry Brown, listening to arguments between Cesar Chavez and his own appointed Secretary of Agriculture, had made up his mind. He would go with Cesar's bill.

In that meeting Cesar described three priorities. "We need a strong agricultural labor act as a lever to get the Teamsters out of the fields,"[1] Cesar told Brown, addressing an issue that weighed heavily on his mind. Since neither man had any clear idea how this might be accomplished, nothing much came of that concern.

"We need you to carry a strong bill for another reason," Cesar went on. "Our 'liberal' friends are fighting with each other over the privilege of sponsoring a compromise bill designed to bring 'peace to the fields.' A strong bill sponsored by you will forestall passage of a weak bill which could truly damage or destroy the UFW."

Cesar then articulated a third priority that he knew would have great appeal to Brown.

"If your bill is good enough," Cesar told the governor, "the UFW will agree to it."

Brown probed a little further, wanting to know if Cesar really meant what he said about agreeing to a bill that was "good enough."

"Are you saying that if our bill was really good for farm workers you would agree to it?" he asked.

Cesar replied, "Yes, but it would have to be a really good bill."

Privately, Cesar doubted that even Jerry Brown could get a sufficiently good bill through the California legislature. And Brown wasn't entirely sure that Cesar had, at long last, dropped his well-known aversion to legislation.

Both knew, moreover, that Cesar's support for the bill would have to be masked, and Cesar had prepared for this. The bill I had drafted with its real and decoy provisions was already "in his hip pocket," and he was ready to move forward with it on an instant's notice. The two men thus agreed that Cesar would submit a public version of our bill to the California legislature just as I had written it. This would be a single bill with its true and false bottom provisions folded into one. Jerry Cohen would send a preview copy to Chatfield, who would pass it on to Brown. In a separate document Cesar would identify which were the "true bottom" clauses.

Cesar would campaign publicly for our inclusive bill, going public with open and vocal opposition to Brown's bill (our real bill). At the right moment, for public consumption, Jerry Brown would closet himself with Cesar, "pound some sense into his head," and emerge with a "compromise" bill to which Cesar would "reluctantly" agree. Brown would emerge crowned as the architect of peace in California's troubled fields.

Very few people would be in on the secret. On our side Cesar, Jerry, myself, and UFW attorneys Sandy Nathan and Tom Dalzell knew about it. On Brown's side, to my knowledge, only LeRoy Chatfield was in on it.

Rose Bird was not. Although she was a woman of undoubted integrity, she had a well-deserved reputation for tending to be rigid and inflexible in her views. On a number of crucial issues these aligned her with the "liberal" block of California legislators who would kill any bill with Cesar's fingerprints on it. Since she was a high-visibility figure in California politics, Governor Brown would have to act skillfully to get his bill passed without an open confrontation with his Secretary of Agriculture.

• • •

A lot, of course, had been left unsaid and unspecified in the secret meeting. Although Brown had made a commitment to Cesar to carry a "really good bill," neither man had said anything about precisely how radical the bill would have to be. It was clear that it would have to be very good indeed to win Chavez's assent. If it wasn't, he would take his case to the people of California the following year.

Yet Brown wasn't giving Chavez a blank check. Brown's commitment would necessarily be bounded by the outer limits of what he considered just, workable, and above all politically feasible. The issues involved were complicated, and the stakes could hardly have been higher. There was no way they could all be addressed, let alone resolved, between the two men in that single meeting.

Cesar and Jerry Brown therefore agreed that Jerry Cohen would meet with LeRoy Chatfield a few days later to identify the provisions of our bill that constituted our true bottom line. Jerry traveled to Sacramento to give LeRoy a copy of our bill and a key identifying its 12 bottom-line provisions. The key was not the full written version of each provision but a succinct summary of each. In a hallway of the California State Capitol, Jerry Cohen ran into Governor Brown. Jerry took advantage of the opportunity to show Brown the key, and Brown looked it over hurriedly:

"No problem. No problem," he said.

Jerry Cohen then went over the details of our bill and key with LeRoy, left a copy of both with him, and headed home.

All systems, it seemed, were set to go.

---

1. Cesar hoped Brown could use a strong farm labor law to bring about negotiations between the growers, the UFW, and the Teamsters resulting in an agreement by the Teamsters to leave farm worker representation to the UFW.

CHAPTER 33

A Near Betrayal

WE had taken it for granted that after meeting with Jerry Cohen, LeRoy Chatfield would forward our bill and its 12-point key to Governor Brown, and Brown would use our key to ensure that his bill contained our essential provisions. Instead, Chatfield sent our bill and key directly to Rose Bird and Herman Levy. Since they were not in on the secret agreement between Cesar and Jerry Brown, they had no idea that the governor had committed himself to carrying our "bottom line" bill.

Working under Bird's supervision, Levy moved forward by collecting all of the farm labor bills pending before the California legislature. After reviewing them all he wrote a compromise agricultural labor relations act for Brown to carry. In doing so, he included some but not all of our bottom-line provisions. Governor Brown, for his part, assumed that Levy had drafted his bill to meet Cesar's requirements.

Governor Brown's bill was scheduled for public release and submission to the California legislature on April 10, 1975. As that day approached, Jerry Cohen became more and more uneasy. He had assumed that at some point we would have an opportunity to review the language in Governor Brown's bill to make sure our 12 points were adequately covered.

Late in the night of April 9, only 12 hours before the Brown bill was to be announced at a press conference, LeRoy delivered it to Jerry Cohen. It was our first look at Brown's language, and Jerry was stunned. The words he was reading were a far cry from what he had expected. Something had gone seriously wrong.

Jerry immediately called Cesar. "There are a lot of things in Brown's bill that are really bad," he said. "They don't mesh with Brown's intentions as he represented them to us. It's a deceptive bill. What should we do?"

"Hold a press conference and call it a deceptive bill," Cesar replied.[1]

Quite suddenly we found ourselves plunged into a byzantine maze of conflicting stories, heated accusations, and bitter cries of betrayal. Things heated up to the point that the whole scheme seemed on the brink of self-destruction.

Immediately after his press conference Jerry Brown and LeRoy Chatfield got on the phone, calling all of the UFW's traditional supporters in the religious, labor, and progressive communities, telling them that his bill was supported by the UFW and represented its true intentions and interests.

This message was directly at odds with what we were communicating to our friends, allies, and the public at large. Cesar denounced Brown's bill and called it a "near-betrayal."

At first Brown believed that Chavez was simply playing out the script that he and Cesar had worked out in their secret meeting and that the rhetoric was for show. Cesar traveled up and down the state attacking the governor in increasingly sharp language, and the governor took to the road assuring our supporters that his was a bill that Cesar really wanted, not suspecting that the differences between the two parties were as deep and serious as they really were.

One of the broadsides that Cesar leveled against Brown hit a surprisingly sensitive nerve. Brown, Cesar said, wouldn't know a potato growing in a field if he saw one. Brown's feelings were clearly hurt, and he was angry:

"Cohen," he told Jerry. "Before you were born I had a victory garden.[2] Do you know what that was, Cohen? I grew potatoes when I was a little boy. I was three years old. You weren't even born. Go tell Chavez that."[3]

• • •

Cesar's opponents jumped on the opportunity presented by the sharp public differences between Chavez and Governor Brown. Among those who now stood against us was Mario Obledo, Brown's Secretary of Health, Education, and Welfare.

Obledo was no errand boy for the growers. He had been seen crying during the film *Fighting for Our Lives*, which showed Teamster goons beating up picketing farm workers. Before Cesar had taken to the road attacking the governor, Obledo had been part of a quiet conspiracy among leading members of Brown's staff to derail Rose Bird and Howard Levy's bill. These Brown staffers had wanted the governor to align himself with the UFW.

Now, listening to Cesar's rhetoric as he attacked Brown, Obledo became convinced that Cesar had set the governor up. "Cesar doesn't really want a bill," Obledo told Brown. "I know him and I know Jerry Cohen. They're crazy crackpots; they're kamikazes who are going to drag you down with them. They're going to destroy themselves, and they'll destroy you in the process."[4]

Brown found what Obledo was saying credible, leaning increasingly to the view that Cesar really did not want a bill. In all likelihood, Brown was thinking, Chavez had told him he would accept a bill that was "really good" at their secret meeting only to avoid being publicly identified as opposed to all legislation.

Now that Cesar was blistering him with hot rhetoric, and Obledo was telling him that Chavez was "crazy" and a "kamikaze," Brown began to lose interest in his bill and to lower expectations that it would get passed. Brown did not want to see his bill go down in flames in the legislature and to be blasted in the process by Cesar Chavez for having "betrayed" the farm worker cause.

---

1. Quotations in Levy, supra, p. 34
2. During World War II, patriotic Americans kept "victory gardens," growing vegetables and keeping chickens to help the war effort.
3. Amherst College Archives, p. 83

4 Quoted in Amherst College Archive, pp. 54-55

CHAPTER 34

Jerry Brown Is One of Us

AS the date set for hearings on Brown's bill in the California legislature approached, Jerry Cohen became increasingly anxious. The original game plan had spun out of control. The public differences between Chavez and Brown were so sharp that Cohen doubted the two parties would be able to reach an agreement in the free-for-all environment of legislative hearings and negotiations. Jerry called me one day at the end of April to get me up to speed:

"We're going to have to meet with Brown in Sacramento really soon, before the legislative hearings start in early May, and cut through the rhetoric. We've got to get back to the terms of Brown's and Cesar's original agreement."

Jerry put in a call to LeRoy Chatfield, asking him to set up a meeting with Brown.

"Tell Cohen to work his issues out with Rose Bird," Brown told Chatfield in response. "His problems are receding on my desk. I've got other more important things to look after."

But on May 1, 1975, Jerry Cohen, Sandy Nathan, and I did meet with Governor Brown, LeRoy, and an aide of Brown's named Jacques Barzaghi, in Brown's celebrated unfurnished apartment. A five-minute walk from his office in the Capitol, the apartment was famous in California because Brown he had refused to occupy the luxurious governor's mansion newly built by Ronald and Nancy Reagan. Brown had chosen spartan quarters that made the sharpest possible contrast with Nancy Reagan's elegant and expensive tastes.

Out of curiosity, I took a quick tour. Brown's apartment boasted a bedroom containing two iron cots requisitioned from a state mental institution, a bathroom on top of whose toilet tank sat a book titled *Zen Buddhism and the Gospel of St. John*, a living room bare of furnishings except for a telephone, and a kitchen furnished with one round table, four chairs, four coffee cups, and a coffee maker.

Barzaghi made the coffee, and when it was ready Brown did the pouring. He gave Cohen, Nathan, Barzaghi, and myself the four cups. He then poured his own coffee into a glass that was hot to the touch, holding it by the bottom to avoid burning his fingers. We chatted pleasantly for about 15 minutes, then moved into the living room to do the serious talking.

Jerry Cohen went straight to the heart of the matter. He had noted that Brown's public statements about his bill, its purposes, and its provisions were quite good. It was the written language in his bill, drafted by Herman Levy, that was bad. Cohen decided to test Brown to see if what he had been saying publicly was what he really meant, or whether he had intentionally left our language out of his bill to gain leverage over us in the final negotiation stage.

"You know, Governor," Jerry said, "If you had just used Tony's language in your bill we wouldn't be having a problem now on the boycott issue. The way we wrote it, it would have accomplished your intent."[1]

Brown did a double take.

"What are you talking about, Cohen?" he wanted to know. "Your language is written right into our bill."

"Not it's not, Governor, and not by a long shot," Jerry said. "Here's our language. Take a look and compare it to the language Levy drafted into your bill."

For the next two and half hours Jerry and I, with occasional input from Sandy Nathan, argued with the governor about the contents of his bill. Brown should have had the opportunity to carefully study our language and proposals long before this. Because of the foul-up, however, it was only at the last possible moment that he was being given the opportunity to so.

It was no easy decision we were asking him to make. The bill we were asking him to maneuver through the California legislature would be characterized decades later as "the most labor-friendly law in U.S. history."[2] Brown had to ask himself whether he wanted to associate his name with a bill that would arguably go farther than any other bill in American history to promote the rights of working people. Clearly, he would have felt a good deal easier carrying something less radical.

He also had to ask himself whether Cesar, Jerry, and I had been literally "crazy" in drafting language that would be struck down in court on constitutional or other grounds, or would subject him to withering criticism from experts in the field of labor relations and/or labor law.

Radical as our bill was, Jerry and I had to persuade Brown that as drafted it was rock solid both as a matter of law and as a matter of policy. The language in our bill giving the union limited rights to carry out boycotts was the most difficult.

"What's wrong with the language in my bill?" Brown asked, hoping he could limit the damage.

"It deals a death blow to farm workers," I replied. "Levy's convinced himself that secondary boycotts are 'immoral,' but a law that gives a union the tools to hold and win elections, but then strips it of the economic clout to win contracts providing living wages and decent working conditions, hasn't done farm workers any favors. What's 'immoral' isn't a law aiming to bring farm workers' wages and working conditions out of the dark ages. It's what keeps them there."[3]

Brown listened carefully to what Jerry and I were saying, clearly taking it in and making detailed written notes. He asked a number of questions about our language, wanting to know how it worked and what its broader implications were. The boycott provisions of our law were clearly the most controversial, and Brown wanted to understand them thoroughly from both a legal and a policy point of view. Jerry and I answered his questions as best we could.

As he got up to leave, Brown turned to Jerry Cohen: "As I read it, Cohen, everything that you're saying comes across to me as, you don't want a bill. And if that's what's going on in my mind, I have to think that that's what's going on in your mind."[4]

Cohen shot back: "Look, you want this bill worse than we do. You're not fooling anybody. You put a lot of political coin into it."

"Not at all," Brown replied. "I couldn't care less about this stuff. Your problem is receding, Cohen. There are other problems, you know, that are more pressing and important than yours."[5]

As he picked up his papers and stood up to leave, Brown added: "I'll read through your stuff and get back to you with my decision. I'll try to get to it sometime this evening."

• • •

Jerry, Sandy, and I left Brown's apartment feeling seriously depressed. Jerry in particular had very bad feelings about how the meeting had gone. The foul-up that had led Cesar to attack Brown's bill so vigorously had raised deep questions in the governor's mind. Did Chavez really want a bill? Had his avowed interest in legislation been posturing all along? The forces opposing Chavez in California were powerful. Brown would have to exercise rare political skill to maneuver a bill as radical as ours through the legislative process. Should he commit himself to doing so, running the risk that he would come up short in the end or, worse, be double-crossed by Cesar Chavez?

We knew that we were in very tough place. Although we had taken a lot of what Brown was saying as negotiating fluff, meant to lower our expectations in order to have more room to maneuver, his problems were very real. During the six weeks he had been marshaling support to get his bill through the legislature, Brown had made commitments to grower associations and agribusiness representatives. If he was to get his bill through the legislative process, he would have to bring all the warring parties—agribusiness, skeptical legislators, and Chavez—together.

After the meeting, I headed back to my home in San Francisco. Minutes passed like hours, and hours like days. I went for a long walk in Golden Gate Park, a short walk from my apartment in the Haight Ashbury. Golden Gate Park never failed to lift my spirits. By supper time I had mostly calmed myself down.

Around 11 o'clock that night my phone rang. LeRoy Chatfield was on the other end of the line: "I've just spoken with Governor Brown. He's gone through all of your language. He also read a law review article on the subject of boycotts, and he's persuaded that you were right. He's decided to go with your bill.

"The governor wants to move forward on this as fast as possible.

We'll start in first thing on Saturday morning. I've called Jerry, and I'll see you and him then."

I put down the phone, stunned and grateful.

* * *

In the end Governor Brown had not relied on the opinion of legal experts supposedly better versed than he on the finer points of labor law. Instead, busy as he was, he had taken the time to read a law review article and had made up his own mind.

Thinking about it later, I could see that Jerry Brown had two distinct reasons for going with our bill. The first is that he was, even then, looking beyond the borders of California for a bigger town in which to exercise his considerable political skills. Winning laurels as the man who finally succeeded in bringing peace to California's strife-torn fields would bring Brown national stature. Brown knew, moreover, that he would need Chavez's support if his national ambitions were to get off the ground.

The second, more personal, reason is that while he may never have physically visited "El Hoyo" in Calexico, he didn't have to. He had seen, from any number of California roadsides, migrant workers toiling in the fields under the broiling sun, and been moved by the sight. He had followed Chavez's movement, and his conscience had been awakened. That was the reason he had been so hurt and outraged when Chavez declared in a public television broadcast that Jerry Brown couldn't identify a potato growing in the fields. Not only could Jerry Brown identify potatoes, he cared deeply about the workers who grew and harvested them.

In his heart of hearts, at this watershed moment in California labor history, Jerry Brown turned out to be one of us. He had decided to throw his political lot in with the migrant men, women, and children he had seen working in the fields, and go for broke.

---

1. Amherst University archives, p. 50
2. Bardacke, p. 422
3. Amherst College archives, p. 54
4. Id., p. 55
5. Id.

CHAPTER 35

The Little Bastard Wrote It Himself

OUR meeting in Jerry Brown's apartment had been an off-the-record affair. As LeRoy Chatfield had told me, a second, on-the-record negotiating session would be needed to work out the actual wording of the new language going into Brown's bill. Rose Bird would have to be present and was not at all happy about it. The main purpose of the meeting would be to substitute our language for the language she and Levy had drafted into Brown's bill.

The meeting took place in the conference room of Brown's spacious office in the California Capitol. Brown had written us into his schedule immediately after the close of his working day. In principle, we would be meeting at what would ordinarily be supper time.

It was no surprise to us, however, that when the appointed hour rolled around Brown was well behind schedule. Few things wear on a person's emotional state as much as the anxiety of waiting around for high-stakes negotiations to begin. Nerves weave themselves into tight knots as you sit around for a seeming eternity before being ushered into the office of the most powerful elected official in the State of California.

Jerry Cohen had foreseen this. To keep us all distracted Jerry took me and a young UFW paralegal named Tom Dalzell out to eat at a popular Sacramento Chinese restaurant.

"We'll give you a call as soon as we're finished with supper," Jerry told LeRoy, giving him the restaurant's name and address. "If you need us in a hurry, you'll know where to find us."

The three of us had a great time, shooting the breeze and eating exceptionally good Chinese food.

After supper, around 7:30, Jerry called LeRoy.

"The governor's still tied up in high-level meetings," LeRoy said. "He probably won't be ready for you for another couple of hours."

Jerry was prepared for this too.

"I think we'll go to the movies," Jerry told LeRoy. "*Young Frankenstein* is playing. It's got great reviews. I'll call you as soon as it lets out."

Jerry, Tom, and I laughed ourselves silly. We were loose, relaxed, happy, and rather full of ourselves by the time we walked out. Jerry put in a call to LeRoy.

"The governor's wrapping up his last meeting," LeRoy said. "Come on back to the Capitol. We should be ready about the time you get here."

By the time Brown and his staff members were finally ready for us it was close to 11 o'clock. The governor and his people hadn't eaten supper, so they ordered in large portions of Chinese carry-out food and dug in. Although Brown had been hard at work since 8 o'clock that morning, he was still full of energy and enthusiasm. He had a great sense of humor, and so Jerry, Tom, and I bantered along with him and his staff until the food was gone. Rose Bird, for her part, was beginning to look a little worse for the wear and did not seem to be enjoying herself. It was close to 11:30 when we finally sat down to business.

Although Bird was there, Herman Levy was nowhere to be seen. In his place she had brought in a team of four eager young labor lawyers.

Governor Brown made it clear from the outset that he wanted his bill enacted into law. The previous day Jerry and I had drafted amendments to Brown's bill designed to bring it into alignment with our bottom line. On a number of key issues, however, Rose Bird was still wedded to the language that she and Levy had written some months before and was not prepared to budge one inch. The governor and his Secretary of Agriculture were thus in deadlocked opposition to each other. One of them would have to back down, and Brown did not want to cram his decision down Rose Bird's throat in an open confrontation. The solution to the problem, as all of us except Rose soon realized, lay in the fact that she was the most visibly tired person at the table. Sooner or later she would either have to leave the negotiations and go to bed or else fall asleep on the table.

Rose was nothing if not determined, though, and so negotiations dragged on.

At long last, around 3 o'clock in the morning, Rose Bird, whose head had begun to droop about a half hour earlier, stood up and announced she was going to bed. With Rose out of the way and unable to object, Jerry Cohen could now reveal our true bottom-line position to Governor Brown and his team.

At 4:35 in the morning on Monday, May 6, 1975—one hour and 35 minutes after Rose Bird had gone to bed—we closed the deal on the most progressive labor law ever written in America.

• • •

Another three weeks of hard negotiations were needed before the bill finally passed both houses of the California legislature and was enacted into law.

After the final vote was announced, Jerry, Sandy Nathan, and I walked out of the Capitol building. A huge crowd had gathered. People were cheering, crying, and hugging each other. Catching sight of Sandy, a very pretty girl named Elaine Esparza ran up to him and, throwing her arms around his neck, gave him a passionate embrace. I've always regretted that Elaine didn't spot me first. For all of us who had worked on the bill it was the equivalent of a ticker-tape parade down Broadway.

• • •

Two and a half weeks earlier Governor Brown had summoned representatives of all major California grower and agribusiness associations to Sacramento. It had not been easy, Brown told them, but he had finally brought Chavez to his senses. If all of the grower representatives in the room would commit themselves publicly to supporting the bill as written, without amendments, Brown said he thought Chavez too would agree.

"Will Chavez agree?" was the big question growers kicked around that night in the room.

"He'll never agree to it, knowing that we've agreed" became the considered opinion of the group.

True to the script that Brown had worked out with Cesar, he too feigned uncertainty.

"This is a tricky one," he said. "Cohen, do you think you can talk Cesar into agreeing? Won't he want the amendments back that he's given up in the bill?"

A few minutes before Cesar was scheduled to come on the phone, a grower representative named Daryl Arnold, shrewder than most, leaned over to Jerry Cohen.

"Cohen," he said. "I'm going to make some good money tonight."

"How do you figure that?" Jerry asked.

"I've got bets riding with a lot of these guys. I say Chavez is going to sign. These guys are persuaded he won't. Why shouldn't Chavez agree? The little bastard wrote the bill himself."

CHAPTER 36

Standing Up for the Rank and File

WITH the fight to obtain a "really good" labor law behind him, Cesar Chavez turned his attention to the other major problem that had burdened his mind since shortly after his successful drive to sign contracts with the Delano table grape growers. The deal cut between Richard Nixon and Frank Fitzsimmons for Teamster locals to stand ready to sign sweetheart deals with those growers at the earliest opportunity, and to follow these with Teamster goons flooding the fields, had come close to destroying the UFW. Cesar had turned to such diverse sources as AFL-CIO President George Meany and Governor Brown for help, but no one had any good ideas. In the end Cesar decided to take matters into his own hands. And so it was that I got a call from him about the time I started drafting the California Labor Relations Act of 1975.

"Tony," Cesar said, "I've got a project I want to talk over with you. I'm heading up to the Bay Area tomorrow morning; I want you to come along, and we'll talk then." For the only time in the years that I knew him I would have Cesar all to myself for the next 48 hours.

No sooner had Cesar's Plymouth station wagon pulled out of La Paz on its way to San Francisco than he turned to me and, with his usual vivid interest and enthusiasm, asked:

"Brother Tony. What is your opinion about prayer?"

Cesar rarely called me "brother." I was the only lawyer in the UFW who was an openly practicing Catholic and, like Cesar himself, had a special attachment to Our Lady of Guadalupe. Cesar launched into a discussion of subjects close to his heart of which I had never heard him speak before.

"The universe is full of unseen lines of communication going in all directions, upward toward heaven and back down again, and also between people everywhere," he said. "Prayer is a communication of this kind. Our prayers constantly flow up above, and flow constantly back down again."

"What do you think about healing?" Cesar asked next. He then launched into a lengthy discussion on the subject of "curanderos," native healers using a variety of herbs, plants, and animal extracts, the faith native peoples have in them, and the remarkable results they sometimes obtain.

After we had canvassed the subject of healing pretty thoroughly, Cesar moved on to another subject close to his heart, monasteries for social activists.

"You know, Tony," he said, "when I retire from the Union, I want to start a monastery for married people and their families. The only kinds of organizations that last over time are those that are based on religious conviction and commitment. Communities that come together for political or ideological reasons fall apart."

I listened attentively, supposing that his thinking about monasteries for married people had been inspired by California's Spanish missions, which held great interest for him. He had taken his wife Helen on a tour of the most famous of these missions on their honeymoon. Although Cesar took the idea very seriously, and at one time even proposed getting the project started with one of his longest-term and most trusted collaborators, Chris Hartmire, it never really got off the ground.

* * *

As we approached the Bay Area, Cesar turned our conversation to his principal reason for asking me to ride with him that day. California's canning industry workers were virtually all under Teamsters contracts, suffering the same kind of discrimination at the hands of the Teamsters Union as they did from their employers, their anger directed in equal measure against both. Over the years many cannery workers had approached Cesar, asking him to take up their cause. He had never been able to do so before, because bringing workers covered by the National Labor Relations Act into his union would have forced him to give up the right to boycott.

Now, however, Cesar's ever-inventive mind had come up with a solution. A Cannery Workers Legal Project created with his assistance, but that was a legal entity separate from the UFW, could bring cannery workers much-needed assistance in their fight against discrimination. Cesar proposed that I head up just such a project, my mission being to bring a series of lawsuits challenging discriminatory employment practices in the canning industry. The canneries and the Teamsters would both be compelled to improve conditions in the canneries.

The project also had a second major objective. For the previous four years Cesar had been obsessively preoccupied with the problem of bringing an end to Teamsters raids of the UFW and its farm worker constituency. His proposed Cannery Workers Legal Project would open a second front against the Teamsters, giving him the opportunity of killing two birds with one stone. Lawsuits that included the Teamsters as defendants would also, Cesar believed, give him leverage in negotiations with the Teamsters to get them to leave organizing farm workers to the UFW. It was ironic that I, a former Associate House Counsel to the International Brotherhood of Teamsters in Washington, D.C., would now be launched into the fight to drive the Teamsters from the fields.

• • •

That night, in Oakland, Cesar and I met with a group of cannery workers who had asked Cesar for help. Their eyes bright with excitement and pleasure, they greeted Cesar warmly, but they were apprehensive as well, unsure of what lay ahead of them. As he always did, Cesar wanted to hear from them what practices in the canneries troubled them most, where they felt the most injustice. He listened attentively to their stories of discrimination and harassment, of opportunities offered to white workers but not to Mexicans.

Cesar then gave them examples of how our project could help them, and I fleshed out the details. I exchanged contact information with the workers, telling them I would get in touch with them in about a month, once I had moved from La Paz to San Francisco. When the meeting was over I took a deep breath. I had just taken an immense leap of faith into a field of the law about which I knew exactly nothing. Precisely how,

I wondered, was I going to climb this intimidatingly high mountain?

* * *

My family and I moved to San Francisco shortly thereafter, where I opened an office midway between the two canning centers of San Jose and Sacramento. Since the Cannery Workers Legal Project was a separate entity, I no longer worked directly under UFW leadership, and I saw Cesar only occasionally. I did stay in regular contact with Jerry Cohen, however, following the progress of our proposed California Agricultural Labor Relations Act, as well as other developments in the UFW, through him. Aside from these periodic contacts with Jerry and Cesar, from this point on in my legal career I was essentially on my own.

Soon after I moved to San Francisco, I began to make the contacts in the Bay Area I would need for getting the project off the ground. I needed two networks, I knew, if it was to have any chance of success. The first would be individual cannery workers or, better yet, organizations of rank-and-file workers with the courage and the imagination to challenge their employers and the Teamsters in federal court. I also sought progressive lawyers and lawyers' groups, always on the lookout for individual lawyers or small law firms that might join together in coalitions to challenge employment practices in one or more canneries.

I got my first break a little over two months later when Ted Smith, a lawyer I had just met in San Jose, called asking me to join him in challenging the settlement of a class-action lawsuit. The suit, which alleged discrimination against seasonal cannery workers, was exactly what I was looking for. The employer, a cannery named "Basic Vegetables," was located in Vacaville, California, and the settlement of the suit had been approved in federal court over the objections of a committee of rank-and-file workers.

Class-action lawsuits are lawsuits brought by a few named plaintiffs on behalf of a much larger class of people. In the Basic Vegetables case, for example, some four or five named plaintiffs had been certified to represent a class which included a thousand or more seasonal Mexican or Mexican American workers.

Class-action settlements are subject to major abuse. The most common form of abuse involves settling such a lawsuit for a small fraction of its true value. The big winners are the lawyers who obtain large attorneys' fees, the named plaintiffs who obtain adequate settlements of their claims, and the employer and/or union, who settle a potentially costly suit at a fraction of its true value. The losers are the vast majority of the class who, in the end, will get either nothing or a fraction of the true value of their claims.

Basic Vegetables differed from many other canneries in that it had a committee of Mexican rank-and-file workers actively fighting discriminatory practices at the company. The suit had been brought and settled without including any members of this rank-and-file committee as named plaintiffs and without consulting them in any way.

On the date scheduled for the court hearing on the issue of approval of the settlement, a large number of employees from the rank-and-file committee showed up. After the attorneys for both the plaintiffs and the defendant had presented their cases, a clamor rose from the rank-and-file workers in the audience. They were asking to be heard. Their spokesperson, Ruben Reyes, stood up and was finally recognized by the judge.

"What's going on over there?" the judge wanted to know.

"This settlement is grossly unfair to the workers at Basic Vegetables," Ruben said. "We weren't consulted, and basically it's a sell-out. We've tried to find an attorney to represent us here today, but so far no one has been willing to take it. We're asking for more time to find a lawyer."

"How long have you been looking?" the judge asked Ruben.

"We only found out about this hearing about three or four weeks ago. We've been looking ever since, but we need more time."

"Exactly what is it in this proposed settlement that you're objecting to?" the judge asked.

Ruben did his best, in the next five to ten minutes, to set forth all of the objections that the rank-and-file committee had to the terms of the agreement. When he finished the judge said, "Sit down, Mr. Reyes. I'm denying your request for an extension of time, and I'm over-ruling your objections as well. I'm approving this settlement."

• • •

Two or three weeks later Ruben Reyes wandered into Ted Smith's office in San Jose. Ted was a solo practitioner with no prior experience of any kind in cases of this sort. He called me up to find out if I knew anything about it.

"I don't," I said. "I have no experience whatsoever in this field either, but I'm willing to give it a try. Let's see if we can put something together." Ted agreed, and we decided to give it our best shot.

* * *

Ruben Reyes, a Mexican-American, was in his late thirties when I first met him. He was tall, smart, good looking, radiating vital energy, and a natural-born orator. He had grown up in rough circumstances in the Sacramento barrio. Most of the boys he had grown up with, he told me, had ended up later being either killed or sentenced to long terms in jail. Ruben himself was already doing seasonal work in the fields and canneries well before he graduated from high school. After graduating he became a full-time cannery worker.

Ruben, who had grown up in an environment where boys and men fought at the drop of a hat for almost any reason, did not take well to discriminatory treatment. He was smart enough to master the provisions of the grievance procedure in the collective bargaining agreement covering his cannery. Since a worker had to go through the union to get a grievance filed, Ruben soon found himself fighting not only with his employer but with the Teamsters Union as well. The Teamsters had a well-earned reputation for winning relatively high wages for the workers they represented but otherwise not hassling employers with employee grievances or any of the other disturbance of dissatisfied workers.

Ruben's success in winning grievances soon caught the attention of his fellow workers, who began to ask him for help with their problems. Under Ruben's leadership the workers formed a rank-and-file committee to press for improvements in working conditions. Ruben's reputation eventually spread by word of mouth to other canneries in and around Sacramento, where workers started their own rank-and-file committees. Ruben went on to found his Cannery Worker's Committee. Representative of rank-and-file workers from a number of Sacramento and Bay Area canneries met regularly to air their mutual problems and to work together for better treatment for seasonal and other workers.

By the time I met him, Ruben had been fired from his job and blackballed from cannery work. He supported himself working at odd jobs while his wife, Hope, brought home a modest but reliable year-round salary. When the settlement agreement at Basic Vegetables came up for hearing in federal court, the company's rank-and-file workers got in touch with Ruben, who agreed to act as their spokesman.

• • •

Ted and I got together and began to explore the mysteries of federal class-action litigation law, looking for precedents dealing with the application of ordinary rank-and-file workers to intervene in pending class-action lawsuits that impacted their lives but over which they had been given no say. We found nothing relevant to our case. In theory the rights of all employees in the class were supposed to be protected by the named plaintiffs who had been certified by the court to represent their interests. In practice it's the rare worker-turned-class-representative who will stand up and fight against a law firm that has assured him or her that under the circumstances they have won the best possible settlement, that litigation would take a long time and could well end in defeat, and that a bird in the hand is worth two in the bush.

Settlement mechanisms in cases of this kind usually provide for a procedure by which workers who are not named plaintiffs make their own individual applications for back wages and other remedies. These employees generally learn of their rights when an official-looking form arrives in their mailbox. The top of the form looks intimidatingly official, with the name of the federal court in block letters at the top, followed by lots and lots of fine legal print, and somewhere in the middle of all this print an explanation of the procedures they need to follow in order to get their claims heard. A large number of employees can be counted on not to read the form through to its end, or if they do, not to understand the hoops they are supposed to jump through to get a hearing. If they do persevere and file a claim, it will eventually be heard by an arbitrator or hearing officer whose selection has usually been influenced by the defendant employer and who can be relied on not to give away large sums of the employer's money.

• • •

Ted and I took the tack that despite the fact that the workers hadn't filed an application for intervention in proper form, Ruben Reyes in the five minutes he had been on his feet had identified major problems with the proposed settlement. Given the short time the rank-and-file workers at Basic Vegetable had had to find a lawyer, the difficulty in finding a lawyer willing to represent impecunious workers pro bono in a difficult federal court class-action case, and the seriousness and complexity of the complaints Ruben had raised, the district court should have given them adequate time to find representation.

My office at this time was located on the fifth floor of a run-down office building at 1st and Mission Streets in San Francisco. Ted and I labored away in my small office, learning the ropes of class-action law and fighting against a tight deadline. These were the days when a young lawyer just out of law school had all the technological equipment he needed to open an office if he or she owned a portable manual typewriter. "Cut and paste" meant that you took a real pair of scissors, cut real paper, and with a real pot of paste attached the latest draft of your argument over the obsolete language in the previous draft.

Ted and I were hard at work as our deadline for filing our appeal came closer. We were still hard at it the very day our papers were due to be filed. Our devoted typist typed and retyped our pages, putting up with Ted's and my obsessive need to craft legal perfection into our brief.

Our appeal had to be filed by 4:30 that afternoon. Eleven blocks separated my office on 1st and Mission Streets from the Circuit Court of Appeals for the Ninth Circuit at 9th and Market. As Ted and I pressed on, the moment finally came when perfection had to give way to pragmatism. If all of our finely honed legal arguments were to do anyone any good, they would have to be filed in court before its doors closed. Court clerks are famous, or infamous, for closing the door on counsel who are still clambering up the stairs five seconds after the clock has struck the deadline hour.

With a little over 20 minutes to go, Ted and I bounded down five flights of stairs, ran the three short blocks from Mission up to Market, turned left on Market, and began to pound the interminably long blocks that separate 1st and Market from 9th and Market. In an effort worthy of the movie *Chariots of Fire*, we rounded the corner at 9th and Market, sprinting through the courthouse doors at roughly 4:29.00. Thirty seconds later we were on the landing in front of the clerk's office. Our watches had not betrayed us. Like Olympians crossing the finish line at the end of a marathon event, Ted and I lunged for the finish line, breaking the tape a full 10 to 15 seconds before the sound of the striking clock resonated through the halls. The clerk stamped our papers. They had been timely filed.

• • •

Ted and I showed up in our courtroom finery the day arguments were to be heard in the Ninth Circuit. Neither of us had argued in a federal court of appeals before, and we were both duly awed and intimidated. Since I was better than Ted at appearing bold and confident when I'm actually quaking in my boots, I went first. Ted followed up. One of the judges on the three-judge panel seemed particularly interested in our arguments, asking lots of questions and listening carefully to Ted's and my answers.

The parties arguing in favor of the settlement, the law firm for the named plaintiffs and the lawyer for Basic Vegetables, went next. The only thing I remember about the plaintiffs' lawyers is that they appeared to be about as nervous as Ted and me. The lawyer for Basic Vegetables, however, was a partner in a major San Francisco law firm located in the financial district. His courtroom finery outshone ours, and he exuded the confidence of a man who regularly represents the great and the mighty before eminent courts such as the Ninth Circuit. He launched into his arguments, which were well honed, in a confident and strong voice.

Very quickly though, things began to go badly for him. The judge who had shown so much interest in Ted's and my arguments began to grill him, taking apart his weakest arguments first before tackling the more difficult issues.

"Your honors," he began, "the petition for intervention herein should be rejected out of hand. It's not in proper form. The federal rules clearly specify the procedures applicable in cases of this kind. Petitioners have followed none of them." He went on to lay out the specific requirements set forth in the Federal Rules of Procedure, point by point, showing how Ruben had failed to meet those standards.

This argument did not go over well with the judge.

"Counsel," he asked, "Would you say that it's a safe assumption that Mr. Reyes has not attended law school?"

"I believe that's correct your honor."

"We may assume, may we not, that under the circumstances he is not familiar with the proper form to be used in cases of this kind?"

"That's a safe assumption, your honor."

"Would you agree with me further, counsel, that a person of average intelligence reading the transcript in the case would have no trouble understanding the gist of Mr. Reyes' objections to this settlement."

"With all due respect, your honor, the standard of clarity in cases of this kind is not what the average person would understand, but what the rules specifically require."

"Counsel, am I to understand that you are arguing, on the particular facts of the case before us today, that matters of form should take precedence over substantive justice, particularly in light of the fact that Mr. Reyes specifically asked for an adjournment for time in order to obtain legal representation, and that the presence of Mr. Gaenslen and Mr. Smith in court today testifies that he did in fact exercise due diligence on that front."

At this point Learned Counsel for Basic Vegetables began to shake visibly. Nor did the judge relent in his attack on the settlement, asking follow-up question after follow-up question that were no easier to answer. By the time it was over my learned brother was sweating profusely.

The decision came out a month or so later. We, Ruben Reyes, Ted, I, and the rank and file, had won out. A few days later the Bureau of National Affairs Labor Law Reporter published its compendium of all labor cases decided that week in federal courts across the country. Our case was the featured "Case of the Week," the case identified by the BNA's editorial staff as the most important development in federal labor law that week.

• • •

Ruben Reyes and I had become good friends during the Basic Vegetables litigation and in its aftermath. He had paid a heavy price for championing his fellow rank-and-file cannery workers. Although he had bought a home while still employed, after being blackballed from cannery work his house had become more and more dilapidated. Poor or not, though, Ruben was generous to a fault.

One day after I had slept over at his house in Sacramento I woke up to find that the weather had taken a turn for the worse and that it was quite cold outside. Since I had been wearing shirt-sleeves the previous day, I asked Ruben if I could borrow a jacket.

"Sure," he said, leading me to his bedroom and throwing open the closet door. His entire wardrobe was inside, consisting of about ten to twelve items of clothing. Two blue nylon shells, each lined with a thin synthetic flannel-like material, hung side by side on the right side of the rack.

"Here," Ruben said, taking one of the jackets and handing it to me.

"Thanks, Ruben," I said. "How can I get this back to you?"

"Keep it," Ruben answered. "I've got two." In that one gesture Ruben Reyes had given me half his winter wardrobe.

• • •

The Cannery Workers Legal Project showed up at an opportune time in Ruben's life, and in mine as well. I could offer legal advice to his rank-and-file workers, speak to them about their rights under the National Labor Relations Act, and bring lawsuits on their behalf when the facts justified it. Ruben offered me access to large numbers of seasonal cannery workers, giving me the opportunity to become thoroughly familiar with the kinds of workplace discrimination and other problems common in the canning industry.

As I traveled from place to place with Ruben, meeting up with cannery worker committees he had started or encouraged, I became aware that approval of a vastly larger settlement agreement than Basic Vegetables was then pending in federal court. The defendant in the case was California Processors, Inc., a consortium of 71 California canneries. As in the Basic Vegetables case, rank-and-file workers felt that they were being sold out. I got my hands on a copy of the proposed settlement, read it through, talked it over with Ruben and a number of workers, and discovered that I agreed with them.

The canneries making up California Processors, Inc. employed tens of thousands of seasonal workers. The scope and potential impact of the case was thus enormous. Fortunately a number of other workers had gotten as worked up over the terms of the agreement as Ruben and the members of his Cannery Workers' Project and had found lawyers of their own. We soon discovered that we had the makings of a coalition of solo practitioners and small law firms, all eager to file a petition for intervention and fight for an improvement to the terms of the agreement.

The decision we had won in the Ninth Circuit in the Basic Vegetables case gave us a road map for the kinds of issues the court considered important when rank-and-file workers challenge a class-action settlement. We attorneys for the Applicants for Intervention divided the work up amongst ourselves and fought hard for the issues we considered most important. High among these was the question of the discriminatory placement of women on the seniority list for seasonal workers. The issue was crucial because the seniority list determined the order in which workers were called back to work at the beginning of each new season.

The problem arose because men had been systematically favored over women for over 20 years. For example, take a hypothetical male named Juan and a female named Juana, both hired in 1946. Juan is #1 on the seniority list, the first worker to be hired when the new season begins. Juana is #220. Numbers #2 through #219 are all men, number #219 having been hired a full 20 years after Juana. In other words, season after season, men hired after Juana were placed ahead of her on the seniority list and called back to work before her.

We Applicants for Intervention fought hard on issue after issue, seeking to dramatically improve the terms of the settlement. The judge presiding over the case turned out, for the most part, to be our ally. He made it clear he would not approve the settlement if it did not address many, if not most, of the issues that we had raised. Defendants had no choice but to agree. Otherwise, the judge would have refused to approve their settlement proposal.

In the end, not wanting an additional set of lawyers cluttering up his hearing room as the case progressed, the judge denied our Application for Intervention. A review of the settlement as a whole, though, revealed that we had won out against our opponents, both the attorneys representing the plaintiff class and the defendant canneries and Teamsters Union, on issue after issue. Federal law at the time provided that plaintiffs who prevailed in employment discrimination cases could collect attorneys' fees from the defendants if they were the party that had prevailed in the case. We decided to go for it, arguing that the successes we had achieved in improving the terms of the settlement made us "prevailing parties" within the meaning of the law. The judge ruled in our favor, awarding us generous fees.

"The Applicants for Intervention may have lost the battle for intervention, but they won the war," the judge wrote. He went on to summarize the many ways in which our intervention had resulted in a better agreement for the tens of thousands of workers employed by Californian Processors, Inc. and represented by the Teamsters Union.

After the decision became effective, well over 10,000 women cannery workers, a goodly number of whom I had gotten to know through my connection with Ruben, jumped more than 200 places on their cannery seniority lists. The shadow that Ruben Reyes cast on the day he had stood up to speak out for rank-and-file workers at Basic Vegetables had proved to be long indeed.

CHAPTER 37

The Ketchup Cases

AMONG the provisions of the settlement agreement in the California Processors, Inc. case had been a procedure for awarding back pay to women who had lost pay season after season when men with less seniority than they had were awarded the year-round jobs. The presiding judge decreed that all such claims would be heard before a single magistrate, Magistrate Woodruff.

I asked a law student friend of mine to attend court the first time such a case was heard and give me his assessment of the magistrate. What sort of a person was he, and where did he seem to lie on the spectrum of pro-employer versus pro-employee sympathies? When my friend called, the report could not have been worse.

"You've got to come down here and see for yourself, Tony," he said. "This guy is out of sight. Workers are going to have one hell of a time winning any favorable decisions in his court."

I made my way to the court to size him up for myself and found that Magistrate Woodruff absolutely radiated the self-satisfaction brought to him by his august station in life. He was such a lightweight intellectually that his ignorance, arrogance, and thinly disguised bias would have been silly if only he didn't have so much power over so many people's lives.

This man, who had jurisdiction over all of the back-pay cases covering all 71 canneries in California Processors, Inc., immediately began giving them all the derisive name "The Ketchup Cases," though very few of the 71 canneries actually produced ketchup. In my case, though, the designation was accurate. I represented five female workers from the Heinz, Inc. ketchup plant in Stockton, California.

Magistrate Woodruff liked to be liked by everyone, though what he appreciated most of all was the admiration and friendship of the high and mighty, such as the lawyers representing Heinz from the prestigious San Francisco law firm of Littler, Mendelson, Fastiff, and Tichy. The firm enjoyed the reputation of being the most aggressive and effective anti-union law firm in the Bay Area, and its lawyers wisely lavished attention on the magistrate.

In truth, I didn't dislike Magistrate Woodbridge myself. Although he was a fop and quite ignorant, his position of authority had not made him mean or demeaning to the people who appeared before him. He was, in fact, always friendly and courteous with me.

Nonetheless it was immediately clear that there was no chance of obtaining justice in "The Ketchup Cases" in that courtroom. In the world that had shaped this man, and to which he still clung, Mexicans existed far below his line of his vision. Plus the many people he knew from the agriculture and canning industries were, he was certain, decent people like him. He could not imagine anyone from his social environment doing anything untoward to their workers. That these Mexicans should show up in his court and demand more than his honorable acquaintances were willing to offer them was simply out of the question.

Since it was clear that Magistrate Woodbridge could not be persuaded to render justice based on either the law or the evidence, I had to fall back on two alternative approaches. The first was to humiliate the magistrate into rendering justice; the second was to coerce him into doing so. I decided to use both approaches.

I thought I had two avenues to exploit in winning a verdict for my clients. The first of these stemmed from the fact that the presiding judge in the California Processors case had made it clear he would not hear appeals in any of the back-pay cases. In other words, Magistrate Woodruff was the court of last resort. This was unusual, but the presiding judge simply didn't want to be overwhelmed with appeals.

Since Magistrate Woodruff's decisions would be insulated from review on appeal, he never put himself through the bother of mastering the law governing employment discrimination cases, a subject about which he knew very little in the first place. Moreover, given his extremely high opinion of the exalted station he held in life, he didn't bother himself with masking his ignorance. On the contrary, he was constantly making off-the-cuff references to the law that were wildly off the mark or just plain dead wrong. I saw my opening.

Because no appeals were supposed to be taken from Magistrate Woodruff's decisions, no court reporter was present taking down all that was said in his court. Court reporters' transcripts constitute the basis from which appeals are made. No court-appointed reporter, no appeal.

But the first day that my case, *Nascimento v. Heinz*, was called, a court reporter showed up and set up her machine. I had paid for her service myself.

Magistrate Woodbridge did a double take.

"Mr. Gaenslen," he said, "I see that you've brought a court reporter with you, and of course she is most welcome. I don't see the point, though. There are no appeals from the decisions in my court."

"You astonish me, Magistrate Woodruff," I replied. "Just when was the Local Rule 64, which does provide for such appeals, suspended?"

A glazed look came over his eyes as he pondered what I had just said. After a few moments, he said, "Very well, then. Proceed."

Herein lay the second vulnerability that I was determined to use to my advantage. Almost anyone else would have guarded against making glib, biased, or outright ignorant remarks in the presence of a court reporter. No such concerns troubled Magistrate Woodruff's mind. By the time our case was ready for hearing on the merits, I had compiled an impressive list of statements in which Magistrate Woodbridge's ignorance of the law was on spectacular display.

Two other lawyers were helping me on *Nascimento v. Heinz*. One of these was my dear friend John (Jack) de J. Pemberton, former executive director of the American Civil Liberties Union and a former attorney for the Equal Employment Opportunity Commission. Jack, a militant on civil liberties issues, was a born teacher who mentored and counseled me as I learned how to argue employment discrimination cases.

Jack and I put our heads together on a plan to thoroughly humiliate and intimidate Magistrate Woodruff. We thus filed a motion to be heard in open court in front of the presiding judge, titling it: "Motion to Instruct Magistrate Woodbridge on the Proper Application of the Law in Employment Discrimination Cases." We highlighted every idiotic statement Magistrate Woodruff had made in his courtroom during the Heinz case, following it with a correct statement of the law. Word that the motion would be made had made the gossip rounds of the San Francisco labor bar, drawing quite a crowd into the courtroom. Magistrate Woodruff had to sit there, his ignorance on display for all to see. In the end, the judge hearing our motion assured us that he had reviewed the applicable law with Magistrate Woodruff and that the magistrate would apply it correctly in his court.

A few days later a friend of mine appearing in Magistrate Woodruff's court gave me a call.

"The magistrate is afraid of you, Tony," he said. "He talked about you a lot in court today. He doesn't know what you've got up your sleeve." Jack and I knew we had him backed into a corner.

• • •

The other lawyer I had brought in to help me with "The Ketchup Cases" was Mandy Hawes, whose office was located in San Jose, home to many canneries. Mandy represented large numbers of migrant and seasonal workers, so she was in court constantly litigating against one cannery or another. Shortly after I associated her into the Heinz case, Mike Whitney, the junior counsel from Littler Mendelson who was actually doing the bulk of the litigation in the Heinz case, told another lawyer:

"Guess who Tony Gaenslen has associated in the Heinz case? Mandy Hawes, the 'Scourge of the Canneries.'" This other lawyer was a friend of mine and immediately passed Mike's remark on to me.

The "Scourge of the Canneries" would play an invaluable role in the unfolding drama of "The Ketchup Cases." Although I am a very competent legal strategist, my dyslexia is a hindrance when I'm faced with myriad unconnected facts. Mandy, in contrast, was a fireball at mastering all the minute details of actual work in the canneries, shepherding such cases skillfully through the courts.

I made an urgent call to Mandy one day shortly before Littler Mendelson scheduled my clients' depositions at their offices in the financial district.

"You've got to help me, Mandy," I said. "They're deposing my plaintiffs. I'll be completely befuddled by the paperwork long before I get to the end of it."

"I'd be happy to, Tony," Mandy said, "but I'll have baby Kyle with me tomorrow, and I can't find daycare for him on such short notice."

"Not a problem," I said. "Just bring baby Kyle along with you. We'll take turns watching him as the depositions unfold."

"What if he needs a diaper change?"

"No problem. We'll call a recess, clear the conference room, and do what needs to be done. It will do these lawyers good to see how the other half practices law."

When Mandy showed up at the reception desk with a baby in a bassinet and asked to be shown to the firm's conference room, the startled receptionist did a double take. She got on the phone and duly cleared Mandy to come in. Once we were there, everything unfolded pleasantly. While the lawyers from Littler Mendelson were rugged opponents, they could not have been nicer about baby Kyle.

An hour or so into the depositions, it became increasingly clear that baby Kyle had loaded his pants and needed attention. Mandy and I asked for a recess and did what we had to do. When the deposition was reconvened, the aroma of baby poop wafted pleasantly through the conference room. By the time it was over, Mandy had deftly steered me through what otherwise could have been quite an ordeal.

• • •

After Jack and I had brought our motion to humiliate Magistrate Woodbridge into rendering justice, we turned to the coercion phase of our plan.

The core issue here was the method for calculating the amount of back pay due to our plaintiffs. Jack had tracked down a statistical expert with degrees from Harvard, Berkeley, and UCLA who had put together a study comparing our plaintiffs' earnings to those of men with similar hire dates and had calculated that our clients were owed approximately $300,000—a very considerable sum in those days.

Heinz had also done a study, going one by one through 20,000 time cards for men with hire dates comparable to our clients'. They contended that our clients were owed only $80,000. They knew that we could never afford to duplicate their study, going through all those cards to locate the errors in their calculations. They were confident that Magistrate Woodruff would rule that their study was more reliable than ours and award $80,000 in damages.

To counter the impact of this likely decision, I threatened to force the magistrate, in open hearings in his court, to go through a card-by-card review of the entire 20,000-card database. I told him that it was my intent to proceed on a card-by-card basis, calling my own witnesses, cross-examining defense witnesses, and the like. As I reminded the magistrate every time he leaned toward accepting the 20,000-card study, it would take several months of hearings in his court to work our way through the entire stack of time cards. I added that I was fully prepared to show up in court for as long as it took to go through the entire study. It may have sounded like a bluff, but I had a plan for putting teeth into this threat.

The women I was representing were all forklift drivers. Every day at Heinz, the forklift drivers—both men and women—were assigned to do, on average, ten different forklift tasks.

The "girls," as my clients had been called when they first began to drive forklifts at the beginning of World War II, were highly skilled at their jobs, having taken over the roles left vacant when the "boys" went off to fight in the war. There was no forklift task the "boys" did that the "girls" had not learned to do just as well.

To knock the back-pay award down from $300,000 to $80,000, the Littler Mendelson lawyers falsely claimed that there were certain jobs the women were not qualified to do. In point of fact the women could do all these jobs as well as the men. One of my clients, in fact, had won a forklift driving contest, outperforming all the men in the competition.

Heinz took the position that the women would not have been called to work at all on any given day that a comparable male performed even a single task for which the woman was deemed (falsely) not to have been qualified. This was the basis on which their study produced such a low number compared with ours.

I countered this ploy by asking my clients if they could identify any one of their supervisors who would tell the truth under oath, even if instructed to do the opposite by legal counsel. The women named one such supervisor, and I subpoenaed him to take his deposition. If he told the truth about my clients' qualifications as forklift drivers, Heinz's case would collapse.

The supervisor in question, when he showed up at my office on the day of the deposition, did not turn out to be quite as honest as my clients had imagined he was. Although he was always honest and decent with them, under direct instructions from Heinz's counsel to misrepresent the facts, he would do so.

The task in front of him was daunting, though. There were well over 100 different tasks a forklift driver might be called upon to do in any given day. This supervisor, having known my clients for years and seen them every day at work, knew perfectly well that they were qualified to do every forklift job in the cannery. If he was to follow the company's and its attorneys' instructions, he would have to "remember" (correctly) which jobs the women could do and "remember" (falsely) which ones they couldn't. As he prepared to perjure himself on the record as the court reporter swore him in, he looked like a man being led to his execution.

I had prepared a stratagem to undermine the witness' ability to keep his lies straight. I anticipated that the witness and his lawyer would expect me to question him about the tasks that were the key to the whole case, the ones for which he would have to falsely testify that the women were not qualified. The attorney would have prepared him thoroughly on this aspect of his testimony.

Instead of doing so, though, I began asking him about close to 50 jobs for which he could truthfully answer that the women were qualified. As one question followed another, an increasingly relaxed expression began to spread over his face; he could tell the truth! This deposition wasn't going to be nearly as painful as he had anticipated.

Around my 51st question, I slipped in the first job on which he was supposed to lie. My ploy worked. By this time the witness had completely forgotten which jobs he was supposed to lie about, and he told the truth. I asked him a couple more questions in which he could tell the truth before slipping in a couple on which he was supposed to lie. The fish was now solidly on the hook. He just went on telling the truth.

I began to move rapidly through the list of jobs about which he was supposed to lie, and he told the truth every time. I was on a tear. Mike Whitney began to squirm anxiously in his chair, slipping a note to his witness.

"Let me see that note, counsel," I shot at him. Mike swiftly pulled it back.

"I've got to go to the bathroom" was his next ploy.

"I've only got a few more questions," I said, lying through my teeth, "and then we'll take a bathroom break." I tore through the questions on my list, the witness telling the truth at every turn.

"I've got to get to the bathroom right away!" Mike shouted out.

"Just a few more questions," I said, ripping through 15 to 20 more.

"I'VE GOT TO GO TO THE BATHROOM!!" Mike jumped to his feet, grabbing his witness by the scruff of the neck, hauling him out the door as he went. He was too late. Tallying up all the answers about which the witness was supposed to have lied, I compiled a list of about 3,500 errors in the company's 20,000-card study.

• • •

I decided to mess with Magistrate Woodruff's mind the next time I showed up in his court.

"Magistrate Woodbridge," I said, "we've just taken the deposition of the defendant's witness, one of the supervisors at Heinz. His testimony reveals that there are some 3,500 errors in the company's 20,000 time-card study. Consider the consequences. As we go through our day-by-day study of these 20,000 cards, and as I put on my case with my own witnesses, and cross-examine the company witnesses as to the accuracy of each one of the 3,500 erroneous cards, you will be compelled to rule in my favor. In the end you will have to do so 3,500 times, since the witness has admitted under oath that there is a total of 3,500 inaccurate cards. Each time you rule in my favor, we will calculate the amount of damages flowing from that error in the study. At some point in this process, Magistrate Woodruff, as the total amount of damages increases, I will become a prevailing party within the meaning of the law, and the defendant here will have to pay my fees for appearing in court. This process could take a very, very long time. It's all right with me, though. My time will be paid for by the defendant."

It took Magistrate Woodruff a little while to absorb the full impact of what I was saying. Turning to Robert Lieber, the Littler Mendelson partner with overall responsibility for the case, he said:

"Isn't there some better way of doing this? A statistical study of some kind?" I kept a straight and solemn face, but inside me fireworks were going off.

* * *

The time soon came to deliver the coup de grace, finishing off Mike Whitney, Littler Mendelson, and Heinz, Inc., in one fell blow. It all came about because of the Heinz supervisor who forgot how to lie when the heat was on. By the time the deposition in my office was over, Mike was a man in a state of near desperation. In just two hours a case that had been dragging on for close to three years and had cost the company over $200,000 in attorneys' fees had gone down the drain. Mike's legal career, he knew, was on the chopping block; lawyers in his position were supposed to crush small-fry practitioners like me. He was now in the position of having to report to Robert Lieber that he had just blown the whole thing.

Mike cracked under the stress of the moment, taking a desperate risk. He ordered a rush copy of the deposition transcript from the court reporter. As soon as it came in, he called his witness at home and went over the transcript line by line, getting him to "correct" his testimony in every case in which he had failed to "remember" the "right" answer. It was a move born of desperation. It backfired.

The witness came into the cannery the following day hopping mad.

"That goddamn lawyer from the company called me at home last night," he ranted. "Spent seven hours making me go over my testimony line by line, getting me to change it over and over again. What the hell does he want from me? I'm not a lawyer. I'm a cannery worker. I told the truth the first time. I want outta this goddamn mess."

One of the workers within earshot of this rant was a close friend of my clients, and he promptly told them about it. The women called me.

I asked them to ask the person who had heard the rant if he would be willing to give me an affidavit under oath, testifying to what he had just heard. He eagerly agreed.

I kept his affidavit in a secret file, waiting to unleash it at the moment it could do the maximum damage. About ten days before the formal part of our trial was scheduled to begin, I filed the affidavit with the court. The *Titanic* had hit the iceberg and was going down like a rock. The only question left was the exact amount of damages for which we would settle. We went for—and got—the full value of the case: $300,000.

Magistrate Woodruff had ruled against the plaintiffs in every one of the 33 previous "Ketchup Cases." Ours was the 34th case he heard and the first workers' victory. I called Jack and Mandy to give them the news.

"It took one hell of a lot of work," Jack said. "But I think we finally managed to teach Magistrate Woodruff a little law."

• • •

As our case had progressed, I kept hearing that the officer in charge of the affirmative action office for all of Heinz, Inc. was a man named Chauncey Depew. He worked out of company headquarters in Pittsburgh and ran a tight ship, keeping on top of all the details as the case developed through the court.

The name Chauncey Depew was familiar to me. An earlier Chauncey Depew had been president of the New York Central Railroad in the 19th century, and later a U.S. senator. Having accumulated a vast fortune, he later became a controversial figure in New York politics.

I loathed the thought that this current Chauncey Depew, no doubt a scion of this wealthy and influential New York family, should be running Heinz's affirmative action office. What did he know about the struggles of the poor? As I imagined him, he would be called from some highbrow party, or would interrupt a cruise on the family yacht, to dispense justice when some poor slob like myself brought Heinz before the bar of justice.

My opinion of Chauncey sank even lower when I learned that he was planning to come to the Heinz cannery in Stockton to personally present back-pay checks to my clients. He and Heinz were thus seizing credit for their largesse in doling out money that would have stayed locked in company coffers had it not been for Jack, Mandy, and me.

I got an unexpected jolt, though, when I learned that Chauncey was planning to come to San Francisco to personally hand over our checks for attorney fees to Jack, Mandy, and me. On the appointed day, I went to Jack's office on the University of San Francisco campus.

When Chauncey Depew came through the door, I nearly fell off my chair. This Chauncey Depew was an African American and, as it turned out, was beyond delighted to be handing out the company's money to us. He congratulated us warmly for our conduct of the case. He asked me a lot of questions about my life and career and, before leaving, wished me the best in all my future undertakings.

There was only one discordant note sounding in the background as I soaked in the euphoria of the moment. Chauncey had dragged Mike Whitney of Littler Mendelson along with him to attend this meeting. Mike sat at the back of the room. The more effusively Chauncey sang our praises, the louder became the peculiar sound emanating from that part of the room. It was Mike grinding his teeth.

CHAPTER 38

The Cornell Eleven

"WE hear you're in Ithaca," said the pleasant, Southern accented, feminine voice on the other end of the line "and we'd like to talk to you." Wondering exactly who "we" were, and why "we" wanted to talk to me, I agreed to meet the woman, whose name was Donna Zahorik, the following morning over coffee.

A few months prior I had in fact moved back to the beautiful upstate New York town where I had gotten my law degree. I had made up my mind to quit working for La Causa quite suddenly in the early summer of 1977 when, coming home from work one day, I found my daughter Elisabeth, two holes in the knees of her hand-me-down pants, crying unconsolably.

"The other kids make fun of me all the time. I hate these clothes. I hate everything about the way we live. I'm never going back to school." On the spot, my mind was made up; my years of commitment to La Causa were over. I had to face the fact that I wasn't adequately supporting my family on the $800 per month salary I had been earning ever since I went to work with the UFW. I would have to hit the hustings and find a "real" job with a "real" salary.

Just about that time I got a call from Jerry Cohen:

"Good news, Tony," he said. "The Teamsters are pulling out of the fields. They're finally feeling the heat we've been putting on them, and besides they've been losing a ton of money in their venture to wipe us out. They're throwing in the towel."

Within a few months I was earning a lawyer's salary commensurate with my experience in a San Mateo labor law firm south of San Francisco. A couple of years later, when my wife got a job offer to teach at Cornell, the time had come for her career to take precedence over mine in our family's life. We loaded our gear into a moving truck and headed East.

I took an immediate liking to Donna. She spoke with a strong Southern accent and exuded all of the warmth and charm I associated with a classical Southern belle. She had a kind and generous heart as well, and for those who were alert to it, her warm and hospitable personality masked a razor-sharp mind and a passion for justice.

"I'm one of a group of academic women at Cornell who have been denied tenure," Donna told me. "All of us feel we've been discriminated against because we're women, and we've come together as a group to fight for our rights. We're calling ourselves the Cornell Eleven, and we've been looking for an attorney to take our case. So far, we've had no luck. Ithaca's isolation works against us, and besides no lawyer or law firm, not even from New York City, has been willing to take on Cornell."

Over the years I had worked with working people, migrant workers, poor people who were both men and women, I thought I knew a good deal about employment discrimination. When I first met with the women from Cornell I was highly skeptical that middle class academic women whose lifestyles didn't differ all that dramatically from mine could suffer comparable forms of discrimination. I was wrong. After meeting with them a number of times I learned that while they hadn't suffered from the kinds of grinding poverty or extreme humiliation I had seen in California or the Old South, the wrongs they suffered were genuine, arousing my sense that serious injustices were unfolding in the pleasant groves of academe.

On coming to Ithaca, and after the daunting struggle to win the Heinz case, I had vowed I would never again take up the cudgel of major federal court class-action litigation. It was too difficult, my opponents too powerful and rich, the firms they hired too massive and aggressive, the outcome too uncertain, the challenge of fighting through to the resolution of the case too exhausting. Now though, facing the stories of discrimination and unjust treatment faced by women like Donna Zahorik, I dug deep into myself and began to think seriously about taking the case.

I knew that if I did so I would be heading into by far the most difficult legal arena I had ever encountered. Cornell University, my law school alma mater, is one of America's great educational institutions. Its student body, undergraduate and graduate, comes from all corners of the world. It enjoys a national and international reputation for excellence. It has both a multi-billion-dollar endowment and an annual budget counting in the billions. I could expect to be facing one the largest and most powerful law firms in the country with an essentially unlimited litigation budget.

At the same time, the many successes I had enjoyed, first in Washington with Arthur Leff and Frank McCulloch and later with Cesar Chavez, Jerry Cohen, and the UFW, had left me with the conviction that I could look any opponent, no matter how rich, powerful, and prestigious, in the eye and take him down. This highly inflated and self-satisfied estimation of myself would soon be tested to the hilt; I agreed to take the case.

When I was first introduced to the women of the Cornell Eleven we all sat around a table in the home of one of the group members. Each woman told me the story of the wrongs she had suffered. Each, quite naturally, hoped for some measure of justice or redress in her particular case. A subtle competition to tell the most horrifying story of injustice pervaded these meetings. I knew that I would have to reorient their energies and their vision of what we could hope to accomplish, applying strategy and tactics I had learned in California with Cesar Chavez and Jerry Cohen.

I began by telling them that if we were going to launch into this struggle, it could only be with the goal of advancing the rights of women as a whole, and not the goal of winning redress of any of their individual rights.

"If you want me to take this case," I said, "you have to understand that I am not promising any one of you that you will get anything out of it personally. Our aim, of course, is for women to win favorable tenure reviews at a far higher rate than they now do, that meaningful appeal procedures are set in place for women denied tenure, and to have more women hired into tenure-track positions. But I can't promise any one of you here today that you will be one of the women to benefit from this suit. I can only promise you that if all of us join in this struggle together, women as a class will benefit from it."

It was a major wrench for the women to take this in. We went through two or more sessions which were repetitions of the first, each woman repeating the story of her particular wrongs. Soon, though, a profound shift in perspective began to take place. Together we began to re-envision the full scope of what we might aspire to accomplish through a lawsuit of this kind.

I began by explaining to the women that litigation under these circumstances bears no resemblance whatsoever to the pursuit of justice as people ordinarily conceive of it, where parties of equivalent size with equivalent resources present their evidence before the judge or jury on an even playing field. A war of attrition would be much closer to the truth. The corporation's litigation team enters the legal arena with the intention of grinding meritorious but underfunded plaintiffs into the ground. The lesson they aim to teach is simple and straightforward: regardless of the merits of a plaintiff's case, litigating against the corporation is a losing proposition. The dynamics we would be facing would be no different from those I had faced litigating against such corporations as Heinz and Basic Vegetables.

This characterization of things was not mine alone. Harry Levin, Dean of the College of Arts and Sciences at Cornell, had warned Donna Zahorik: "Don't litigate against the university, Donna. They'll destroy you emotionally and financially. They've done it to others, and they'll do it to you."

Dean Levin had well described the predatory legal environment in which the women would be litigating their case. As I use the word "predator," the term refers to someone who subverts the "rules of the game" on which the ordinary citizens of a community and its ordinary citizens conduct their affairs. The predator subverts these rules in order to gain an unfair advantage. For example, an ordinary citizen living in an ordinary small or midsized town who believes she has suffered an injustice naturally and reasonably assumes that its courts of justice are places where she can have her claim heard and resolved on the merits.

Predatory corporations, and the predatory law firms which serve them, are in the business of assuring that this never happens. Long before the matter reaches trial, the unsuspecting plaintiff's claim will have died in a legal maze of delays and obstructions. Exhausted emotionally and financially, the plaintiff will have no option but throw in the towel or settle for pennies on the dollar.

"There are," I went on to explain to the women, "few things more debilitating for an individual plaintiff, or even a group of plaintiffs, than to enter the predatory arena to resolve what is in essence a matter of justice. You plaintiffs have lost your jobs and hence your source of income. Defense counsel are masters of the art of dragging out cases. Hearing after hearing goes by with precious little progress, punctuated by your lawyer's periodic requests for more payments into his escrow account. In the end, should the case actually make it to trial, you're buying an unknown judge's notions of where justice lies in your case and what the remedy should be. Plaintiffs often end up profoundly disappointed, if not disillusioned. They waste away, give up, die on the vine. We, however, are not going down that road."

"In the first place, by constituting yourselves as a group into the Cornell Eleven, you have laid the foundations for a truly revolutionary approach to academic litigation. We will make time work for us instead of against us by organizing ourselves at the local, regional, and national levels. You will tell your stories, raise consciousness about the nature of discrimination against women in general, and its particular manifestations in academic environments such as those that prevail at Cornell University."

"The women who have been denied tenure and lost their jobs cannot finance an undertaking of this sort. At the same time that we raise consciousness, we will be raising our litigation budget from our growing network of supporters. Those of you who are still employed will have to contribute generously, and reach out to family members, friends, and Cornell alumni."

I went on to describe the kind of financial commitment they would have to make if I was to take on the case. No small-town lawyer operating an ordinary practice could undertake a case of this kind and hope to survive the war of attrition. I was willing to do it because I was unemployed at the time. I didn't have a practice to maintain or other clients to serve. I would have only one case on my agenda and could devote my full time to it, but I would need a monthly stipend to survive financially over the years of litigation we would be facing. It would have to come, not from the unemployed plaintiffs themselves, but from the support group. I would hope to make up the difference between this survival stipend and a living wage with an award of attorney fees at the end of the case if we prevailed.

As I delved into the evidence with the women's assistance, it became clearer and clearer that we had the makings of a very strong case. Statistical evidence showed that Cornell was at the bottom of the Ivy League in the percentage of women on its faculty and that it had the lowest number of women at the tenure-track level of assistant professor and the lowest net gain in women faculty in the Ivy League over the last five years. We had, moreover, a well-developed theory and compelling evidence of the mechanism for explaining these results. The three named plaintiffs, Donna Zahorik, Judy Laws, and Antonia Gasse, whose cases raised the issue of denial of tenure, would all make powerfully compelling witnesses at trial.

I was, nevertheless, taking on a very long shot. I personally had never faced such intimidating odds against so formidable an opponent at any previous time in my legal career. Any reasonably sensible person might well have concluded that it was an insanely bold undertaking. Over and over in my life, though, I have taken on such challenges. I do believe that fortune favors the brave, or as the Latin saying on which it is based has it, fortune or good luck rushes in to assist those who act boldly and take courageous initiatives. In the Cornell case, I would seize the initiative and trust that the breaks would go our way.

• • •

While all this was going on, I was back in the trenches, reviewing all of my clients' tenure denial files and putting together the essential elements of my complaint. I was fortunate to have some of the best academics in the country orienting me in a field about which I knew nothing. In the end, we decided to go straight for the heart of the tenure evaluation system. We alleged that unconscious evaluative bias fatally skews the way men see and evaluate women, systematically downgrading them and their achievements.

Among other things, we cited studies showing that when identical hypothetical job applications were circulated, half bearing the names of imaginary men, the other half imaginary women, men were offered jobs at the associate (tenured) professor level, while women at the assistant (untenured) position. Similarly, identical professional articles attributed to men were rated higher than those attributed to women. "Larry" was judged to have responded more rationally than "Linda" to the same situation. A strong performance by a man was more likely to be attributed to innate ability, in a woman to luck or hard work.

Qualities such as assertiveness and competitiveness were perceived as being desirable in men, leading to excellence. This was not true of the same characteristics in women. Competitiveness in men is enjoyed by other men but in a woman can result in her ostracism. A written comment in Donna's file reflected this view.

"The problem with Donna is not that she is female," the report read. "The problem is that she is feminine." The writer went on to describe the ways in which Donna was an ineffective presence in the internecine struggles within her predominantly male department.

Surprising to me also was research given to me by my clients showing that the highly competent woman is the person maximally affected by pro-male evaluative bias. Although everyone prefers competent others to incompetent ones, males prefer competent women only at a distance, when observing them. That preference disappears when they have to interact with women, whether cooperatively or competitively. Workers clearly prefer working with highly competent men over highly competent women. This form of evaluative bias was particularly germane in our case, as my clients were among the most gifted scholars nationally in their respective fields.

The very heart of our complaint lay in our allegations that evaluative bias is maximized when evaluative criteria are vague, and evaluations are carried out in a perfunctory, careless, or haphazard way. We alleged that there was a pervasive pattern of evaluations of this kind at Cornell.

With a lot of assistance not only from my clients but also from Jack Pemberton, whom I brought into the case and consulted with on the phone several times a week, I put together a complaint and filed it in Federal District Court in Syracuse on Halloween Day, 1980. Although I hadn't intended to hand Cornell a "trick or treat," it did end up that way.

The complaint that the Cornell Eleven and I put together ended up being a singularly hard-hitting document. It alleged that tenure reviews at Cornell, at least those involving women, were often conducted loosely and carelessly. The heart of the tenure review process lies in accumulating a complete and thorough record of the scholarly and research record of the candidate in question, a lengthy and time-consuming process. We alleged in support of our theory that evaluation bias pervaded the academic scene and that a review of the cases of highly competent women revealed a pattern of inadequate documentation and a summary or sloppy review of their accomplishments. The remedy we fought for was a far more rigorous elaboration of the standards to be followed in tenure reviews and the creation of an internal appeal procedure so that women alleging that they were wrongfully denied tenure would not have to resort to litigation in adversarial courts of law redress their wrongs.

* * *

Cornell would be represented by Bond, Schoeneck & King out of Syracuse, the largest law firm in central New York. Very shortly after I filed the suit, Bond Schoeneck filed a motion to dismiss my complaint on the basis of a truly frivolous legal theory. I couldn't imagine why the motion was filed, but I soon found out.

The judge we had drawn in the case, Judge Munson, was conservatively inclined. Judged on its merits, the motion deserved very short shrift. Indeed, if Judge Munson had been ill-advised enough to grant it, I would almost certainly have succeeded in reversing it on appeal. The appeal process, though, would have taken about a year, dealing a devastating psychological blow to my clients.

I soon discovered that there was a method behind Bond, Schoeneck & King's madness. The case was argued for Cornell by the president of the Syracuse Bar Association, one of the chief adornments of the Syracuse legal community. I, in contrast, was a newcomer to upstate New York, an utter unknown who had never before appeared in federal court in Syracuse. Bond Schoeneck had managed to get the case scheduled for a special hearing after the lunch break on the Wednesday before Thanksgiving. It was the only case on the calendar that afternoon, and Judge Munson wasn't happy to be hauled back into court to spend the first hour of his Thanksgiving break listening to counsel argue this late-filed motion. Unfairly, but not unexpectedly, he took most of his aggravation out on me.

Bond, Schoeneck & King, in a word, had played its home-court advantage to the hilt. I rather imagine that somewhere at some time some judge with the approximate mental acuity of Magistrate Woodruff had granted such a motion, and Bond Schoeneck decided to take a shot at it themselves.

Bond Schoeneck went first. I was stunned to hear Judge Munson appear to take its lawyer's arguments seriously, and even more stunned when he laced into me when I stood up to argue. His fundamental difficulty was not with the technical merits of the motion, which he fully realized he should deny summarily, but with his larger concern over the prospect of a great university such as Cornell being dragged into court by an unknown like me. We were challenging the very heart of Cornell's claim to academic pre-eminence by calling into question the integrity of the tenure-granting process by which Cornell claimed to select the best scholars in the country into its ranks.

The argument teetered back and forth for a full hour. Judge Munson was sorely tempted to grant the motion, thereby ridding himself of the problem of presiding over a case for which he had absolutely no enthusiasm. Towards the very end of the hour, in a fit of utter frustration and aggravation, he finally let the cat out of the bag.

"Counsel!" he yelled at me. "Don't you realize that the reason why our forefathers came to this country was that they believed in the principle of individual initiative and individual excellence?" There it was! If Cornell had promoted these men to tenured positions, Judge Munson clearly believed, they had obviously displayed a sufficient measure of individual initiative and excellence to deserve it. Who was I, and who were these women, to challenge this sacred principle? I saw my opening and went for it.

"Your honor!" I shouted. "I too believe in the principle of individual initiative, and that's why I'm here. All I'm asking for is for my clients to have their day in court so that they can prove to you that they are better than the men that Cornell promoted."

"I'm going to give you that chance!" Judge Munson roared. "Motion dismissed."

"YOUR HONOR!" shouted the president of the Syracuse Bar Association, leaping to his feet. It was no use. Not only was Judge Munson's mind made up, but he was not about to put his Thanksgiving break off one minute longer to hear counsel rehash the matter.

Cornell University and Bond, Schoeneck & King had paid the highest possible tribute to the quality and impact of the complaint we had filed by sending so distinguished a figure as the president of the Syracuse Bar Association to face off against me in arguing its motion. Precisely how good a lawyer he was, though, I would never learn. Cornell fired Bond, Schoeneck & King from its position of lead counsel in the case after he lost the motion. The university continued to retain the firm in the wholly secondary role of local counsel. The mantle of lead counsel was taken over by Hogan & Hartson, the largest, oldest, and most prestigious law firm in Washington, D.C. Decidedly, we would be in for quite a ride.

* * *

When Hogan & Hartson filed their appearance in the case, I learned lead counsel in the case would be one of the firm's most senior and prestigious attorneys. I no longer recall his name, but he was fourth or fifth from the top of the Hogan & Hartson letterhead. I will simply call him Number Four.

In keeping with large firm practice, though, Number Four would simply enjoy the overall supervisory role in the Cornell litigation. The name of the partner actually litigating the case appeared about halfway down the Hogan & Hartson letterhead. I will refer to him as Number 44.

Number 44 made his appearance in the case shortly after Bond, Schoeneck & King's failed attempt to knock me out of the box. Like

Bond Schoeneck, Number 44 had concocted a plan for decking me early on, based on a subterfuge designed to mislead the inexperienced litigant. It might have succeeded but for the kind and unexpected intervention of a complete stranger.

The Federal Rules of Procedure provided that plaintiffs bringing class-action lawsuits had to file their Motion for Class Certification within a very short time after filing their complaint. In the normal course a plaintiff's attorney in my position, after filing his complaint, would pull books off the shelf, look up the law, discover that he had to prepare his Motion for Class Certification in short order, or else move for an extension of time which, under normal circumstances, would be readily granted.

About a week after I had won the motion before Judge Munson the phone in my office rang.

"Is this Tony Gaenslen?" asked someone I whose voice I didn't recognize.

"Yeah, it is," I said.

"You're the attorney who's taking on the Cornell University discrimination case?"

"Yeah, that's me."

"My name is Kerrigan. I'm a partner in a Washington, D.C., law firm that does a lot of plaintiffs' side discrimination litigation. I got a call from Judy Laws, one of your plaintiffs. We're old friends, and she wanted to talk her case over with me. I've got a head's up that I want to pass on to you, so I asked her to give me your phone number."

"A number of the major defense firms are using a stratagem for knocking inexperienced lawyers out of the box early on in class-action cases. The stratagem is to lure you into blowing the deadline for filing your Motion for Class Certification. Opposing counsel will give you a call proposing a massive schedule of depositions that will tie you up for several months. If you're not aware of the class certification deadline and blow it while you're buried in depositions, they'll file a motion to dismiss the class-action aspects of your case. Surprisingly, they're having a good deal of luck with this. A number of judges have granted their motions."

"If you get a call from opposing counsel proposing a lengthy deposition schedule, don't agree to it unless you get counsel to stipulate to an extension of time on the motion for class certification." I thanked him profusely for his kindness and advice.

A few days later my phone rang again. Number 44 was on the other end of the line, his voice hearty and cheerful.

"Tony," he said. "I'd like to schedule the depositions of your clients. I've got a proposed schedule I'd like to go over with you."

"Fire away," I said.

Number 44 outlined an ambitious schedule that would have had me up to my neck in depositions until well after the deadline for filing our motion for class certification.

"I don't have any problem with that," I said. "Of course, you'll have to stipulate to an extension of time for us to file our motion for class certification."

A sound like air hissing out of a punctured tire whooshed through my telephone receiver.

"Yes," said Number 44 in a decidedly less hearty tone of voice. "Of course."

Thus, through the consideration of a man I had never met and who only spoke to me once in his life, I survived to litigate another day.

• • •

When an attorney like Number 44 attempts to gain a decisive advantage over an opponent by misleading him, or resorting to other methods leaving something to be desired on the ethical front, and it misfires, he or she may well open up an unexpected opportunity onto which alert opposing counsel can pounce. In this case Cornell University paid dearly for Number 44's failed attempt to take advantage of us.

By scheduling my client's depositions for an early date, I had to place them at the top of our litigation agenda. I devoted long hours to preparing each of my clients for her deposition, thereby gaining vast amounts of detailed information about their life stories that I would otherwise not have had so early in the case. When Number 44 actually took the depositions, we went through the stories a second time. Not only did I all but learn their stories by heart, I also got a detailed opportunity to assess the strengths and weaknesses of their case early in the litigation.

All of this paid high dividends when the time came to file our Motion for Class Certification, which had been put off until mid to late summer of 1981 to make room for the depositions. I now had a vastly greater and more detailed body of information about my clients' cases to draw on in putting together our Memorandum of Law in Support of Motion for Class Determination.

Not only that, but I had a team of a nationally ranked women scholars, all of them behind-the-scenes supporters of the Cornell Eleven, advising me. During the lengthy period of time it took to go through all the depositions, we were able to put together a truly impressive study of the history and nature of discrimination against women in colleges and universities, and the considerations that had led Congress to bring them within the protection of the Civil Rights Act. Consequently, by the time we finally filed our memorandum of law in support of our motion for class certification, it was a vastly stronger document than it would have been if Number 44 had simply allowed litigation to follow the course contemplated by the Federal Rules. In that case, we would simply have had to file a less comprehensive and well-researched memorandum of law at an earlier date. As my friend Peter McClelland, a tenured professor in the economics department, put it after reading our memorandum:

"It hits you with the force of an express train."

Peter was sufficiently impressed with our memorandum to recommend it to a number of other male faculty members who were friends and acquaintances of his but who had remained dubious about the merits of our case. He also put a copy of our brief on reserve at the Cornell University library, accessible to anyone who wanted to read it.

With this powerful weapon in our hands, we decided to take advantage of it to educate a much broader network of potential supporters and friends about the merits of our case. Thus, in addition to filing our motion and supporting brief in court, we printed some 300 copies of the "express train." We circulated copies to everyone who had demonstrated an interest in our cause and to a select number of influential alumni. We used the "express train" to raise consciousness about the nature of unconscious bias and its discriminatory impact on women academics. Additionally, we built up our network of support, raised money for litigation, and got the word out locally, regionally, and nationally, thus furthering the women's strategy for maintaining the initiative and making the passage of time work in our favor. Though he no doubt would not have appreciated the compliment, I owed Number 44 a large debt of gratitude for his role in bringing the "express train" into being.

Looking at it analytically, which I did, Number 44 was in a much more difficult position than I. He was on the letterhead of one of the nation's truly prestigious law firms, charged with the responsibility of representing one of the nation's great universities in an effort to bring an early end to a dangerous lawsuit. He was facing off against an unknown, solo, small-town legal practitioner who was nevertheless proving to be an exceptionally troublesome and tenacious aggravation, embarrassment, and expense to Cornell. Number 44 was under great pressure. He had to knock me out of the box at the earliest possible date. If he failed, or otherwise blew the case, he would fall from a very great height. In contrast, the odds against us were so long that my clients had no extravagant expectations of me. If I were to be pushed off my pedestal I would fall no more than three feet onto the flower bed outside my office window.

Number 44 was additionally hamstrung by the fact that he was practicing formula law as laid down by Hogan & Hartson, the formula universally followed by "megalaw" firms retained by powerful corporations to represent them against weak, vulnerable, and underfunded opponents. Consequently, Number 44 was being asked to use his personal legal ingenuity or skill in a very limited and proscribed sense. He was expected to follow the established formula for grinding small litigants like myself and my clients into non-existence, and knocking us out of the box when the opportunity arose. If he deviated from that formula to take bold action on his own initiative and it backfired, his career would take a serious hit. He was hemmed in by these constraints, placing him at a distinct disadvantage in facing off against a free-wheeling operator such as myself, ready to take advantage of any opportunity that came my way.

• • •

Quite early in the deposition schedule I took time off to pay a personal visit to an attorney who had become legendary in the field of academic litigation. He had won in the early stages of his case, representing a woman denied tenure in a prestigious Ivy League university.

"It's pretty simple," he told me. "A lot of these guys are unbelievably careless about what they say and what they write. Their bias, prejudice, and often disdain for women is right there in the files. You need to subpoena all the documents you can get your hands on, and go through them with a fine-tooth comb. Believe me, you'll come up with some telling stuff. I settled my case when I came across a memo in my client's tenure file which read: 'Laura has great tits. It's too bad she can't have tenure in our department.'"

My new-found friend's account brought home to me that I was litigating in a very different environment from the one I had faced in California. There, if my client's name had been Maria, Esperanza, or Guadalupe, no one would have blinked an eyelash at such sexist commentary, or indeed at far more outrageous forms of sexual harassment and humiliation. When brought into the bright light of day in the environment of the Ivy League, though, these comments were terminally damaging.

While the statement in and of itself did not establish that Laura actually met the standards for tenure at this university, it betrayed a level of sexist bias that should never taint the tenure evaluation process. The university could never allow such testimony to surface into the bright light of judicial and public scrutiny. It would have to settle the case immediately, and did so.

The comparable testimony I would be presenting at trial was not quite as dramatic, but it was telling nonetheless. I was highly confident that the university would settle the case long before Dean Levin could be called to the witness stand to testify to exactly what he meant when he told Donna Zahorik that the university would destroy her emotionally and financially if she chose to litigate. He would be grilled as well on the names of the women he had in mind when he told Donna, "They've done it to others, and they'll do it to you."

I had other land mines waiting in my files as well. One day, sitting in my office, my phone rang.

"Are you the lawyer for the Cornell Eleven?" asked the voice at the other end of the line. When I said that I was, he went on.

"My name is Eric Smith. Something just happened which might

interest you. I'm a research associate. The chairman of my department just visited my office with a tape measure, and measured its dimensions."

"What's going on?" I asked him.

"Our department has hired two new assistant professors for the coming academic year, one a man, the other a woman. He's just making sure the man gets the larger office."

• • •

The deposition of Keith Kennedy, Provost of Cornell University, also yielded startling evidence.

One of the Cornell Eleven had told me:

"Some time ago I sent an anonymous note to Provost Kennedy alerting him to the fact that Professor X, who played a key role in denying Donna Zahorik tenure, was then sleeping with a woman graduate student on whose thesis committee he served as chair. He had, moreover, previously slept with another young woman thesis candidate on whose committee he served. I asked Provost Kennedy to look into this blatant violation of university rules and ethics. So far as I know, Provost Kennedy has done nothing about it."

I used this lead when I took Provost Kennedy's deposition.

"Provost Kennedy," I asked. "Do you recall receiving an unsigned note alleging that Professor X was sleeping with two of his graduate students?"

"Yes, I do," Provost Kennedy answered.

"Did you do anything about it?" I asked.

"I certainly did!"

"Could you tell us what that was?"

"Why yes! I went straight over to Professor X's office, and I said to him, 'Professor X, is there anything to these allegations of your having improper relations with your graduate students?' And he answered: 'No.'"

"Is that it?" I asked. "Is that all you did?"

"Why, yes," answered Provost Kennedy in some surprise. "Well," he added, "I did go and see the chair of his department and talked to him about it."

• • •

Dean Levin yielded another stunning admission when the time came to take his deposition. I was questioning him about another named plaintiff,

Antonia Glasse. Antonia's tenure file contained letters from a number of the top scholars in her field. They described her as the finest candidate for tenure in her field in the entire country. She had, nevertheless, been denied tenure.

"Dean Levin," I asked. "How could it be that a candidate like Antonia Glasse, recognized by a number of leading experts as the top candidate in her field in the entire country the year she came up for tenure, could nevertheless be denied?"

"You have to understand," Levin replied, "that Cornell University is a great university. Our standards are very high. It may be that in any given year no candidate in a particular field, not even that year's top candidate, meets them. To be good enough to be promoted to tenure at Cornell, a scholar may have to be a 'once in three years' or 'once in five years' candidate."

"That's most interesting, Dean Levin," I said. "Could you help me out by telling me just what those criteria are that a scholar at Cornell has to meet to warrant tenure here?"

"Certainly," Levin replied. He went on in a very helpful manner to explain the seven or eight criteria Cornell looked for in a world-class scholar. I was a most respectful and interested audience, eager to learn from Dean Levin just what the outstanding characteristics were that warranted tenure at Cornell. When he finished listing them, I followed up:

"Is that a full list, Dean Levin?"

Levin gave it careful thought. "Yes, I think so."

"Thank you, Dean Levin," I replied. "I'd now like to ask you to go through the list you've just provided me with and tell me how Professor L, a male who was promoted to tenure in Professor Glasse's department just a few years before her, meets each of those criteria."

Dean Levin had not seen that question coming. Taken aback, he paused for a few moments, trying to collect his thoughts, and then answered in a straightforward manner:

"I don't think he does."

It was a stunning admission. Harry Levin didn't have it in him to prevaricate, obfuscate, or lie. He simply told the truth. Antonia, Donna Zahorik, and I went back to Donna's house when the deposition was over, opened a bottle of champagne, and toasted each other.

• • •

During this time I kept the initiative in our hands, continuing to collect evidence and prepare for an eventual hearing on the issue of class certification. To take back the initiative, on four separate occasions Number 44 filed motions in court that would have, had they been granted, burdened me in a variety of ways and seriously delayed the advancement of the case. To maximize his advantage, Number 44 always brought these motions, on which Hogan & Hartson had spent weeks if not months preparing, on an "order shortening time." Such orders are granted when the moving party (in this case Hogan & Hartson) alleges the existence of an emergency requiring a much shorter time to respond than is normally provided by the rules of court. Obtaining orders shortening time is a common practice resorted to by large law firms. When used against solo or small practitioners, it often compels them to rush into court either ill-prepared or unprepared.

Number 44, however, sought to gain an additional advantage by having Bond, Schoeneck & King personally deliver the motion to Judge Munson's clerk in Syracuse on a Friday morning, but only serving my copy by mailing it to me from Washington. Consequently, just about the time Number 44's motion was delivered to my desk in Ithaca on the following Monday afternoon, I would get a phone call from Judge Munson's clerk telling me to appear in his chambers the following afternoon. With little to no time to prepare, I burnt the midnight oil getting up to speed.

These hearings in Judge Munson's chambers were always nerve-wracking events. Initially Judge Munson would appear to take Number 44's arguments seriously, weighing the arguments for granting them. As Number 44 and I argued the points back and forth, though, the judge would always pull back to the broad middle ground. In the end, none of Number 44's motions ever did us much damage except for emotionally draining me.

• • •

While I was toiling away on the legal side of the case, the Cornell Eleven women were hitting the road. They built up networks of support locally in Ithaca, regionally in central New York and its Southern Tier, and nationally. They lectured on the nature and extent of unconscious bias against women in general, and in academic settings in particular, describing telling examples taken from learned studies and their own personal experiences as well. Since Ithaca is a small town (the city and the university each boast a population around 30,000 today), gradual shifts in perceptions began to sift through the university's permeable borders.

But the women's most dramatic single success came at the national level. I discovered that an old friend of mine from my Cornell student days, Peg Downey, had become an administrative assistant to the president of the American Association of University Women (AAUW). Peg spoke to her about us, and as a result the five named plaintiffs and I were invited to Washington. There we all spoke to representatives of the AAUW and to the leadership of other prominent women's advocacy groups. The plaintiffs were all compelling speakers with dramatic and all-too-familiar stories of discrimination to tell. They were received warmly. A number of them received invitations to return to the nation's capital and further spread their message.

Capping all these efforts was the creation of the AAUW's Legal Advocacy Fund (LAF). Founded in 1981, the year after we filed our complaint, its first contributions were made to our cause. The Cornell Eleven women's struggle went on to cast a long shadow. Today the LAF is the largest legal fund in the United States devoted solely to sex discrimination litigation involving women in higher education.

• • •

Well over a year after I filed our Motion for Class Certification, it finally came up for hearing in front of Judge Munson. Among other things, Number 44 had argued that our motion should be dismissed because it was not supported by sufficient evidence. To my surprise, Judge Munson agreed with this position. He did not dismiss the motion. Fair-minded as he was, he offered me more time to gather and submit additional evidence.

I had to do some very quick thinking. I could, of course, have had the women collect and submit an impressive amount of additional evidence, but I didn't think it would significantly alter the overall picture of the case. We had quite naturally put our strongest foot forward. Additional evidence might have added strength to our motion, but not dramatically. It would have had a cumulative, but not a dramatic, effect.

In the five to ten seconds that I had to think my way through this problem, I decided to reject Judge Munson's offer. I asked him, instead, to render a decision on the evidence before him. I knew full well he would turn us down, but I had considerations of my own for wanting him to render a decision and commit his reasoning to writing.

Judge Munson was clearly a fair-minded man. At every turn, when Number 44 had tried to gain procedural advantages over me, Judge Munson had ruled in my favor. On the substantive side of the case, though, I sized him up as an old-school male. Fair-minded and considerate though he may have been, he belonged, as I saw him, to that population of men who would have been astounded and offended to be told that their attitude towards women was distorted by various forms of unconscious and not-so unconscious bias.

If he ruled against us the case would be heard on appeal in the Second Circuit Court of Appeals, one of the most liberal federal courts of appeal in the nation. While I expected the Second Circuit to rule in our favor on the class certification motion, I had an additional, deeper motivation for wanting them to hand down a decision. I counted on the Second Circuit to address the larger question of academic sex discrimination law raised by the case. Its statements would not be binding rulings, but what lawyers call dictum: non-binding views on legal issues arising out of the larger context of the case. In a word, I counted on the Second Circuit to give us a "road map" we could use to keep Judge Munson on track as we litigated our way into the case's substantive issues.

Another consideration, though, weighed heavily on me. I was beginning to burn out. In one memorable stretch not long before, I had arrived at my office at 9 o'clock in the morning and worked until midnight for 30 consecutive days. It wasn't something I could keep up indefinitely. Not only that, but on the financial side it was becoming clear the plaintiffs could not count on their support network coming through into the indefinite future. I thus had compelling reasons for wanting the case pushed to an early resolution. If the Second Circuit ruled in our favor, I would use the immense leverage that victory gave us to move to settle the case.

• • •

At the same time that we prepared our appeal to the Second Circuit, I began work on a motion intended to strike a major blow at Cornell's enthusiasm for ongoing litigation and to prepare the ground for settlement. This was territory of a kind I had often approached in earlier cases. Whatever the ostensible reason for the motion, my real intent was to draw the client's attention to just how the case was being litigated on its behalf and just what it was getting for its money. In all of my previous cases I had had to guess at what point the client was beginning to chafe at the high cost of the legal representation it was getting.

In the Cornell case, however, an unknown ally had given me hard evidence that the university had spent massively in prosecuting its end of the suit and would want to know what it was getting for its money. One day in the fall of 1983 an unmarked envelope arrived at my office. An anonymous ally in Cornell's treasurer office had sent me a copy of the university's litigation invoices. Glancing over them, I saw that Cornell had spent close to $3 million in litigation fees. We had spent slightly more than $100,000. At today's rates, the comparable amounts on our side would be on the order of $750,000, and on the university's between $15 and $20 million. We were being outspent over 20 to 1. The time was ripe on financial grounds alone. My overall strategy, though, was to invite closer university scrutiny of Number 44's conduct of the case as a whole.

I aimed to so thoroughly discredit Number 44 that he would be bumped out of his role as chief litigator for Cornell. I had done so successfully in some of my previous cases, and I trusted it would work here. If I did succeed in getting Number 44 bumped down, I expected that the next phone call I would receive from Hogan & Hartson would be from Number Four, exploring the possibilities for settlement.

While I would make it my business to file a motion that would call into question the overall competence of Number 44's litigation strategy, I now intended to take maximum advantage of his underhanded tactic of mailing me papers from Washington that had been hand-delivered to Judge Munson's chambers earlier in the day.

Had Number 44 lived in Ithaca and pulled stunts of this kind on his fellow attorneys in town, he would not have lasted long. It was the kind of shoddy behavior that destroys an attorney's reputation in his home community. Number 44 could think of getting away with it with me because, from the lofty heights from which he practiced law in a remote and prestigious location, I was an insignificant speck on a distant horizon.

I achieved my end by delivering a broadside attack on the way Number 44 had been dragging out the case in order to deny my clients substantial justice during their day in court. I was also fiery in my indignation about his shoddy, underhanded tactics, imputing them not only to him but to the university as well. Why, I seethed, the university's legal counsel had sunk so low as to repeatedly file motions for shortening time that were so outrageous that I ended up with less than 24 hours to prepare my defense against motions on which counsel had had weeks if not months to work. Did a great university such as Cornell really have to sink so low, I asked, to seize an unfair advantage over its women academics?

* * *

My strategy worked! Well, it half-worked. The university did drop Number 44 from his role as its lead counsel. Hogan & Hartson, though, had a deep bench. I had thoroughly expected that when Number 44 was sent to the showers, the university would open settlement negotiations. And indeed, Number Four was now called up from the bullpen. It was not, however, to negotiate a settlement. He took over active prosecution of the case and began to smoke hardballs across the plate fast enough to take your breath away. He was good, and I knew it.

Number Four was, however, far from an entirely happy camper. He had any number of vastly more important matters on his mind back in Washington than dispatching a small-town lawyer and his clients into litigation oblivion. He resented being dragged away from his busy and demanding practice to fly up to Ithaca in noisy, badly heated puddle jumpers. The schedules flown by these cramped propeller planes were frequently cancelled in cases of inclement weather. When and if the plane actually took off, the passengers could look forward to a bumpy ride through turbulent air currents as they jolted their way towards centrally isolated Ithaca.

The relationship between Number Four and Number 44, moreover, verged on the sulfuric. In Number Four's estimation Number 44 had seriously compromised the case, and with it Hogan & Hartson's reputation. Number 44 heartily resented being bumped in favor of Number Four, feeling humiliated in his new role as Number Four's briefcase carrier.

Number Four's was a truly remarkable character. Although he would run me a merry chase, his manner was friendly, open, and talkative, and I got to know him well. We found each other fascinating and enjoyed each other's company.

Number Four was also astoundingly open in describing his feelings about discrimination against women.

"My wife is a big feminist," he would tell me. "I'm getting all sorts of hell at home for taking on this case."

He was also an old and close friend of Kate, wife of the director of Cornell United Religious Work.

"I had dinner over at Bob and Kate's last night," Number Four would tell me. "She roasts me for defending the university every time I see her." Roasted or not, Number Four had dinner with Bob and Kate every time he came to Ithaca.

Number Four told me he had been legal counsel in the White House during the presidency of Lyndon Johnson. He had impressive names to drop and did not hesitate to drop them. When he mentioned "My partner, Senator Fulbright" in Judge Munson's chambers the effect was immediate. Despite the prominence of his firm and the client he represented, Number 44 had failed to win any home-court advantage with Judge Munson. If anything, the advantage in that department lay with me. With Number Four though, that edge shifted rather dramatically to the other side.

• • •

Despite his surprising openness, Number Four came into town meaning business, and he set about it straight away. He had no interest of any kind in formula law or in delaying matters. He wanted to get the case out of the way as expeditiously as possible and by the most direct route. The all-important issue of certification of the class still remained in the balance, and Number Four wanted to go to the mat on it. The arena would be the Second Circuit Court of Appeals in New York City.

I would not be arguing the case in the Second Circuit myself. While I consider myself to be a highly competent legal strategist (that is what I mean when I describe myself as a "litigator"), I do not have fancy moves as a trial lawyer in large, complicated cases in open court. I had tried to fill that gap by recruiting a powerful New York law firm with a strong trial department into our case, but none of the New York firms I or my clients contacted wanted to take on Cornell.

I solved the problem by contacting Martha Tonn who, while still a student at Cornell Law School, had been extremely helpful and supportive working with me on the case. She now worked for a major Chicago law firm specializing in anti-trust litigation. Her supervising attorney was a woman named Fay Clayton, and Fay agreed to bring the Cornell Eleven case to the attention of the senior partner in the firm, Lowell Sachnoff.

Thanks to Martha Tonn, a remarkable and dedicated young woman, I got to know Fay Clayton and Lowell Sachnoff. They were both extremely intelligent and highly gifted advocates, practitioners at the top of their field. They were exceptionally warm and supportive people as well. (They were good friends at the time I met them, and they later got married.) Lowell immediately agreed to sign on to help us, with Fay and Martha taking the laboring oar in the day-to-day working of the case.

Fay argued the case superbly in the Second Circuit. A number of attorneys sitting in the courtroom at the time walked out after she finished and gathered around her, congratulating her on a brilliant job and wanting to know who she was. One of them offered her a job with his firm on the spot.

We were therefore devastated a few months later when the Second Circuit denied our appeal. I well knew that civil rights law had been rapidly eroding after Ronald Reagan became president. He appointed very conservative judges to the bench with no ideological sympathy whatsoever for cases of this kind. I had warned my clients that we were in a race against time and had to win before the law became too badly eroded. I had thought, though, that we had more time.

The denial of our motion for class certification came as a terrible blow. It meant that the denial-of-tenure case was reduced to the claims of the five named plaintiffs, not women in a class consisting of all women at

Cornell. The salary discrimination case still remained alive, but my clients were disheartened, and our ability to continue raising money to litigate was seriously compromised.

I knew that we were in a weak position. The time would soon come when we would have to settle on the best terms we could get. I called Jack Pemberton in San Francisco, and together we crafted one last bold initiative. We filed motions for the depositions of key witnesses on both the East and West Coasts, giving the appearance that we were still going hell-for-leather on the remaining issues in the case. Having filed our papers, we waited expectantly for the phone to ring with what we hoped would be a substantial settlement offer.

Time passed though, with no call coming from Hogan & Hartson. I had to face the fact that I might have to make the opening call, a move I wanted to avoid if at all possible. The opposing party always takes such a call as a sign of weakness and counters with a dramatically less satisfying offer.

The moment drew closer when I could no longer put off making my call. I knew, moreover, that a settlement offer coming from our side at this time would result in a counter-offer for the "nuisance" value of the case: the amount of money Cornell would be willing to pay to make a tiresome nuisance like myself and my clients go away. The Cornell Eleven women had calculated that if we settled the case for $50,000 we could pay off all our existing debts with a token amount left over. To get the $50,000, I would have to open negotiations at $100,000, a sizable sum in those days, backing down to $50,000 as an absolute bottom line. I was still dithering around, putting off the call, when the phone in my office rang. It was Number 44.

"Tony," he said in that hearty voice that always spelled troubled. "We're wondering if you might be interested in settling the case. The university is prepared to offer $50,000."

Number 44 had blinked first and was making a "nuisance value" settlement offer. It was the last mistake he would make in the Cornell Eleven case.

"Fifty-thousand dollars?" I shot back. "My clients would never under any circumstances consider settling for so low a figure. But I will relay your offer to them to see if they're interested. If they are, I'll get back to you with a serious proposal."

I put in a call to Fay Clayton and Lowell Sachnoff to relay this information. Lowell told me to catch the next train to Chicago to meet with him, Fay, and Martha. When I got there, Lowell had a plan.

"Tony," Lowell told me, "I know Number Four quite well. We served jointly as counsel in a major anti-trust case a number of years back and became good friends. He's a fine lawyer and a good man. I'll put a call in to him and talk settlement with him. I'll tell him I've met you and that you're a nice kid, but that you're a litigating fool who doesn't know when it's time to stop. You keep on charging on into the fray long after the time has come to talk settlement. I'll tell Number Four that I think I can pound some sense into your head, but he's going to have to make it worth our while. You, Fay, and Martha put together a complete settlement proposal. I'll call Number Four with the proposal and a settlement figure of $300,000. I'll tell him that we're not gandy-dancing. That's our bottom line."

• • •

Lowell did put in his call to Number Four and settled the case for $250,000, approximately $2 million at today's rates. I was more than grateful to Lowell Sachnoff for making that call. His eminent position as senior partner in a prominent Chicago litigation firm gave him leverage I would never have had.

From the beginning it had been our intent to ensure that larger numbers and a larger proportion of women were hired into tenure-track positions and received tenure at the end of their probationary period, and that those denied tenure had meaningful appeal rights. Cornell had recently instituted just the kind of internal appeal mechanism we had been fighting for and was making progress on all the other fronts. In his negotiations with Number Four, Lowell had argued that our lawsuit had been a major force in bringing these internal appeal procedures into being, and claimed credit for it. He had solid grounds for doing so. During my deposition of Provost Kennedy, I had asked him:

"Provost Kennedy. I understand that Cornell University has now set in place a new appeals procedure for women denied tenure, as were the women in this case. Is this correct?"

"Yes, it is."

"Was this appeal procedure instituted, in part at least, as a response to the issues we've raised here in this case."

"Yes," the Provost answered. "It was." He paused for a moment, and then added. "In part, at least."

It was a remarkable piece of candor. In the four and a half years since we had filed our complaint, the Cornell Eleven and our lawsuit had in fact played a significant role in bringing about a sea-change in the way women were perceived and treated not only at Cornell but throughout the academic world. Moreover, after Cornell instituted its appeals procedure I personally coached more than 15 women through its procedures, winning tenure for more than half of them. A substantial number of other women who had been active in the Cornell Eleven support group and who had initially been denied tenure requested that their departments grant them an extension of time in which to review their cases, and a majority of them won tenure too.

Because Donna Zahorik and the other Cornell Eleven women had stood up and been counted, they had not been destroyed either emotionally or financially. On the contrary, Lady Fortune had rushed to their side with a veritable phalanx of allies. We all became part of a nationwide movement for social justice. By standing tall, Donna and the other plaintiffs became leaders in that movement, spearheading the changes that came to Cornell. They were noble women; it had been my privilege to represent them.

• • •

Number Four, Number 44, and I all gathered in Judge Munson's chambers after the settlement was negotiated to sign the final agreement and bring the case to a formal end. The ball had taken a truly remarkable bounce after I filed the papers that resulted in Number 44 being driven from the case. Number Four had turned out to be a formidable adversary. But once he accomplished what he had come to Ithaca to do, he negotiated a settlement that was more than generous. Ironically, a motion that could have turned out to be the biggest blunder of my professional career, bringing the opposition's terminator to the mound after I had driven his predecessor to the showers, turned out to be one of the most successful moves I ever made. It's a strange and wonderful world.

By now the case had dragged on for nearly five years, and as is common in such cases, the lawyers and judge were more than relieved to put it all behind us. A kind of camaraderie often invades such situations. Attorneys who have been adversaries let their hair down and behave like ordinary human beings for a change, trading anecdotes they would never share while still in the trenches.

Judge Munson in particular was feeling good at the settlement of such an important matter, and not unhappy to be associated with a case that was being widely reported in the papers. He was in fine fettle. Picking up a pack of filtered cigarettes he drew one out and, tapping it lightly on the table, declared expansively:

"There are two things I don't like. Cigarettes filters that are tightly packed, and women's sweaters that aren't."

Truly, the measure of success we achieved in his court had defied all the odds.

PART 4

AN AWAKENED HEART

CHAPTER 39

Hitting the Wall

I WAS done in by the end of the Cornell Eleven litigation, running flat out into the wall of a full-blown midlife crisis. At one point in that litigation I had spent 30 straight days in the office from 9:00 a.m. until at least 11:00 p.m. I was 44 when the case finally settled. I no longer had the stamina needed to survive in such a demanding environment. Neither my body nor my mind could take that kind of punishment any longer.

There were other, deeper considerations bearing down on me as well. For the last ten years I had woken up night after night, tossing and turning for an hour or two, obsessed with figuring out just where my opponent's jugular lay, and when and how to go for it. In the Darwinian environment of large-scale litigation, where only the fit survive, I was determined to come out on top. For years I had studied the differences between the named partner at the top of a prestigious mega-firm's letterhead and the partner or associate actually trying the case. When I launched my counter-attack, aimed at decimating the associate's conduct of the case, that person's career often took a hit. In some cases associates lost their jobs.

Situations like these created an inner turmoil, which came into sharp focus when I met an elderly Quaker woman named Althea Postlethwaite in the early 1980s. I had become a Quaker about a year before, and I met her at a conference. Althea, who might have stepped right out of a Norman Rockwell illustration of Quaker life, minced no words. After introducing herself she asked:

"What do you do for a living?"

"I'm a lawyer," I answered. "I practice labor law. I've been doing a good deal of large-scale federal class-action litigation on behalf of working people in the last few years."

"Just how do you reconcile practicing law with your Quaker convictions?" Althea wanted to know, looking me squarely in the eye.

I was so new a Quaker that I wasn't even aware that I had Quaker convictions that might be hard to reconcile with practicing adversarial law.

"It's not a problem," I said. "I litigate on behalf of women, minorities, migrant and seasonal workers. I fight for social justice."

The look in Althea's eyes told me that I hadn't made a sale. The following dream, which came to me shortly after my conversation with her, shows how right she was:

> *I have been on a long, hard journey through a desert. Suddenly I see to my left a beautiful monastery built in the shape of a Greek cross, its white dome gleaming in the bright sunlight. The jovial abbot greets me at the door and gives me a tour. At its conclusion we sit in the refectory in the center of the monastery, directly under its gleaming dome. Four wings containing the monks' cells extend like a cross in the four directions of the compass. Looking down each wing I see a monk sitting upright in each of the cells. All of the monks are dead.*

The dream was startling. It forced me to recognize that I had long been troubled by the life I was leading. As a college senior I had thrown myself into the Civil Rights movement in order to dedicate my life to the nonviolent struggle for peace, justice, and compassion. Since then, I had become a movement heavy. To all outward appearances I gleamed with the reflected glory of the movement's many accomplishments. But inside me, all the monks in my monastery were dead.

• • •

The dream also forced me to face death's influence on my life—particularly the damage it had done when my Aunt Polly died. Some 20 years earlier, when I was in law school, the phone rang in our apartment. My dad's brother Richard was on the line, and the news he shared was stunning.

"The girls are both dead," Uncle Rich told me. "Polly and Ann have killed themselves in a joint suicide pact."

Aunt Polly, my father's youngest sister, was my favorite aunt. Other than Grandpère, she was the only adult member of my family who saw the inner part of my being as it really was and noticed my accomplishments. She was the only one to notice how quickly I learned to read English after leaving France, for example, or to comment on my encyclical memory for historical names and dates. She was a rarity, an aunt young enough at heart to be trusted with the secrets of small boys bound on adventures their parents would surely disapprove of.

Case in point: when my cousin David and I were about ten, we decided to emulate our heroes, Tom Sawyer and Huck Finn, by smoking in the nearest available graveyard. Finding a cemetery was the easy part, since there was a large one about ten blocks from our grandfather's house in Milwaukee. For tobacco, we pilfered a pack of Aunt Polly's Pall Malls, concealing them in a paper bag with a box of matches. We were scampering out the door when Aunt Polly appeared.

"What have you got in that bag, boys?" she asked.

"Nothing, Aunt Polly," David and I said in shaky voices.

"Where are you going, boys?" she asked.

"Nowhere, Aunt Polly," we said in even shakier voices.

"Do you boys have a pack of my cigarettes in that paper bag?" Aunt Polly wanted to know.

"Yes, Aunt Polly." By now David and I, heads bowed, mumbled all but inaudibly.

"You're planning to go to the cemetery and smoke them?" she asked. We had been caught red-handed. What frightful retribution, we wondered, would fall upon us when Aunt Polly reported our crime to Dad and Uncle Duane?

"Yes, Aunt Polly," David and I croaked.

"Well," Aunt Polly said, "run along and have fun."

When my aunts died, Dad flew in from France for the joint funeral. I had flown in from Ithaca the day before. Uncle Rich and I met Dad at the Milwaukee airport. Rich told us what had happened:

"The two girls told their husbands they were going off for an overnight jaunt at Port Washington. Instead, they parked Ann's car a few blocks away, came back to her house, took an overdose of pills in a side-attic room, and lit up cigarettes. When the police found Ann's car a couple of days later they notified Ann's husband Duane. He searched the house and found them. They must have lost consciousness very quickly. They were holding the burned-down cigarettes between their fingers when they died."

Dad, Uncle Rich, and I stood silently together for quite a while after Uncle Rich finished telling us the story of my aunts' death. Neither then, nor later, did anyone in my family speak about them again.

Something inside me died along with Aunt Polly. I experienced vivid death and dying dreams, and I felt that part of me had turned into wood. It was all too much to take in. I thrust the tragedy of my family into some dark dungeon in my unconscious mind and bolted the door shut. Never again, I vowed, would I let those demons run free. Twenty years later, though, the demons were clamoring to be let out.

With the Cornell Eleven case behind me, I had to confront the troubling realities to which my archetypal dreams pointed. I wandered around aimlessly, stunned at the prospect of having to rebuild my professional life from the ground up. I knew I couldn't go back to California and relive my glory days there, and I had neither the experience nor enthusiasm to open a general practice law office in Ithaca. I soon had to confront the fact that I could never match either the excitement or the recognition I had won working with Cesar Chavez. Those days were forever behind me.

CHAPTER 40

"You Made a Difference"

AFTER a number of false starts, I finally opened an office representing injured workers in workers' compensation and Social Security disability claims. Many workers' only capital asset is their bodies, which break down, often when they are still quite young, through hard use. Many of them face the pain and deprivation of work-related injuries like native-born philosophers, with courage, resilience, and humor. A case in point is Rich, a client of mine in his late 40s whose body was badly broken down. Despite the fact that he had what I considered to be clear-cut cases for benefits, he had been turned down for both workers' compensation and Social Security disability. Although he was in constant pain, Rich was cheerful and uncomplaining as he told me his story:

"I'm a dumb shit," he said. "I was too dumb to read instructions or construction plans, that sort of thing, so I never could break into any of the trades. The only thing I knew how to do was bull labor, throwing myself at stuff. I'm small, too, and took a lot of hard hits. That's how my body broke down."

Since Rich was only semi-literate, I had his wife come into the office to execute some legal documents. To my surprise, she was about ten years younger than he, very pretty, and quite smart.

"I wonder what she sees in him," I asked myself, watching her walk out the door.

"I wonder what she sees in me." It was Rich speaking, his voice interrupting the flow of my thoughts. "I adore her, though," he added. "The guy she was married to before me used to beat the holy hell out of her."

"We've got a daughter," Rich added. "But she ain't dumb like me. She takes after her mother. She's smart, has lots of friends, and she's doing real well in school. She's going to make something of herself. We're real proud of her."

I took Rich's workers' compensation and Social Security disability cases and won them both.

Because of Rich and people like him, I found a new passion in my work. I loved putting injured workers on the witness stand to tell the stories of their lives, the way they had become injured, and the consequences that flowed from it. Poor people for the most part live well below our radar screens. We don't see them, and for we imagine that if they are poor, they more or less have it coming. I made it possible for them to have their day in court, creating a space in which they could be heard and, if they and their stories were persuasive, win their cases.

Most people, poor people included, have no real idea of how to present their stories and their cases effectively. What seems most important to them is usually pretty marginal to the facts that both make up a good story and are legally compelling. I took huge pleasure in my new job description, namely as the producer and artistic director of theater productions starring my clients' real-life human dramas. They almost all had compelling stories to tell and, for the most part, richly deserved to win.

• • •

For a number of years after the Cornell Eleven case settled, I coached women through its newly instituted internal appeals procedure. Word got around, and people who had been denied tenure in other schools in the area contacted me.

A number of my academic clients, once they had won tenure, gave me a wide berth whenever they saw me, lest members of their departments or other colleagues infer that they would not have gotten tenure without my help. Not all of them, though. Some of them thanked me over and over again every time we crossed paths.

Dave was one such client. He had been turned down at a neighboring college due to the personal antagonism of his chairman. I found a way of exposing the chairman's false claims and statements about Dave, and he won his tenure. He went on to have a highly successful career. For years afterwards, whenever he saw me, Dave always took the time to tell me how grateful he was. I then lost sight of him for a number of years. Not long ago, though, I heard a familiar voice saying, "Hello, Tony." It was Dave. Standing next to him was his son, who was about 12. Turning to him, Dave said:

"Mike, this is the man I've been telling you about. He's the one who saved my career."

• • •

Two other clients who have stayed in my heart are Owen and Alice. They told me the story of how they met:

One day, after 20 years of addiction to alcohol, having vainly tried to find a homeless shelter for the night, Owen was at the end of his rope. He drifted into a Catholic church and sat through several masses. Eventually a kind stranger came over, asking if he needed help. The stranger found a bed for him that night in a shelter, drove him there, and picked him up the following morning to take him to an AA meeting.

At that meeting Owen met Alice, a drop-dead gorgeous red-head. Alice had woken up a few days earlier to find that her head was propped up against a toilet bowl and that she was soaked in her own vomit. Sick of it all, she staggered into AA.

Owen and Alice fell in love. Neither one of them ever again drank a drop of alcohol. They became mainstays of AA, telling their stories over and over again, and being there for countless other people whose lives were as desperate as theirs had been.

A few months after Alice and Owen moved in together into a small, low-rent apartment, a developer bought their building and began to turn it into condominiums. He was in a hurry, driving existing low-rent tenants out by means both fair and foul.

One morning two burly men showed up at Alice and Owen's door with a message that terrified them. If they didn't clear out of their apartment within three days, the men said, they would find themselves locked out of their apartment and all of their furniture on the sidewalk. Owen and Alice were just beginning to get on their feet. Eviction under those conditions would have devastated them. They came to my office for help.

I called the developer:

"Is this Bill Smith?" I asked. "I'm Tony Gaenslen. I'm an attorney and

I represent Alice and Owen. They tell me that a couple of your goons just threatened them with forcible eviction. If I hear that Alice, Owen, and their furniture have ended up on the sidewalk outside your building, I will sock you with a lawsuit that will shut your operation down for at least a year. I'm big hearted, though, and I'll cut you a deal. Sign a year's lease with Alice and Owen guaranteeing their rent at its current rate, and I'll give your sleazy operation a pass. Mess with them though, and you'll wish you hadn't."

Alice and Owen got their lease. They invited me over for supper in their apartment, and I went with them to a number of AA meetings. For more than 20 years thereafter Owen sent me a card every Christmas. One year he sent me a copy of John Grisham's *Street Lawyer* with the words "He reminded me of you" written in the flyleaf. Owen had always been a man of few words, simply signing each card "Alice and Owen." A few years ago, though, he added the words "You made a difference." It was the last card I received from him.

• • •

Workers' compensation law, particularly in a small town, isn't very adversarial. The lawyers on both sides of the fence handle so many cases together that they get to know each other and the judges quite well. For the most part we enjoyed a certain kind of camaraderie. So too with the insurance adjusters, whom I got to know by name. We treated each other as human beings and enjoyed the practice.

I also had absolute calendar control in this practice. If I went on vacation or wanted to take time off, I simply called the calendar clerk and blocked off the time. For the first time in my adult life, I went out of town when I felt like it and enjoyed life with family and friends.

And so I left the practice of high-level adversarial law. A true child of the Sixties, I dropped out, tuned in, and turned on to the life of a very ordinary small-town lawyer. I crossed paths with Althea Postlethwaite some years later:

"You were right Althea," I told her. "It's very difficult reconciling the practice of adversarial law with Quaker principles." I added that I had found a way of practicing law that, for the most part, could be readily reconciled with my Quaker convictions.

CHAPTER 41

Where Mother Went Wrong

ALTHOUGH I felt quite proud of my practice of law, I couldn't deny that its financial side justified my mother's oft-repeated lament that I had taken a wrong turn somewhere, and that she had been a failure as a mother. For 24 of the 42 years that I practiced law, my income placed me in the bottom quartile of all lawyers in the United States. There were years when I scraped the bottom of the bottom quartile. My parents had sacrificed so much to position me at the pinnacle of my profession that I could not help feeling a sense of loss and regret at this poor showing. Young lawyers just getting out of prestigious law schools such as Cornell made more in their first year of practice than I made in all but a very few years of my entire career.

My mother never recovered from the wrong turn I had taken in life and from what she had done, or failed to do, that brought it about. The year before she died she organized a family gathering of the Dior clan by the ocean near Granville. She wanted everyone who had been important to her to be there. Dad, who never came to these reunions in France, made this one. Mom ardently wanted to be with her grandchildren, and so Nancy and I came with our daughter Elisabeth, who was 5, and son Max, who was one and a half, staying with her in a rented villa. She and Christian's sister Jacqueline had grown up almost as sisters, and they laughed and joked together as only sisters can.

One night, as Mom and I were doing the dishes together, she became pensive. Turning to me, she asked the question that had troubled her so deeply for so much of our life together:

"Where did I go wrong with you, Tony?"

It was a heartfelt and anguished question. Mom desperately wanted to understand just where and how the adventure of our relationship together had wandered so far off the path. Where did mother go wrong with me? It was a good question and deserved an answer, but I was too angry to answer it.

"I know you find this hard to believe, Mom," I said in a voice laden with heavy sarcasm, "but I could conceivably have turned out even worse than I did."

Mom, taken aback, fell silent. The following morning, though, contrite and hesitant, she sought me out.

"You are kind, Tony" she said. "You're honest and hard working, and even though you're stubborn, one can always reason with you." Mom had stitched together a few other virtues that she added to her list, but her heart wasn't in it. She loved me, and it grieved and burdened her that her grand plan for bringing about the very best for me had gone so badly awry.

The following year she was diagnosed with a ganglion on the outer edge of her brain, which caused her to lose her sense of balance. She decided to undergo experimental surgery at the Cornell Medical Center in New York rather than face eventual confinement to a wheelchair.

The surgery itself succeeded, but the blow to my mother's metabolism was too great. Over a period of three weeks I saw in her something of the haughty, determined imperiousness of her Viking ancestors as she fought for life. My mother had a passion for life, and she did not reconcile herself easily to the idea of dying. She was not one to go gently into that good night. But in the end, she succumbed to a heart attack.

My presence during those last three weeks brought my mother little comfort. I had no power to save her or even to bring her much relief. She blamed herself for having been a bad mother, and that guilt weighed heavily on her Catholic conscience as she stood on the threshold of judgment before her God, in whose power it lay to cast wretched sinners into the fires of everlasting hell. All her life my mother had prayed earnestly to Jesus, Mary, St. Anthony, and her favorite Norman saint, St. Theresa the Little Flower. Now the time had come for Jesus to step in and save my mother. It was no easy task.

Jesus' duly delegated emissary, the harried and overworked priest assigned to bring the consolations of the Church to patients dying in the Cornell Medical Center, failed to save Mom. It wasn't that he didn't try: he reached her name on the list of patients he was scheduled to visit just a few hours before she died. He rushed through the sacrament, hurrying on to administer last rites to the next dying person on his list before it was too late. Overworked as he was, he didn't have time to linger and bring my mother the spiritual comfort she longed for.

But where the priest had failed, my father stepped in. Dad was at the hospital doors every morning at six o'clock, waiting for them to open, and he stayed until he was thrown out at midnight. He stayed at Mom's side 18 hours a day, holding her hand, comforting her, telling her he loved her, telling her she was the best thing that had ever happened in his life.

The last day of Mom's life I was at the hospital with Dad, and we decided to take a break. I said goodbye to my mother for what would be the last time, telling her how much I loved her. She took my hand in hers with an extraordinarily strong grip and said, with great intensity:

"Thank you. Thank you."

* * *

Years later, I would face the loss of my father as well. His memory began to fail when he reached his late seventies, and when he could no longer read the newspaper and get riled up about how the Democrats were tearing down the country, he became a dear, sweet, affectionate, trusting, and dependent child; we became very close.

One day, as I was talking with Dad about the "wrong turn" I had taken in life that had so burdened my mother's conscience, he quite suddenly cut me short, saying:

"You're a fine man, Tony. You're everything I could want in a son."

Dad also revealed himself to be a nature mystic in his last years.

"Look, Tony! Look!" he would exclaim with great excitement. "The trees . . . the sky . . . the flowers . . ." Dad would say, unable to find words to express what he was feeling. He didn't have to. I could read it in his expression, his voice, and his eyes.

One day, as I Dad and I were driving, it occurred to me that sometime in the past year Dad must have spoken his last complete thought to me. I wished I had remembered it and had written it down. As I was pondering this, Dad's voice cut into my thoughts:

"I guess there are people who don't believe in God," Dad said, returning to a question that had occupied his mind most of his life.

"That's right, Dad," I said. "There are people who think that way."

"They just don't get it," Dad said. "If there's a creation, there has to be a Creator. It's just that simple." It was the last complete thought my father ever spoke to me.

He died of complications from pneumonia about six months later. He lit up when I walked into his hospital room for the last time, and we spent about an hour together. I told him what a wonderful dad he had been, how generous he had been, and how much I loved him. Dad couldn't speak, and he had intravenous tubes in both arms, but he clapped his hands together to show me that he understood what I had said and that he felt the same way. I kissed his forehead before leaving for home.

Around midnight, I awoke to a sense of presence in my room. Looking up, I saw Dad standing in the doorway. He looked as he had in his prime, dressed in his field clothes and eager to be off. He had always stopped in to say goodbye before heading out for his seven-week treks into the desert or jungle. Now, though, he had a universe to explore and galaxies to roam. He lingered in the doorway for no more than a minute, and then was gone.

CHAPTER 42

The Woman of My Dreams

LOOKING back over the course of my life, I came to think of myself as the victim of a perfect education. That my parents loved me I of course took for granted, but it wasn't the kind of love nor the kind of education that equipped me well, if at all, for the two tasks that I eventually came to think as the two that truly mattered—how to be a loving husband and a good father. While I got glittering grades on the formal side of my education, I largely flunked the course on the other two.

Nancy and I fell in love in the wake of a shared pilgrimage to Chartres Cathedral, organized by the Catholic Chaplaincy of the University of Paris. Our Catholic faith was the great attraction and the principal glue that brought and held us together. We were married two years later in June, 1964 at St. Malachi's church, deep in the heart of North Philadelphia's African-American ghetto where I had founded Joseph House. Nancy had been one of the very few of my friends to support my decision to plunge into the Civil Rights movement. Our daughter Elisabeth was born one year later, our son Max four years after that.

The happiest years of our married life would be spent in Washington, D.C., during the years that I worked for Arthur and NLRB Chairman Frank McCulloch. While I spent long weekday hours at the office, Nancy and I spent most of our week-end time with Elisabeth and Max, visiting museums and parks, playing, camping, and hiking in Washington and in the Virginia countryside. I read *Winnie the Pooh* to Elisabeth most evenings, playing often with Max and freeing him when he got into such scrapes as locking himself into our second floor bathroom. I scaled an outer wall with an extension ladder, climbing through the window to make the rescue.

While I leapt at the opportunity to work with Cesar Chavez in California after being fired by the Teamsters, my family would pay a heavy price for the years I spent devoted to the cause of migrant workers, the poor, the discriminated against, the exploited. The battlefront conditions which govern large-scale litigation took as large a toll on Nancy, Elisabeth, and Max as they did on me. My basic work-week was six days, roughly nine to six or seven, and often much, much more. There were years when I ended up taking no vacation. When up to my neck in class action law suits I thought about little else, spending hours in the middle of each night obsessing about just where my opponent's jugular lay, and how best to go for it.

In many ways the moment that for me defines the nature of my relationship with my family during the years we spent together in California came the night when I was scheduled to speak to a gathering of several hundred cannery workers. Since I was gone most nights, neither I nor any member of my family seemed to take much notice of it. On this night, though, Max desperately wanted me to stay home. "Don't go, Daddy, don't go" he sobbed. I stayed with Max for half an hour past the time I was scheduled to leave, and then left to make my speech—the sound of Max's voice ringing in my ears:

"Don't go, Daddy. Don't go."

How many times in the ensuing years have I longed to relive that moment, stranding the audience of 300 in order to stay with my little boy. In the end all four of us bore scars and paid the price for those years of passionate devotion to La Causa on the one hand, and neglect of my family on the other.

• • •

After we moved to Ithaca in late 1979 Nancy and I became friends with Babs and her husband Larry. A Jungian psychotherapist, Babs was insightful, kind, and compassionate. In March 1984, I had three powerfully disturbing dreams in quick succession. I decided to invite Babs to lunch and tell her about the dreams.

In the first dream, as I was looking at the face of a friend of mine, someone began to strangle him. His face grew whiter and whiter until, on the very brink of death, the strangler released his grip. A thin trickle of blood began to rise into my friend's features, and I woke up.

Two nights later I dreamt that I was part of a cult-like group of 15 people listening to our leader speak. He instructed us to drink poison, and we did. Six months later I returned to the site and was able to locate my own grave among the 14 others. I spotted a piece of paper lying on it and picked it up. It was a love letter written in red ink to an unknown woman. The letter was half-finished; I had died before completing it.

Two nights later, in my third dream, I had gone to a Quaker retreat center high in the California redwoods. As I came out of my room after dropping off my bag, a beautiful young woman took me by the hand and, leading me outside, made love to me under the redwood trees that towered over us like the vault of a great cathedral. Midway through our love-making I let out a great cry of mingled agony and ecstasy, and I woke up.

Describing this third dream to Babs, I said: "This prostitute took me by the hand, led me outside, and made love to me."

"Why do you call her a prostitute, Tony?" Babs wanted to know.

"Well," I said, "we weren't married."

"That woman isn't a prostitute, Tony," Babs said. "She's offering you the gift of love. There's been entirely too much agony in your life, agony which you haven't been willing or able to face. She's offering you the gift of healing which can only come from true love. Beneath the agony and death layering over the surface of your life lies a great, even explosive, natural capacity for ecstasy and love. Both halves of your nature came together with her in that moment of love-making; it was their collision that made you cry out. Your head and your heart have become separated from each other, Tony. This woman came to you to offer you the gift of healing, bringing both halves of your being back into harmony with each other."

As Babs spoke, my heart began to pound, harder and harder, until it felt like a sledgehammer trying to pound its way out of my chest. It kept on pounding ceaselessly that way for the next three days. "If this keeps up," I thought, "I'm going to have a heart attack."

The night of the third day I caught a train to Milwaukee to visit Dad. Waking up in my sleeper bunk the following morning, I found that my heart was still pounding. A thought popped into my mind. "I'm in love with Babs" it said. Immediately the pounding stopped, and my heart began to beat normally once again.

• • •

I immediately told Nancy what had happened, and we agreed to work with a couples therapist to try to put our marriage back on track. We separated and filed for divorce before the year was out.

A few months after Babs and I began seeing each other in earnest, trying to figure out how to put our lives together, she was diagnosed with breast cancer. Although our relationship was still very new, I couldn't allow her to face this terrible disease alone. We moved in together in the fall of 1987, and we were married two years later on Bastille Day, July 14, 1989.

On our very first date Babs had given me a Jerusalem cross on a chain to hang about my neck, long enough so that the cross hung just midway between my head and my heart. "This is to bring your head and your heart together," Babs had said. From the very beginning she undertook to do just that, insisting that we engage fully in a meaningful relationship.

For the first time since I had begun practicing law 20 years before I had a wife who insisted that I be home in time for dinner, unless there was genuinely pressing business at the office. It was a stretch, but I learned to finish what I had to do by 5:30 and come home.

I am, moreover, terminally absent-minded. When I actually arrived home from work, my mind was usually absorbed with something far removed. Babs demanded that I be present and accounted for in the present moment.

"Speak to me," she would demand. "Say something intelligent." Jerked back into the present from some distant mental landscape, I would often need a full five minutes to collect my scattered wits enough to think of something even vaguely cogent.

Slowly, I began to change. I became less self-involved and made a conscious effort to cut short the long stories I was in the habit of telling other people. Bab wasn't into what she called "popcorn relationships." She wanted people to be real with each other, beginning with us, and she made it happen.

The mother archetype was writ large into Babs' psyche, and I soaked it up. We were always together, since there was no one else I would rather be with. She became the incarnation of the woman who, in my archetypal dream, had taken me by the hand to make love with me under the towering trees. She set me on the path to healing the split between my agony and my ecstasy, my head and my heart.

* * *

For nearly ten years Babs experienced a remission in her breast cancer, and we were beginning to feel that the remission was permanent. We felt extraordinarily blessed, counting on a long life together. In the late fall of 1997, though, Babs experienced a recurrence. Her cancer had metastasized to bone and liver. I put the practice of law, and everything else, on the back burner to be with her through every stage of the disease. In September 1998, I turned my legal practice over to my friend Peter Littman and to my secretary/paralegal Tracy so I could be with Babs 24 hours a day, seven days a week.

There were times when Babs suffered intensely. When she cried I would cry too, pained to see her hurting so much. She faced her death with enormous faith and courage. I was filled with admiration and with broken-hearted love.

One day as she neared her end, Babs said to me:

"You will be loved by another woman, Tony. She won't love you the way I've loved you, though. She will love you in her own way."

Three nights later, as I took her to bed, I placed three oil lamps on the window sill by our bed, lighting two of them.

"Those lights are so pretty," Babs said. "Light the third one." And so I did.

Babs had wanted to die in my arms, and so I took her gently in them. She died just before noon the following day, February 5, 1999.

* * *

I was half-crazed after Babs died. I had lost the person with whom I spent most of my waking hours and the one person I would have turned to for help, guidance, and support to get through a dark time. Babs had been the great love of my life.

In September, 1999, seven months after Babs' death, I bought a 26-foot cruising sailboat and set off, solo, for Annapolis, Maryland. I had never sailed anything larger than a daysailer before, but I felt a desperate need to throw myself into the teeth of the gale and prove, to myself at least, that I was still alive and on the planet. Even after running into a hurricane, and surviving, what I mainly proved was how much I hate being alone.

Back in Ithaca, I called my friend Susan. "I'm so lonely the intensity of my loneliness terrifies me," I told her.

"I know someone who's dying to meet you," Susan said. That "someone" was Annie Wexler, but she wasn't actually dying to meet me at all. All she wanted out of life at that moment was to find a hiking partner.

"He loves to hike," Susan had told Annie. It was a bald lie; I never hiked. I was intrigued, though, by the idea that this woman was dying to meet me, so I told Susan to have her give me a call.

When Annie's call came I picked up the phone. "I hear you love to hike" said a pleasant feminine voice. "What kind of a ploy is this?" I wondered. "The woman's dying to meet me, and here she is talking about hiking."

"I've never hiked a day in my life," I replied. After an awkward pause I added, "I walk."

"I know a really nice three-hour hike," Annie said hopefully.

"Two hours is my limit," I replied.

On the hike with Annie, I talked nonstop about Babs. When we parted, we both knew we would never see each other again.

The following week, though, driving across town to spend an hour with a friend of Babs who was stricken with terminal cancer, and passing by the turn-off to Annie's house, I felt an irresistible urge to make the turn and see her. Back home I picked up the phone.

"I think I could manage a somewhat longer hike," I said.

Lonely as I was, it was much too soon for me to meet anyone. On our first New Year's together a few months later, Annie came to my house, cooked a delicious dinner, and put it on the table. Hearing Annie work in the kitchen that Babs had so recently abandoned was so intensely painful that I told her it was all too much for me, and I asked her to leave. She went home immediately, the dinner uneaten.

Soon after we met I had told Annie that all I wanted or expected to get out of life was to find someone who was kind and gentle. Annie is that and so much more. She hung in with me for more than a year until I could be fully at peace with myself in her presence. By the end of that time she had me hiking 3,000 feet up and 3,000 feet down on the same day in the French Alps. On my side, I took her sailing up Lake Cayuga to the Erie Canal, across Lake Ontario, and down the St. Lawrence River's 1,000 Islands.

Falling in love with Babs had the felt experience of a bolt of lightning striking to my very core. With Annie, our love grew with the passage of the years like a gradual awakening, until I was—and still am—filled with all the love my heart can hold.

CHAPTER 43

Child of the Light

I HAD become a Quaker shortly before moving to Ithaca. Because worship in most Catholic churches had become dead for me, I had wandered for a while from church to church, searching for a Catholic community in which the vibrant spirit I had experienced decades earlier was still alive. One Sunday, I stumbled into San Francisco's Quaker meeting. When an elderly white-haired woman named Madge Seaver rose midway through the meeting to speak out of the silence, I was profoundly moved:

"That woman is in touch with God," I said to myself.

I started attending the meeting regularly, and not long after I had a mystical dream:

I am in an orthodox church attending a funeral mass. Although the priest should be wearing white vestments (symbols of hope) when celebrating a funeral mass, the priest is wearing old-style black vestments, and the church is draped in black.

At the moment of consecration in the mass the priest, who normally lifts up a wafer that has become the sacramental body of Christ for all to see, instead goes down to the casket and raises up the corpse of the dead man. I see that the dead man is me; I am attending my own funeral. I leave the church and, walking across a large, barren parking lot, enter a huge warehouse that has recently been refurbished and whitewashed. Although the building is mostly empty, I spot chairs arranged in a circle at one end. Approaching, I see that they form a circle around a large, life-size mosaic of a figure in white standing on a cross of light. It is the resurrected Jesus who, like a Christian-Jewish Buddha, embraces all humanity in his look of tender and infinite compassion. I know that I am in a Quaker meeting house and that every piece in the mosaic has been set in place by a different person coming from a different part of the world, and that together they represent all the different faiths on earth. Tears fill my eyes, and I say, "At last, somebody sees what needs to be done and is doing something about it."

I woke up to find real tears in my eyes.

Never before had I ever seen a representation of Jesus that reflected such universal and all-embracing love and compassion, and I was deeply moved. Soon after having this dream I became a Quaker.

A couple of years later, while on a visit to Paris, I paused at the display window of a religious-articles store and found myself looking at a reproduction of the extraordinarily compassionate face of the risen Christ that I had seen in my dream. I went into the store and bought the icon; the inscription on the back stated that it is a detail of a larger 16th-century icon. No one in the store could tell me anything more about it.

Much later, with Google's help, I tracked it down to the Icon Museum in Recklinghausen, Germany. Titled "Resurrection of Christ and the Harrowing of Hell," the icon was an exact reproduction of my archetypal dream, with the sole exception that the "Harrowing of Hell" had numerous other people in it, while in my vision the only figure was Christ's. The icon's artist and I, it seems, had both tapped into the same archetypal source, lodged deep in the collective human psyche.

* * *

The path that led me into my first Quaker meeting marked the culmination of an eight-year struggle with dark depression, beginning not long after Aunt Polly's death. There were days when my depression had been so intense that it took everything I had just to force my feet out of bed and onto the floor.

Almost immediately after my first Quaker meeting I plunged into reading the foundational documents of Quakerism, beginning with the Journal of George Fox, principal founder of the Quaker movement. I soon discovered that Fox's own spiritual journey had begun with a four-year period of intense depression, and that early Friends had all begun their journeys in their new religion with an intense period of inner scrutiny and self-transformation, well described by Quaker author Hugh Barbour in a book chapter entitled "The Power and Terror of the Light." It read:

"The Lamb's War began for most early Friends with a hard, slow, inner conflict; only afterwards could they call themselves Children of the Light. This opening struggle shaped the meaning of their new lives and gave color to all they thought or felt about the inward Light and the Spirit of God. The serenity and trust and the sense of daily direction from the Spirit finally became the most characteristic part of the Quaker way of life."

Inspired by Barbour's words, I began a daily meditation practice of my own, wanting to transform myself in the way early Friends had. I would begin every morning by turning toward the Inward Light within me. After 20 minutes or so the feelings of depression and agitation with which I awoke every day would begin to lift. Slowly but surely, I began to experience greater and greater measures of inner peace, as though I was being resurrected day by day from the caskets and graves of my archetypal dreams by the light and life within me. In time depression became part of my past.

I also made a practice of observing each shift in my consciousness as I walked the path of the inward light and began to think of my life as a longitudinal study of my own states of awareness. Barbour's article had encouraged me to believe that early Quakers crossed this threshold after five or six years of inward struggle; I anticipated the same thing for myself. In point of fact, I would not fully cross it for close to 40 years.

• • •

My archetypal dream had taught me that each piece in the Resurrection mosaic had been set in place by a different person, and together they represented all the religious faiths of the world. For this and for other reasons I eventually came to the conviction that Quakerism is both a Christian and a universal faith. Over the 40 years that I meditated on the Inward Light I also grew into a deeper understanding of different world religions and the teachings of such enlightened figures as Moses, Socrates, the Buddha, Lao-Tze, Mohammed, Gandhi, Black Elk, the high religion of ancient Egypt, and the Gospel of Mary Magdalene,[1] among others.

My relationship with Annie led to a very practical application of these developing beliefs. During my years in the Civil Rights movement I had often met and been inspired by many progressive Jews, some of whom had become dear friends. None of them, however, ever spoke to me about their religion; it had remained, for me, a closed book.

All that changed after I met Annie, who is Jewish. Through her I came to know, practice, and love Jewish religion and the Torah as much as I love my Quaker faith and the Sermon on the Mount. I learned to read Hebrew, the better to follow prayers, songs, and Torah portions. For me it came to make as much sense to separate the "Old" from the "New" Testaments as it would be to put a new head on an old body. The two constitute for me a single *Histoire Sainte*, or Sacred Story.

Annie and I worship together with our Jewish congregation on Fridays and with our Quaker meeting on Sundays, each enriched by the other's traditions and finding great happiness and fulfillment with dear friends in both.

I had always thought that when I finally crossed over the threshold into the consciousness of a Child of the Light, it would come in a flash of illumination or deep insight. It wasn't that way at all. Indeed, on my 75th birthday, I was surprised to discover that I had crossed over this threshold some time before without actually knowing it.

Annie had organized a birthday party with a dozen of our dear friends. She always makes up funny songs for celebrations like this, using elements of my life as fodder for her lyrics. I have always been guarded, keeping the most vulnerable part of me safe under Tex's protective presence, and finding ways to discount or divert other people's expressions of love or care for me. That day, though, as I looked into my friends' eyes as they sang Annie's song, I could see their love and affection, and I let it penetrate into the core of my being.

Enlightenment turned out not to be a big deal at all; it was the smallest of deals. St. Paul had written: "When I was a child I spoke as a child, I understood as a child, I thought as a child but when I became a man, I put away childish things." I reversed Paul's formula, healing myself instead from the disease of thinking like a man. It was as though I stood once again at the gate of the Chalet de Caux when Dad dropped me off there, only to awaken to the miracle of the incomparable beauty of the Swiss countryside, the glorious profusion of small mountain flowers growing in the fields, the tall evergreens and towering mountains behind them, a pretty little girl who had special eyes for me, "Grande Marie" who took us all into her protective 8- or 9-year-old arms, the girls' club, the older children—big, fine, beautiful, kindly, and protective of the small fry we then were, and the promise of what we might grow up to be.

It was as though love had taken me by the hand and guided me through the darkness to a bright land. Once again, as when I was a small child, I saw that all of life is sacred and eternal. To see it and touch it, though, we must first learn to look out on reality with our hearts and see it anew through the eyes of a small child. The universe is a benevolent and good-hearted place, and all living things—trees, birds, plants, flowers, animals, are all good-hearted, too. We, her children, are capable of great things. When the spirit moves us, there is nothing we cannot do.

"Every heart sings a song," Plato writes, "incomplete until another heart sings back"

1. The *Gospel of Mary Magdalene* is a fifth-century document written in Sahidic Coptic, the original having been written in Greek in the second century. It teaches that the Resurrection came as a vision to Mary and that its core teaching is that the indwelling spirit, or consciousness, of Jesus awakens in us in order to "make us fully human." See *The Gospel of Mary Magdalene,* Translation from the Coptic and Commentary by Jean-Yves Leloup, English translation and Notes by Joseph Rowe, Inner traditions, Rochester, Vermont.

CHAPTER 44

The Courage of a Few

IN July 2011, I decided to return to Savigny le Vieux to visit the *berceau* or ancestral village of the Dior family. As a child I had grown up on stories of the Diors having been in Savigny for close to a thousand years. And so I went to visit the village of my ancestors and say a prayer at the grave of my great-grandfather Louis Dior and his wife Anne. I was stunned, when my cousins and I came to the village square, to see a plaque that had not been there on my previous visits. It read:

HERE IN SAVIGNY LE VIEUX
SOME THIRTY JEWISH CHILDREN
WERE WELCOMED AND PROTECTED
THANKS TO THE COURAGE OF A FEW VILLAGERS
AND THE GOOD HEARTEDNESS
OF THE VILLAGE COMMUNITY.
LET US REMEMBER THE HUMANITY
TO WHICH THE MEMBERS OF THIS VILLAGE
GAVE PROOF.

I had tears in my eyes. As my cousins and I left the village, I made three resolutions. The first was to find one or more of the children whose lives had been saved in my village. The second was to discover who were the courageous few who made this possible. The third was to meet members of the village whose families had saved Jews.

Back home, my research attempts came to nothing. I had pretty well given up when I told the story to my friend Sherry Burford, who said, "Maybe I can help you."

Sherry returned to my house a couple days later with a box of note cards she had bought at the Holocaust museum in Washington, decorated with watercolor paintings by a Jewish boy who had been hidden in France.

"Maybe he was hidden in your village," Sherry said.

It was a long shot, but I skimmed the pictures in the box. One in particular caught my attention. It shows a man harvesting wheat with a scythe. In the corner of the picture is the spire of the village church, and next to it the red roof of a large house. The spire, in fact, belongs to the village church of Savigny, and the red-roofed house belonged to my great-grandfather Louis Dior and his wife Anne. The name of the Jewish artist was Simon Jeruchim, and I soon discovered that he and his wife Cecile live in Pomona, New York, three hours' drive from Ithaca. We met them a few weeks later and quickly became dear, close friends.

Who were the few in Savigny whose courage saved 30 Jewish lives? To answer that question, we have to go back to July 17, 1942, one of the darkest days in all French history. On that day agents of the Gestapo, with the active support of the Vichy regime and the Paris police, made a sweep of 12,884 Jews—men, women, the elderly, children, babies—and herded them into the Velodrome d'Hiver (the winter bicycle arena) with no sanitation facilities, holding them there for deportation to Auschwitz. Jews had been arrested before in Paris—isolated men in 1940, larger groups in 1941—but never before on this scale. It was France's Kristalnacht. For the first time, the people of Paris awoke to the horrors that were unfolding in their midst.

One example. When my cousin Eric Dior, a prominent left-of-center journalist in Paris, asked his grandfather, my cousin René, if he remembered the Vel d'Hiver roundup, René answered:

"Who can forget it? It was terrible. I could hear the cries and screams of my Jewish neighbors and their children as they were being dragged from their apartments." He then added, "They should never have done that. Those were our Jews."

Immediately after the Vel d'Hiver arrests, an organization of young women recruited from the ranks of teachers, nurses, and social workers sprang into being. Calling themselves "Organization de Sauvetage d'Enfants" ("Organization to Save Children"), these courageous young women rescued Jewish children orphaned by the arrest and deportation of their parents by ferrying them to homes and villages in the remote French countryside—in the distant provinces of Brittany and Normandy.

The plaque in the Savigny village square tells us that these 30 Jewish children were saved thanks to the courage of a few villagers and the watchful benevolence of the village community. Who were the courageous few, and what did this watchful benevolence of the village community look like?

In the summer and fall of 1942, as the French Resistance spread out through the countryside searching for villages willing to shelter Jewish children, the first people it contacted would be the village priest and its mayor. In Savigny these would be Abbe (Father) Perrin and Mayor Adolphe Rigaud. Once these two men agreed that their small village of 1,000 inhabitants could shelter as many as 30 children, they made it the Norman village that would hide the largest number of Jewish children during World War II.

Did the Savigny villagers hide these children knowing they were Jewish? Some no doubt did, while others did not; in most cases there is no way of knowing for sure. One woman who did though, welcoming a little girl who had just come from Paris, opened her suitcase and began to sort through her belongings. Coming to a jacket that had the yellow Jewish star sewn on it, she took a pair of scissors and began cutting it off.

"Don't cut that star off," the little girl cried anxiously. "I'm supposed to wear it."

In 1942 the spiritual leadership of this devout Norman community fell to Abbe (Father) Perrin, who was fully aware that the children he and his fellow villagers were asked to shelter were Jewish. He deeply believed that he and the villagers had an all-but-sacred trust not only to save these children's lives but to safeguard their Jewish identity as well. This is well revealed in a conversation he had one day with Marie Louise Blondel, who was sheltering 7-year-old Lucien Berkowicz. Marie Louise, who had come to love Lucien deeply, asked Abbe Perrin if she could adopt him.

"That's not possible," Abbe Perrin replied. "Lucien would become Catholic. That would betray a trust which I can't allow. And although

Lucien is only a child, he fully understands this and what it means."[1]

In Paris, as in all major urban centers, most Jewish lives that were saved came about through the unexpected, timely, and compassionate intervention of strangers. Such was the case with Simon Jeruchim, his sister Alice, and their brother Michel. The morning of the Vel d'Hiver roundup, Simon's mother kept an appointment she had with her dentist.

"I've got terrible news, Madame Jeruchim," the dentist told her. "A patient of mine, a policeman, just told me that the Germans and the French Police are under orders to arrest all Jews in the city and will be coming for you and your family this very night. You must go into hiding immediately."

That night the Jeruchims' cleaning lady hid all five members of their family, and another Jewish family of four, in her tiny apartment. The following night the owner of the local hardware shop, who earlier had befriended 13-year-old Simon, agreed to hide the Jeruchim family in a back room in his store. Later the three Jeruchim children would be sheltered by a Protestant French family named Bonnieux until the day a Mme. Mounier came for them. As Simon describes her, Mme. Mounier was a cheerful, warm, pretty, and very courageous young woman of about 20. Like hundreds of other young women in the Organization de Sauvetage d'Enfants, Mme. Mounier repeatedly ferried Jewish children from homes or safe places, crossing Paris on foot or in the metro to the train station that would carry them to Normandy. Leaving the Bonnieux home, Simon, Alice, and Michel turned to look back on their parents for the last time. Both would perish at Auschwitz.

Annette Fruchmanne is another example of a Savigny child saved through the courage and compassion of strangers. Since Annette's father Jankiel allowed himself to be persuaded that only Jewish men would be rounded up, he was the only member of the family who went into hiding after the Nazi invasion. Jankiel's concierge hid him in a dark corner of their building's basement while his employer continued to send him work and pay him. Annette, her brother Maurice, and their mother Riwka were thus utterly unprepared when the Germans came for them and took all three to the Vel d'Hiver. The wife of Jankiel's employer went to the Vel d'Hiver, raising holy hell. "If you don't keep quiet, madame," one of the officers told her, "we're going to have to arrest you too." The woman only raised more and more commotion until, at last, the frustrated guard let Annette, Maurice, and Riwka go, one of the very few families to escape from the Vel d'Hiver. Riwka, who was pregnant, died a few days later, but Annette and Maurice were saved in Savigny.

• • •

Not all children who came to Savigny had easy or happy experiences, at least not initially. Simon Jeruchim was 13 years old when he was hidden there. The husband of the woman who took him in was a prisoner of war in Germany; she looked at Simon primarily as an available hand to work hard on her farm. Simon, who was a sophisticated young Parisian teenager, had to get used to wearing the rough, hard, wooden sabot or shoes of French peasants; living in a peasant hut with no running water; using an outhouse; sleeping in the hay in a barn; and putting up with another boy who made unwelcome advances. His memories of this place are not happy. Mme. Mounier came back to check on him after a few months and, discovering that he was unhappy, moved him in with Mme. Prim, who was already hiding a young Jewish girl named Annette. Simon's sister Alice, meanwhile, was hidden by a Mme. Ledauphin whose husband was also a prisoner of war in Germany. Alice and Mme. Ledauphin became very close. After the war Alice and Simon returned many times over the years to visit with Mme. Ledauphin and her son, Wilfrid. The two families would remain close for more than 70 years. Not long ago Alice's granddaughter returned to Savigny to spend a week in the village that had saved her grandmother's life.

• • •

Seven-year-old Lucien Berkowicz woke up around 4:00 one morning in January 1943 in the Guy Patin orphanage for Jewish children. Hungry, he went downstairs to scrounge for food. There he spotted two young French women about 20 years old, and with them about a dozen children ages 12 to 14. The group, which had been talking animatedly when Lucien came downstairs, fell silent when they saw him. After a long silence one of the young women suggested to the other, "Let's take him with us."

"My little brother is upstairs," Lucien told the women. "I can't leave him here." One of the women went upstairs with Lucien and found and dressed René, then age 6. As dawn broke, the group made its way through Paris' deserted streets to a monastery temporarily sheltering a large number of young people.

Two weeks later, after a home could be found for them, another young woman ferried Lucien and René by train, bus, and finally horse to Savigny and the small home of Marie Louise Blondel. Lucien Berkowicz, renamed Lucien Blondel, would live for the next three years with Marie Louise, her sons Pierre and Gustave, another Jewish boy named Maurice, and a newborn daughter Simone. Lucien writes:

"I had the privilege and good fortune of being immediately accepted by a family which took me in as one of theirs. All members of the family treated me with affection; I was never bullied or maltreated."

In October 1987, more than 40 years after leaving Savigny, Lucien and his wife Nili returned to renew their connection with surviving members of Marie Louise's family. Pierre Blondel, Lucien learned, now lived in Moulines, a hamlet three miles from Savigny. No one being home, Lucien wrote Pierre after his return to Israel. Lucien received a response written by Pierre's daughter, Annick. Pierre had been a reluctant scholar at best when he and Lucien lived together in Marie's tiny house and now, Annick wrote, "Dad doesn't write, it's not his strong suit. Now that we have telephones in the village he only communicates by phone."

Annick, who inherited the full measure of Marie Louise's kind, loving, and compassionate heart, invited Lucien and his family to return to Savigny. It was only upon meeting Lucien that Annick discovered for the first time that her grandmother had hidden Jewish children during World War II. When Annick asked her mother about it, Mme. Blondel replied, "Why yes. In fact, there were some 15 Jewish children that I know of hidden in Savigny. There may have been more, but I don't know who they are or which families took them in."

On the spot, Annick resolved to recover the history of Savigny during World War II, which she did with the help of Georges Crochet, son of the village schoolmaster who had given Simon Jeruchim his first watercolor set. The Berkowicz–Blondel bond was renewed. Lucien invited

Annick and her husband Eric to spend time with them in Tel Aviv.

"You're my daughter," Lucien told Annick. Turning to his children, he said:

"You owe your lives to her."

On May 24, 2011, 24 years after Lucien first came to Savigny to renew his bonds of friendship with the Blondel family, and thanks to the efforts of Annick Davy, Georges Crochet, and Nicholas Leboulanger, Commemoration Day was celebrated in the Savigny village square. The commemorative plaque was unveiled by Yael Berkowicz, Lucien's daughter, and by Fabrice Davy, great-grandson of Marie Louise Blondel, both of whom, by different paths, owe their lives to Marie Louise. Whoever saves a single life, goes the Jewish proverb, saves the whole world. Marie Louise was an obscure Norman peasant in 1942, but her name is now written in the book of life.

Lucien Berkowicz was unable to make the trip to Savigny for the commemoration, but his written "Homage to a Village" was read by his daughter Yael. Lucien writes:

The village of Savigny has remained as wise as it was the day of our arrival, my brother René, and I, Lucien Berkowicz, after a long voyage to find a refuge and safe haven.

At that time France, our fatherland, was in one of its greatest shipwrecks; it had lost the three principles of the great Revolution of 1789; Liberty, Equality, Fraternity.

But this village welcomed us with a great deal of fraternity. It treated us with equality, surrounding us with warmth and embracing us as do fathers, mothers, brothers.

We orphans, after this victory, left this benevolent community to search, often in vain, for what was left of our families. We succeeded in creating a future for ourselves, without ever forgetting the debt we owe the people of this small, benevolent village.

For long years after the war we, often fatherless and motherless, spread out over the planet. We each lived our own lives, started families, built our future . . . But we have never forgotten that we too are, and forever will be, Savigniens.

This journey back to Savigny has allowed each one of us, and our families, to thank from the bottom of our heart this courageous community to which we owe nothing less than . . . our lives.

• • •

When my cousins and I saw the commemorative plaque in Savigny in July 2011, it had been installed just two months before. My search for answers led me to Simon and Cecile Jeruchim, and through them to lasting bonds of friendship with Annick and Eric Davy, and Georges and Pierrette Crochet. With these friendships enriching Annie's and my life, I gave little further thought to the village of Savigny itself. It remained for me what it had always been, the *berceau*, or cradle, of the Dior family, the home of my ancestors.

In 2017 though, as rhetoric around the Trump wall began to heat up, I saw a people I had come to know and love being slandered for economic and political gain. Their children, torn from their parents' arms, linger forgotten in heartless detention centers scattered throughout our land. Thinking of them, I often remember cousin René's anguished cry: "They should never have done that." These are, after all, our children. What was true then is true now. What, I had to ask myself, can I do about it?

My thoughts returned to Savigny, and what had been accomplished there and in small towns and villages scattered throughout France in the dark days of the Shoah. And so I invited one of the Jewish children who had been saved in Savigny, and descendants of those who had saved them, to America to tell their story. In October 2018 Simon Jeruchim, Annick Davy, and Georges Crochet came to Ithaca to do just that. They spoke to a capacity audience which, deeply moved, gave them a standing ovation.

At the time of the German invasion of France in 1940 there were 340,000 Jews living in France. The Gestapo, acting in collusion with the Vichy government, succeeded in exterminating some 72,500 of them, just under 25 percent of the total, in death camps such as Auschwitz. More than 75 percent were saved. Of the 72,000 Jewish children in France at the time of the Shoah, 12,000 died. Some 60,000 lived on.

In 1942 Savigny-le-Vieux was a very small and very ordinary village in occupied France. Joining hands with other communities and individuals no larger or more distinguished than they, together they saved thousands upon thousands of precious lives.

This is the story of Savigny. This is the story I have to tell.

Today, as we stride into the early decades of the Third Millennium, we are facing challenges as great as and greater than those lived through by the Civil Rights and Peace movements: mass incarcerations of black men; widespread poverty, discrimination, and exploitation; unimaginably brutal and inhumane treatment of migrant workers and their families and children; devastation of the life-support systems of our fragile planet; the nigh-fatal mortgaging of our children's future in the interest of short-term gain.

Shakespeare knew that "what's past is prologue." What the Civil Rights Movement and other great movements in our history teach us is that when "we the people" dig deep into ourselves and face our challenges with courage and devotion, we shall, indeed, overcome.

We of the Sixties generation did what we could in our time. I hope this book inspires you to fight for justice in yours. The time to jump in is now. Your story is waiting.

---

1. Berkowicz, Lucien. *L'histoire de la Survie de Lucien et René Berkowicz*, p. 12

Epilogue

MY friend Aloja Airewele and I visited Dorothy Cotton just one week before she died, and we found her with her spirit undiminished. Dorothy had always loved to break into song, often in the middle of a conversation, as the spirit moved her. Her favorite songs had always been "This Little Light of Mine," "Wade in the Water," and "I'm Gonna Do What the Spirit Says Do." She sang all three now, and each time she did, all voices in the room stilled to listen to her sing. Over and over, she came back to the one that was her very favorite:

> I'm gonna do what the Spirit says do
> I'm gonna do what the Spirit says do
> What the Spirit say do,
> I'm gonna do oh Lord!
> I'm gonna do what the Spirit says do!

It was her valedictory to me, and to the world.

—TONY DIOR GAENSLEN
MARCH 16, 2020
ITHACA, NEW YORK